MW00615716

A Brief History of Doom

A Brief History of Doom

Two Hundred Years of Financial Crises

Richard Vague

PENN

UNIVERSITY OF PENNSYLVANIA PRESS

PHILADELPHIA

Copyright © 2019 University of Pennsylvania Press

All rights reserved. Except for brief quotations used
for purposes of review or scholarly citation, none of this
book may be reproduced in any form by any means
without written permission from the publisher.

Published by
University of Pennsylvania Press
Philadelphia, Pennsylvania 19104-4112
www.upenn.edu/pennpress

Printed in the United States of America
on acid-free paper
10 9 8 7 6 5 4 3 2 1

A catalogue record for this book is available from the
Library of Congress.
ISBN 978-0-8122-5177-7

CONTENTS

PROLOGUE

In the mid-2000s, I was a CEO of a large consumer lending bank and had been a banker since the late 1970s. I'd seen my share of financial chaos. My most formative experience was the banking crisis in the Southwest in the 1980s when oil prices collapsed. It was my job to know risk.

We were national credit card lenders, but as a routine part of our credit and risk analysis, we'd look at loan volumes in many different consumer sectors. "Private debt," the subject of this book, means the whole range of business and personal debt, including credit card debt, commercial real estate loans, energy sector loans, student loans and, by far the biggest slice of the private debt pie, mortgages.

In 2005, I began to notice that mortgage sector growth was extraordinary, having accelerated from $6 trillion in mortgage loans to $9 trillion in just three years. It was a chilling discovery. It's difficult to exaggerate the enormity of that kind of increase. Unprecedented. Alarming. To create a sense of scale, credit card debt at this time totaled a comparatively small $730 billion.

With that kind of growth, we could surely anticipate that there would be major delinquency problems in mortgages. I wasn't a mortgage lender, but I assumed that this magnitude of delinquency would cascade into my business too. We discussed this with other lenders and economists, who mostly maintained that we shouldn't worry about the growth in mortgages because consumer asset values—that is, the value of stocks and houses— were even further ahead.

This was, in part, why I left the lending industry. I'd come to see that the view from Wall Street, the corner office, the Federal Reserve, the ivory tower, and Congress is markedly different from the experience of those who borrow and lend. From my perspective, with runaway mortgage debt like this, we were in trouble no matter what. Yes, things seemed fine for the moment, but if the value of houses dropped, then much of the debt would go bad. And even if house values remained high, debt service for many would be so high that they would be forced to sell those houses to pay the debt.

Although I moved on, I never forgot a hunch that I'd been developing about private debt: if wildfire private debt growth was behind the 2008 economic crisis, then maybe it lurked behind other crises, too, including the Great Depression. So I went to find private debt data on the Depression, a far more challenging task that I had imagined, and my hunch was confirmed. In the late 1920s there had been an explosive, though rarely mentioned, growth in private debt, right before the all-too-frequently invoked stock market crash of October 1929.

Maybe this was a bigger factor than generally believed.

I began to think about Japan's crisis in the 1990s, and when I retrieved data, I saw the very same pattern: runaway growth in private debt had come before the bust and the fall. I was hooked on the project and wanted to see whether my hypothesis applied more broadly. So I convened a team of researchers and analysts to assist in this quest. I also began talking to economists at every opportunity. By now I have spoken to hundreds. These conversations have been invaluable but also troublingly consistent in one regard: for most, private debt is a secondary or peripheral topic and barely mentioned. In fact, private debt wasn't even a component of most economic forecasting models before 2008.

That shouldn't have surprised me. I had been a lender for over three decades, had sat on the boards of both Visa and MasterCard, had aggregate industry statistics on debt at my fingertips, and had reviewed hundreds of economic forecasts. How could *I* not have known this? It's a devastating paradox: while private debt is a necessary component of an economy, rapid private debt growth may be the most crucial variable explaining financial crises—and also the most overlooked explanatory factor.

As my team and I embarked on years of research, I pondered why other economists hadn't emphasized private debt. Perhaps it's because the generation of economists in positions of power and prestige in 2008 had grown up during that prolonged period from 1950 to 1980 when private debt was so low that it truly wasn't much of a factor in economic outcomes. Perhaps it's because they minimize or neglect the role of private debt in creating new money and thus heightening demand. Another factor might be the outsized influence of the Federal Reserve itself, which historically has not made loans directly to the private sector and thus tends to view the world through the lens of government debt and reserve accounts. Finally, private debt may be overlooked because there is a constituency with the wealth, means, and incentive to promote an unfettered laissez-faire outlook, and there is no well-funded constituency to promote an alternative viewpoint—namely, that unfettered private debt can and often does get out of control.

If readers take one lesson from this book, I hope it is this: when it comes to financial crises, we're not in the grip of unseen and hopelessly complex forces. Such crises are neither inevitable nor unpredictable. Runaway private debt and the resulting overcapacity does a better job than any other variable in explaining and predicting financial crises. It is our job to heed those danger signs.

)

Introduction

The Anatomy of a Financial Crisis

Imagine a future country of Oz, in the year 2030. It was in this imaginary country that citizens became captivated by a radical new invention—heliocars. These cars ran on stored sunlight, could be constructed out of ultralight material, and traveled on monorails at four hundred miles per hour.

Entrepreneurs scrambled to form dozens of companies that built these monorails, which promised to revolutionize travel. These companies were all heavy users of cash since they needed to buy air rights and right-of-ways, build monorails and heliocars, hire operators and technicians, market the service to customers, and more. Stock sales alone weren't sufficient to provide the needed capital, so these companies looked to borrow.

That's where "infrastructure banks" (IBs) came in. They had been authorized by the Ozian Parliament twenty years earlier to aid capital-intensive, long-term infrastructure projects. Unlike conventional banks, IBs had minimal capital requirements and key tax advantages, and could obtain funding through the tax-free infrastructure bank bonds secured by their loans. They were regulated by the Ministry of Commerce, which had a lighter regulatory touch than the conventional bank regulator, the Central Bank of Oz.

Heliorail stocks were the darlings of the stock exchange and soared upward, and the value of the land and associated air rights went up rapidly with them. The more IBs lent, the more monorails were built. Since their loan collateral was increasing in value, IB executives grew bolder and vied with each other to lend larger amounts in this sector. If heliorail stocks were hot, IB stocks were hotter. Some heliorail founders got rich; a handful became billionaires. They hired thousands of new employees, many of whom became rich, too. This spilled over into the broader economy and quickened the pace of gross domestic product (economic or GDP) growth. New heliorail startups appeared, further crowding the field. Everyone from the virtual-reality repair guy to the lowly eSports equipment manager was looking for the latest tips on heliorail and IB stocks.

The commercial real estate (CRE) industry projected that hubs with heliorail service would grow rapidly, so CRE developers began building major new office parks at key points adjacent to these lines. Conventional banks, envious of stratospheric IB growth and profitability, jumped into this lending game. With employment rising, mortgage lenders became more aggressive too.

Photos of heliorail executives were plastered on the front of every e-magazine and news blog in the country. Conventional banks and IBs who wanted in on their loans hesitated to scrutinize their financials for fear of being shut out. Heliorails hired armies of lobbyists to defend and expand their legislative and regulatory turf and became major contributors to the campaigns of the most influential members of Parliament.

The economic boom brought higher corporate tax receipts, and the government's budget turned to surplus. The prime minister of Oz took full credit, claiming, "Oz has entered a new era of prosperity due to the policies of our administration." But there were now fourteen heliorails serving the capital, Emerald City, alone. None were yet profitable. Firms had vastly overprojected growth in passengers.

In mid-2033, regulators at the Ministry of Commerce began to express concern about the underwriting standards of IBs, but members of Parliament intervened successfully on their behalf, warning the press that any intervention would interfere with the market and could slow the economy. But with concerns of their own, the investors buying industrial bank bonds began to pull back. Without this needed funding, IBs had to curtail their lending. Executives dismissed this concern, but the change was real. Without new funding, heliorail growth began to decelerate. Some pulled back on service. Companies stopped bidding for air right-of-ways, and those values began to decline.

Disappointment followed disappointment, but the stock market was slow to absorb the trends. Then in June 2034, the highly respected investment firm of Emerald Sachs warned its clients: "We do not see the possibility of meaningful profitability for any heliorail company as long as this large of a number of companies continue to operate in the sector."

In contrast, the CRE office-park boom continued unabated. The CRE industry and conventional banks assumed any problems would be limited to the heliorails. IBs began lending to the CRE industry to try and diversify away from their overreliance on the heliorail industry. Unspoken was the fact that both conventional banks and IBs needed the lucrative fees and interest from CRE loans to offset the emerging problems in their heliorail portfolios.

Then came a shocking announcement. Yellow Brick Heliorail, the third largest in the industry, reported that after unsuccessfully seeking strategic alternatives, it was discontinuing operations. Other, smaller heliorail companies soon followed. In October, the Ozian 500 stock index, which had gained 64 percent in the previous three years, took a tumble, dropping 38 percent in three weeks. The stock market collapse meant that heliorails could no longer raise funds through stock sales.

By 2035, enough loans had soured that Oz's largest IB lender, the First Industrial Bank of Oz, was compelled to disclose a massive multibillion-ozbuck loss. Sixty percent of its loans were heliorail loans. The Central Bank of Oz had been precluded from intervening in IB regulation or supervision, but alarm over the heliorail industry now prodded Parliament to grant it the power to intervene—along with a 375 trillion ozbuck war chest to provide liquidity and capital as needed.

More failures and near-failures of IBs followed, along with the near-failures of several notable conventional banks that had also been swept up in the craze. But the Central Bank was soon committed to stemming the damage and intervened by infusing institutions with new funds or hastily arranging acquisitions by stronger banks. These years brought massive layoffs at heliocar companies and IBs. Oz's unemployment rate shot up, and its GDP dropped. CRE activity finally peaked in 2036 and then plummeted when tenants for new office parks failed to materialize, affecting conventional bank-loan portfolio quality. The rapid growth in mortgage loans was followed by rising delinquency and losses, and those lenders pulled back as well.

The Tinman Political Party—in power during the crisis—was voted out and the Lion Party ushered in, though neither party foresaw the crisis or had any real insight or remedies for it. Government economists viewed it as a "black swan," an unpredictable event. Legislation was passed with a surfeit of new regulations designed to prevent the next crisis, many of which were misguided. Time heals most wounds. Memories of the crisis faded, and by 2037, Oz's economy was growing again.

This hypothetical case describes well any number of crises over the past two hundred years: Britain in 1825, Germany in 1873, Japan in 1907, China in 1999, the United States in 2008, and many others.

This book is a brief history of financial crises. It emphasizes in particular the rapid growth in loans—which we refer to as private debt—that preceded them. It concludes that almost all financial crises follow a simple if ultimately agonizing equation: *widespread overlending leads to widespread overcapacity that leads to widespread bad loans and bank (and other lender) failures.* This is the essence of a financial crisis.

In simplest terms, a bank fails when it makes too many bad loans—for example, when it makes far too many loans for buildings when there aren't enough tenants to fill them, so the buildings sit empty for years. You might think that this would be a rare blunder, but as you will see, it happens often and has been happening for centuries. When it occurs, most often there is a run on that bank's deposits and funding, or a regulator steps in, and that bank is closed or is rescued by the government. A financial crisis happens when a lot of banks and other lenders in a given country fail or come so close to failure that they have to be rescued. To truly qualify as a financial crisis, these failures must be so widespread that they involve a significant number of lenders and affect a country's economic growth.

Bad loans almost never come in this quantity unless those loans bring widespread overcapacity in one or more of the largest sectors in that economy. In the nineteenth century, that sector was railroads and the associated land purchases and real estate construction; in the twentieth and twenty-first centuries, it has been housing and commercial real estate. When lending leads to too many buildings for the number of tenants available, for example, the owners of those buildings will struggle to repay the loans.

The formula is straightforward: overlending leads to overcapacity, which makes those loans bad. It's never subtle. There have to be far, far too many new houses or office buildings or some other "something" built for a crisis to ensue. Overbuilding and overcapacity are at the very heart of a financial crisis because vast overbuilding and overcapacity are only possible through an equally vast amount of overlending. It almost always occurs in a few short years. Building one new high-rise condominium in a given neighborhood in a single year is not a problem, but building ten is, since there are not enough tenants in that short span to support the excess. Overlending itself, because it creates overcapacity, can turn initially good loans bad.

Almost every financial crisis examined in this book was preceded by extraordinary growth in private debt, especially in ratio to GDP. In comparison, periods of benign private debt growth, such as the in the United States in the late 1960s, the United Kingdom in the 1990s, France in the 1970s, and

Germany in the 1980s, have not provoked financial crises. Notably, the government (or public) debt of major, advanced economies has not been much of a factor in financial crises until after the collapse.

Once a crisis has occurred, repair only comes through time and new capital—time enough for natural growth to absorb the overcapacity and new capital to repair damaged lenders and companies.

This book's primary goal is to show that financial crises tend to follow the same plotline. Since the global financial crisis of 2008, there has been heightened interest in how to prevent or mitigate future financial crises. Unfortunately, it is the special purview of regulators, economists, and policymakers in power at the time of a financial crisis to later assert that crises cannot be predicted or prevented and that when a crisis happens, we are in the grip of economic complexities that we can neither foresee nor prevent nor entirely understand. But this betrays those millions who did not cause the crisis but were badly damaged by it, as well as the governments and political systems that were badly disrupted. This book argues to the contrary that financial crises, across time or place, have measurable prerequisites and a predictive indicator—once we start paying attention to lending.

I examine financial crises over the last two hundred years, primarily in the United States but with detours into the United Kingdom, Germany, France, Japan, and China—which together were the six largest economies on the globe during that span—totaling roughly 50 percent or more of world GDP for that period. I focus on the last two hundred years because it has been a unique era. From the Industrial Revolution onward, both economic and population growth have exploded beyond anything previously seen.

Financial crises deserve heightened attention because among the major types of economic crisis, they are the most damaging to major economies. As part of their excellent work, economists Carmen Reinhart and Ken Rogoff have listed six different categories of crisis: external sovereign debt crises, internal sovereign debt crises, currency crises, inflation crises, stock market crises, and financial (or banking) crises. Looking at them since 1960 and taking into account the size of the country, the three most prevalent by far have been financial crises, currency crises, and stock market crises.[1] And among these three, the one that has caused the most impairment to major economy GDPs has been the financial, or banking, crisis. Sovereign debt and inflation crises have been comparatively rare, even though these have drawn disproportionate scholarly attention.

Table I.1. Major Financial Crises

	United States	United Kingdom	Germany	France	Japan	China
1819	*					
1825		*				
1831				*		
1837	*	*				
1847		*	*	*		
1857	*	*	*	*		
1866		*		*		
1873	*		*	*		
1882–1884	*			*	*	*
1893	*					
1901			*			
1907	*		*	*	*	
1910						*
1914	*	*				
1925						*
1927–1931	*		*	*	*	
1930s						*
1987	*	*				
1990s					*	*
2008	*	*	*	*		

Table I.1 shows the crises that are covered in this book, if not in detail, at least in passing. This list is derived from a number of excellent lists compiled by noted economists.[2] For convenience I have designated a specific year for each crisis, although most have unfolded over a period of several years.

These and other financial crises have been explained by and attributed to many factors, separately and in combination, including interest rates, gold policy, trade, greed, deregulation, global savings gluts, and lack of confidence, to name just a few. All of these factors and more can play a part in a crisis. We'll discuss them briefly throughout, as appropriate, although a full review is beyond the scope of this book. The research presented in this book demonstrates another thesis. *Private debt is key, and the story of financial crisis is, at heart, a story of private debt and runaway lending. Time and again it is a story of lending booms in which bankers and other lenders make far too many bad loans.*

The importance of private debt is minimized altogether by some, who reason that for every borrower paying more interest and therefore reducing spending in a given period, there is a lender receiving interest as income and increasing spending in that period, and it all nets to zero. In practice, however, this tends not to be true since lenders need not increase their spending by the same amount that distressed borrowers are forced to cut back. And even if it does increase the spending of the lender, that usually happens later. In the economy as in business, the timing of spending is everything. More important, it does not capture the duress of those borrowers forced to constrain their activity because of overleverage, and the crippling impairment to lenders when too many loans are not repaid.

But financial crises recur so frequently and are so often linked to rapid increases in lending that we have to wonder why lending booms happen at all. The answer is this: growth in lending is what brings lenders higher compensation, advancement, and recognition. Until a crisis point is reached, rapid lending growth can bring euphoria and staggering wealth. Lending booms are thus caused by an intense desire to win, to prevail, and to increase wealth. They are driven by a ferocity of ambition that is ever present and incites, compels, and pervades these booms. It's no different than a computer company's desire to sell more computers, a coach's desire to win championships, or, for that matter, a king's desire to conquer new territories. Lending booms are driven by competition, inevitably accompanied by the fear of falling behind or missing out.

In a lending boom, optimism pervades projections of earnings and valuations, and credit standards around such things as debt ratios, down-payment requirements, and past credit issues get relaxed. Hence delusion, especially self-delusion, is also a prerequisite for a financial crisis, even if it is delusion couched in carefully extrapolated graphs and serious, high-toned presentations. *Property values will continue to rapidly rise. Housing demand will continue to increase. Corporate earnings will continue to strengthen.*

Time and again, a financial crisis emerges directly not just from ambition but also from this capacity for self-delusion and deceit, intended or unintended, official or unofficial. Time and again, lending is the platform for that delusion. This intense ambition is impossible to overestimate and crucial to understanding business and economics in general, not just booms and crises. To seek to explain booms solely through impersonal, technical factors is to miss their single most important characteristic. It is to miss completely the fact that economics is a behavioral and not a physical science.

It is to miss the essence of financial crises.

In an accelerated lending boom, the ones that concern me in this book, resistance of lenders to the siren song of accelerated loan growth is rare. These lenders tentatively depart from conservative lending to make loans that have somewhat greater risk, and as they do, the economy gets better, asset values rise (since lending helps cause these valuation gains), and employment and growth trends improve. The compensation of these lenders and their companies' stock price both get better. Other lenders take note and are judged unfavorably if their lending trends fall behind. Bit by bit, most respond by accelerating their own growth, and soon enough, a large swath of the lending industry is locked in competitive overdrive, making incrementally riskier loans. Most often, borrowers are happily complicit. Many times in my career, I have seen companies borrow more simply because loans were so readily available. The saying has always been that "the time to borrow is when lenders are lending."

A lending boom feels great while it is happening. The economy gets better because certain core forms of lending, especially bank lending, actually create new money and thus create more demand. At the moment when a bank makes a loan and deposits the funds in that borrower's account, new money is created. Businesses that receive these loans accelerate spending and hiring. Employment increases, far more than dictated by organic demand—the demand that would exist without this lending boom. Consumer borrowers increase their spending. Government revenues go up since businesses and individuals are making more money and therefore paying more taxes. The impact of this excess lending spills outward. New jobs abound, unemployment plummets, incomes go up, housing and other asset values go up, and the government debt profile usually improves.

Why do lending booms happen? Having spent a lifetime in the industry, I can report that there is almost always the drive to grow loans aggressively and increase wealth, and lenders, as a practical (and sometimes perilous) matter, are usually not greatly constrained in the amount of loans they can make. So the better and more profound question is, why are there periods in which loan growth *isn't* booming?

Lending doesn't boom when regulators or risk managers have the upper hand and when lenders are chastened—often in the years following a crisis. In fact, a few countries have gone so far as to enact explicit limits on credit growth. Lending also tends not to boom in phases when businesses and other borrowers are overleveraged and not in a position to rapidly increase their borrowing. Apart from those periods (which include calamities such as wars, most notably World War II), the era covered by this book is one in which private debt always outgrows GDP, and often by a wide margin. It's the rule rather than the exception. It's endemic to developed economies.

The United States had lending booms in the 1830s, 1850s, late 1860s and early 1870s, late 1880s and early 1890s, mid-1900s, 1920s, 1980s, and 2000s—and all resulted in a financial crisis. This list is not exhaustive. Lending booms have preceded almost every financial crisis.

Financial crises are calamitous enough that in one sense it's surprising that they recur, and lenders touch this hot stove time and again. Yet gradually, after a crisis, memories of earlier troubles fade, and lenders can point to a lengthening accumulation of years in which problems have not occurred and begin to accelerate lending and slacken lending standards once again. "This time is different" rationalizations—or amnesia—set in.

Soon enough, a new lending boom begins.

The germ of financial crisis begins with overlending in a sector or sectors big enough to pose a systemic risk to the economy. In recent decades, residential and commercial real estate (Figure I.1) have become the largest lending sector and the ones most susceptible to rapid expansion through lending. Mortgage loans alone went from $5 trillion to $10.6 trillion, or 44 percent of all private loans, during the 2008 crisis in the United States. If 10 percent of those loans were bad, it would equal more than $1 trillion in an industry that only had less than $2 trillion in capital at that point. In contrast, it would be hard to create enough bad loans in the consumer staples sector to create a national crisis since loans to that sector are less than 2 percent of all private debt.

As lending in a sector increases, the value of that sector's assets go up because that lending increases demand. This is especially true in real estate. Lenders believe that they are following a trend when, in fact, their loans are *driving* a trend. This becomes a feedback spiral: because more lending results in more borrowers, it results in rising real estate prices. This increase in prices boosts lenders' confidence that they have lent wisely, which translates into even more real estate lending and development. It's a self-reinforcing cycle and a self-fulfilling prophecy—at least for a time.

Booms do not just happen in banks. The initial lending boom often comes from a secondary type of financial institution with less regulatory scrutiny.

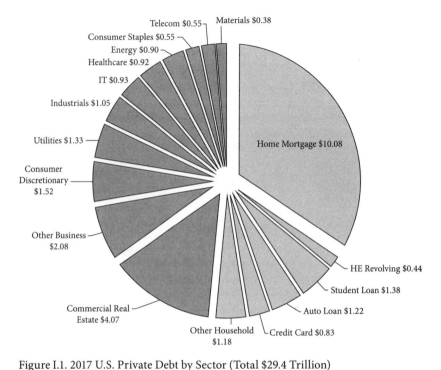

Figure I.1. 2017 U.S. Private Debt by Sector (Total $29.4 Trillion)
Note: Business debt is dark gray, household debt is light gray.
For all data sources for charts throughout the book, please visit www.bank ingcrisis.org.

For example, mortgage banks played an outsized role in 2008, savings and loans in the 1980s, trust banks in 1907, *Baubanken* in 1873 Germany, and so on. Another portion of this lending occurs outside of regulated banks and savings institutions altogether, in an area often called "shadow banking" that includes insurance companies, hedge funds, private equity funds, and more.

The crisis is inevitable before it is obvious. "External shocks," a phrase popular with economists to describe disruptive factors, often emerge but are not required to ignite the crisis at the point when massive overcapacity is reached. Overlending and overcapacity themselves can bring a crisis. At some point the tragedy begins. Participants gradually realize that too many of these loans will not be repaid. Lending is curtailed. Building or other business activity will then likely decline. Lenders soon find themselves in a crisis trap: the only way to maintain prices is to continue to make real estate loans using high valuations, but that continued lending creates more bad debt. Yet if lending abates, values decline, which exposes problem loans. The good times that these lending booms bring are so good, and the bad times that a reversal will bring are so bad, that those benefiting the most are highly reluctant to accept the troubling news as it emerges.

Financial crises don't often happen at a single point in time. They unravel over years. In Japan, overbuilding occurred in the late 1980s, stocks crashed in 1990, real estate values plummeted in 1991, and yet the government showed unusual forbearance and did not widely recapitalize banks until 1998. For the crisis of 2008, housing construction peaked in 2005, building slowed and housing prices declined in 2006, the stock market unraveling started in the fall of 2007, and the famed Lehman Brothers failure came in 2008. (Stock market crashes are a symptom—admittedly sometimes the most luridly visible one—and not a cause of financial crises. But they can compound the downward pressure.) Lenders that have made too many bad loans—bad loans that approach in amount their total capital and reserves—fail or have to be rescued. Even banks not as far gone can fail because depositors and funders will "withdraw now and ask questions later." Banks operate at much higher levels of leverage than most other types of businesses and are thus inherently more vulnerable to adversity. Lending totals often (but not always) slow or decline. The economy slows. Large-scale layoffs follow.

This is the onset of phase two, the bust after the boom. All booms look more or less the same—very rapid growth in private debt and widespread overcapacity—but recoveries do not. The duration and severity of bust periods that follow vary widely, depending largely on the policies employed to combat them. The sheer size of the problem means that often only the government is large enough to rescue the troubled institutions. And as these chapters show, government response at this point can range from passive and hands-off to active and interventionist. Institutions can be allowed to fail or be rescued. Typically, active intervention means a softer short-term impact on the economy but an economy that remains overleveraged. Conversely, less intervention can mean more short-term distress but greater deleveraging. There are, of course, a variety of government responses between these two extremes.

Crises often happen at similar times across several countries. In 1837, 1857, and 1873, to cite just three examples, a crisis erupted in both Europe and the United States. This should not surprise us. Bankers on both sides of the Atlantic had strong financial ties to each other, often overlaid with family ties. The Warburg banking family of Hamburg was related to the Kuhn and Loeb banking family in New York. There were Morgans in New York and London. Technologies tend to develop simultaneously in different locales as well. This was especially true of the railroads that were at the root of so many nineteenth-century crises. Railroad building, and almost inevitable overbuilding, occurred simultaneously in several countries. Price or volume swings in such commodities as wheat and copper in one market rippled around the globe, sometimes compounding crises. And the core forces of competition and envy that motivate lenders' ambition do not know national boundaries. They affect lenders across borders, just as they do within.

Rapid growth in lending is the key harbinger of financial crisis. In examining financial crises from 1945 forward, a period for which we have more complete data, I've found that a financial crisis is highly likely *if the ratio of private debt to GDP grows by 15 to 20 percentage points or more in a five-year period and the ratio of overall private debt to GDP reaches or exceeds 150 percent.* This is a general guideline, to be applied with reflection and judgment. The deeper issue is how much overcapacity is being created and that country's policy accommodations for lending institutions. For example, China is well over these thresholds but is uniquely situated since its government owns or controls all the relevant components of crisis—lenders, borrowers, and regulators. Nevertheless, when we apply this rough formula to a database of forty-seven countries in the postwar period for which we have relatively complete data, this straightforward formula predicts a "calamity" roughly 80 percent of the time—where *calamity* means a financial crisis or a 2 percent GDP decline, or both. This rapid debt growth is the measurable residue of overcapacity in the making. At the very least, most of the worst financial crises are those preceded by credit booms. (This analysis can be found on this book's website, www.bankingcrisis.org.)

It is important to note that only in rare cases have financial crises occurred when *not* preceded by rapid private debt growth.

Rapid debt growth can also bring overcapacity in countries with less than 150 percent private debt to GDP, as we will see often in this book, especially in the 1800s. However, at this lower overall ratio, rapid private debt growth results in crisis far less certainly, since that low ratio may indicate undercapacity, as was the case in the United States after World War II. In other words, whether rapid debt growth results in a crisis has much to do with how much capacity existed before the lending boom—be it housing or office space or some other category, as well as the nature of the policy response. Private debt levels of 150 percent or more of GDP implies ample existing capacity, which would mean that a lending boom that rapidly adds more capacity will likely bring too much. Further, as Steve Keen has shown, when overall private debt is higher, a drop in new lending results in a drop in total economic demand; when it is lower, it does not.[3]

As far as hypotheses go, this book won't have quite the emphasis on gold (or silver) in crises in the 1800s and early 1900s that most accounts do. As I will elaborate in the chapters to follow, lending booms could and did happen without additions of gold reserves. And while withdrawals of gold could and did bring contractions of loans and often exacerbate a crisis, withdrawal of gold was not the primary issue: it occurred after the damage from profligate lending and overcapacity had already taken place.

Nor will the book emphasize the role of the central bank (or some surrogate) as the lender of last resort since the role of the lender of last resort comes only after the lending misbehavior has occurred and the emphasis of this book centers more on that misbehavior itself. Though as we will see, a lender of last resort can make a profound difference in how a crisis plays out once it has begun.

The story told here is not entirely new, but it has been widely overlooked and ignored. Some observers as early as the 1800s attributed their financial crises to profligate lending. The hypothesis and explanation most in keeping with the story I tell here comes from economist Hyman Minsky (1919–1996). He powerfully articulated something close to the theory of private debt that I espouse in this book.[4] I learned from and relied on much of what he has written as I developed my own theories and observations.

Minsky held that the mechanism that pushes an economy toward an inevitable crisis is rampant speculation and the accumulation of debt by the private sector (investors, banks, and companies). Minsky claimed that in prolonged periods of prosperity, actors take on more risk, and a speculative euphoria develops.

Minsky's view was that lenders start first with "hedge" loans, loans where interest and principal can be repaid from cash flow. Next, they move to "speculative" loans, where cash flow can service interest but not principal, and then lastly to "Ponzi" loans, where cash flow can repay neither interest nor principal and the asset or business must be sold to repay the debt. When a preponderance of the loans in a sector is closer to this Ponzi category, a crash becomes highly likely. This movement of the financial system from stability to fragility followed by sudden major collapse that brings a crisis point is often called the "Minsky moment."

I would annotate Minsky's thoughts in the following way: lenders don't have to believe that they are making this speculative Ponzi type of loan for it to end up as one. They may truly believe they are making a hedge loan if, caught in the euphoria, their projections for a borrower's future cash flow were too optimistic or if competitive circumstances changed adversely after the loan was made.

To test, discover, and develop this thesis, my team and I collected comprehensive private debt data for the several years before and after each financial crisis listed above. This was a very different approach, not only because private debt gets overlooked but also because historians, especially those of older crises, have tended to minimize or gloss over the several years leading up to each financial crisis. They focus on the dramatic facets, such as bank failures, stock market declines, commodity price collapses, and the agony and ruin that follows, not the preceding years of accelerated lending, new bank formation, skyrocketing prices, and pervasive euphoria.

Records on rapidly escalating private debt have especially been neglected.

One goal of this book is to remedy that, though there are unfortunately still significant gaps in the data for many crises. I have made these assembled data for each crisis, along with other schedules and analysis covered in this book, fully available at www.bankingcrisis.org.[5] Though my team and I have read hundreds of books and articles, hoping to find new sources or snippets of data, much data remains elusive, especially data related to private debt. Records on private debt have not been well kept, in large part because economists and historians did not deem the subject of high importance. In some cases these records may never be found or reconstructed.

The United States sets the standard globally in data collection, though it still has important omissions in sector data and derivatives. Japan has remarkable data from the Meiji restoration forward, although it lacks key sector data for the post–World War II period. The United Kingdom, Germany, and France did not keep records in the 1800s as well as one might have expected. I would also note that I have a lower level of confidence in all aggregate data and statistics, such as GDP, prior to 1945, based not only on incomplete data but also the reliability of the extant data.

All in all, it was a research adventure. These data are available to anyone who wishes to download, view, add to, or challenge them. I have a comment section where we invite and welcome new data submissions or corrections to the assembled data. We hope these data sets continue to improve through time. I encourage readers to study and pursue their own conclusions.

In each chapter or introduction to a new financial crisis, you'll see a chart that I call a "crisis matrix." It distills into one visual display the dividends of my team's efforts to find data on private debt for a given country and crisis. It contains data selected from the much more comprehensive set of data found on our website. The crisis matrix chart in each instance shows the growth in private debt, government debt, GDP, and select other data during the most relevant five-year period before a crisis, along with that same data in key years after the crisis. Where a crisis matrix for a given country is not shown in the chapter, in most cases I have provided the broader set of data on the website.

At the bottom of each matrix, I also express these data as a percentage of GDP, to help with comparisons through time within the same crisis, as well as comparisons between crises. For periods in which we have no private debt data, we have included other key economic data, such as construction spending or capital formation, which serve as a proxy for private debt data. All numbers in the charts and tables throughout this book are nominal unless indicated otherwise.

The following chapters tell the story of financial crises, first through the major financial crises for which we have the most, and most reliable, data. We start with what many economists think of as the important crisis and the one for which they deem to have the most elusive explanation—the Great Depression. This chapter excavates data on housing, commercial real estate, and other sectors to tell a surprising new story about this iconic financial crisis: at its heart, it was a real estate crisis brought on by rampant private lending and debt. We then move to the two major crises that followed, one in the 1980s United States and the other in 1990s Japan, to show how the same pattern of financial crisis played out.

After these first three chapters, the grim logic that underlies financial crises will be clear.

A reader might wonder, however, if the patterns of financial crises as private debt and real estate crises apply to earlier eras. Have we discovered a plot of financial crisis since the industrial era began, in other words, or only a plot of relatively recent crises?

To settle the matter, I move in the next two chapters back in time to test our hypothesis further on the frequent, yet quantitatively murkier, global financial crises of the 1800s. We find the very same pattern. In Chapter 4, I take a look at the crises of 1819, 1825, and 1837, while Chapter 5 looks cumulatively at the many crises of the "railroad era," from roughly the 1840s to the early 1900s. I argue in these chapters that the crises confirm our core findings: while commercial real estate and home mortgages could, and did, bring down the U.S. economy in the 1930s and the late 1980s and Japan's economy in the 1990s, in the 1800s, it was the behemoth railroad sector of the economy along with associated construction that was large enough to inflict that kind of damage. The proliferation of railroads—forged by private debt—is the key to this extraordinary period in U.S. and global economic history.

With fresh eyes, and this narrative in place, we return to the recent past in our last chapter, on the 2008 crisis. We establish that the crisis of 2008 was inevitable as early as 2005. In fact, it should readily have been predicted.

One final disclaimer: Because we spend so much time in this book on the pernicious effects of private debt, with such debt almost serving as the economic villain of financial crisis, it is crucial to note that private debt is a necessary and positive element of an economy and is one of the fundamental ingredients of growth, trade, profit, and investment. Take away private debt, and commerce as we know it would slow to a crawl. The world suffered crisis after crisis in the 1800s, but per-capita GDP increased thirtyfold in that century, and private debt was integral to the growth. Many of those nineteenth-century crises were rooted in the overexpansion of railroads, but they left behind an impressively extensive network of rails from which countries still benefit. China's unprecedented and extraordinary rise since 1980 has been largely built using private (nongovernment) debt. And though there has been calamity along the way, and more likely yet to come, the rapidity and breadth of the country's rise would have been impossible without it.

Private debt is indispensable but becomes a problem when it grows too fast or gets too large in relation to the economy. That is the paradox of debt. And as many studies have shown, if an economy's private debt-to–GDP ratio is high but not rapidly growing, then that private debt dampens GDP growth.[6]

Life goes on after a crisis. An economy that had been growing will sometimes simply resume its course, as was the case for the United States in the nineteenth century. Yet understanding the anatomy of financial crises is a critical obligation we have to the governments and political systems that are disrupted, and even more to those millions who do not cause the crisis but are badly damaged by it. Predicting financial crises should be our *duty*. My hope is that if we better understand financial crises by focusing on the neglected yet vital matter of lending and private debt, as the following chapters amply illustrate, then much of the damage that comes from them can be avoided.

CHAPTER 1

A Jazz Age Real Estate Crisis

The Great Depression

From the distance of more than eighty years and in the cold light of economic analysis, it is easy to forget the death and despair of the Great Depression. Historian Adam Hochschild describes a country that "simmered in misery," with thirty-four million Americans living in households without a breadwinner. He writes of unemployed steelworkers living inside idled coke ovens with their families and rummaging through the garbage bins for food, of riots, and of men in cloth caps waiting outside churches and charities for quickly depleted food supplies.[1]

The Great Depression brought a level of misery rarely seen in American history. Oceans of ink have been spilled to explain why the bust phase of the Great Depression, with the collapse of GDP, was so protracted, painful, and deep. For economists, explaining its cause has sometimes been referred to as the holy grail of macroeconomics. But largely absent from the most widely read books on the Depression is its one central cause: runaway private debt.

Those who do mention private lending, such as Milton Friedman and Anna Jacobson Schwartz in their iconic *Monetary History*, misrepresent the phenomenon. Though Friedman and Schwartz had a number of pivotal insights about the collapse in the 1930s, they said little about the overlending of the 1920s. "If there was any deterioration at all in the [pre-Depression] quality of loans . . . it must have been minor," they wrote, and "any [pre-Depression] deterioration in the quality of loans . . . was a minor factor in subsequent bank failures."[2] By dismissing private debt, Friedman and Schwartz didn't just miss its contribution. More fundamentally, they missed the human factors involved in a crisis: the competitive intensity, the drive for wealth, the pervasive hubris, and the self-delusion.

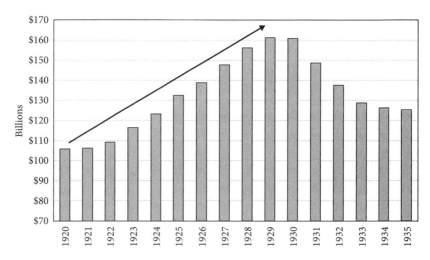

Figure 1.1. United States: Private Debt, 1920–1935
In the United States, private debt increased 52.7 percent from 1920 to 1929.

John Kenneth Galbraith's *Great Crash of 1929* glossed over the national real estate boom beyond Florida. In his final chapter on "causes," he only briefly mentioned lending, noting mostly that in the late 1920s "money was tight," even though loans were then growing at a robust 6 percent per year.[3]

The misery that unfolded from 1929 to 1933 was a story of rampant and unsound lending followed by widespread loan contraction that contributed the lion's share of the cataclysmic GDP contraction. The Great Depression was a massive residential and commercial real estate crisis. The financial records of the 1920s, which have largely been overlooked, indelibly show this. During the 1920s, annual housing and commercial real estate construction almost *tripled*—and nearly all of it was financed by debt (Figure 1.2).

This explosion in residential and commercial construction lending, augmented by lending for utilities and stock purchases, created the euphoria of the Roaring Twenties, the jazz age of robust spending and celebration. Companies used the new money from loans to expand and employ more people.

The acceleration in construction resulted in such extensive overbuilding that by the final years of the decade, before the stock market crash, thousands of newly erected office buildings, houses, and apartments sat empty. Office vacancy rates rose, and residential mortgage foreclosures nearly doubled in the final years of the decade.[4] As in other cases, this crisis was inevitable before it was obvious. The only question, and the only area where the president

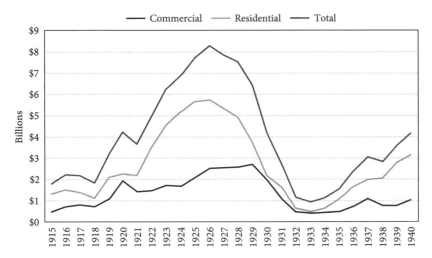

Figure 1.2. United States: Construction Spending, 1915–1940

and the Federal Reserve could still have a discretionary impact, was the length and severity of that correction.

The Great Depression, like most financial crises, can be thought of as occurring in three distinct phases. The first, from 1923 to 1928, was the runaway lending boom that led to the avalanche of terrible loans that brought so many banks to failure. The second—the great contraction—lasted from 1929 to 1933, when GDP fell by an astonishing $48 billion, or 46 percent, and brought 30 percent unemployment. The third phase began in 1934, when the economy ceased contracting and slowly struggled forward. (There was a notable new recession outside of the scope of this book that began in late 1937.)

The state of the nation's housing had become a national issue in 1921, when Secretary of Commerce Herbert Hoover began to advocate for increased home ownership as "the foundation of a sound economy and social system." In 1923 he wrote, "Maintaining a high percentage of individual home owners is one of the searching tests that now challenge the people of the United States."[5] This argument—that the homeowner was a more committed and responsible citizen—would recur in the 2000s. Hoover urged homebuilders to become more efficient and lenders to become more generous.

New tax incentives supported home construction. Historian Donald Miller writes that no legislation boosted New York City's construction industry more than the 1921 exemption from real estate taxes for ten years of residential construction. "In the 1920s," he writes, "New York City would account for fully 20 percent of all new residential construction in the country. Builders of large apartment houses were the pacesetters. In 1926, 77 percent of all new residential construction was given over to apartment dwellings."[6]

Banks, building and loans, bond houses, and other lenders responded to Hoover's call. As Robert M. Fogelson reports, Albert E. Kleinert, Brooklyn's superintendent of buildings, reflected the frenzied pace of the era when he said, "They [the speculators] are now selling property between twelve and one o'clock and then at two o'clock they notify their tenants that the rent will be raised, and then when they show an income gain on paper, they sell again. More often than not, the new owners repeated the process."[7]

In a financial crisis, it is typical for lenders other than conventional commercial banks (those that are less regulated or unregulated) to play a leading role in the preceding lending upturn, and so it was here. The number of building-and-loan associations—savings institutions whose primary purpose was home lending—grew from 8,000 to 13,000 during the 1920s.[8] Builders and developers chartered many of them to finance their own projects in a brazen conflict of interest, especially by using low down-payment, long-maturity loans. As one example, to help fund their expanding real estate business, two Florida banker-developers succeeded through political connections in getting bank regulators to create sixty-one new national and state banks in which they took a stake. Others gained charters by extending loans to regulators.[9]

In addition to bank loans, real estate bonds were a major source of building finance. Many were sold to the general public, some in denominations as low as a hundred dollars. Billions of dollars in bond funding were raised—for apartments, hotels, office buildings, and more. Unlike bank loans, institutions that sold these bonds did not have risk of loss if the underlying real estate didn't perform; they therefore embraced looser credit standards.

Much of this bond activity was unaffiliated with banks, but a number of banks sidestepped limitations on underwriting and trading in bonds by launching securities affiliates, which grew in number from 10 in 1922 to 114 by 1931.[10] On a per-capita basis, the U.S. housing boom of the 1920s was every bit as large the housing boom of the 2000s.

Overbuilding in commercial real estate, while smaller in dollars than housing, was still vast and more visible than overbuilding in houses. Between 1925 and 1931, office space increased by 92 percent in Manhat-

Table 1.1. U.S. Crisis Matrix: Portrait of the Great Depression

Billions of Dollars	1923	1928	1931	1923–1928 Change
GDP	$85.3	$97.0	$77.4	$11.7
Federal Debt	$22.4	$17.6	$16.8	$(4.8)
Private Debt	$116.4	$156.4	$148.6	$40.0
Business Debt	$62.6	$86.1	$83.5	$23.5
CRE (est.)	$12.1	$16.7	$18.8	$4.6
Utility (est.)	$12.2	$17.2	$18.3	$5.0
Household Debt	$53.8	$70.3	$65.1	$16.5
Mortgage	$27.3	$39.9	$42.1	$12.6
Memo: Broker Loans	$1.6	$6.4	$2.1	$4.8
Bank Suspensions	646	499	2,294	−147

As Percentage of GDP				1923–1928 Change
Federal Debt	26%	18%	22%	−8%
Private Debt	136%	161%	192%	25%
Business Debt	73%	89%	108%	15%
CRE (est.)	14%	17%	24%	3%
Utility (est.)	14%	18%	24%	3%
Household Debt	63%	72%	84%	9%
Mortgage	32%	41%	54%	9%
Memo: Broker Loans	2%	7%	3%	5%

In the five years leading to 1928, private debt grew by $40 billion or 34 percent, far greater than the GDP growth of $12 billion. Sectors with the greatest concentration of overlending were household mortgages, commercial real estate, utility debt, and broker loans. Together they comprised 68 percent of the increase during this period. Government debt actually declined.

tan, 96 percent in San Diego, 89 percent in Minneapolis, and 74 percent in Chicago.[11] In New York alone, approximately 235 new buildings were constructed in this critical period, almost all debt financed. As Daniel Okrent maintains—and as our data indicate—more "buildings taller than 70 meters were constructed in New York between 1922 and 1931 than in any other ten-year period before or since."[12] Historian Robert Fitch estimates that between 1921 and 1929, "developers had added 30 million square feet of office space to the Manhattan inventory—an amount and a rate of increase that approaches the eighties office expansion. . . . They kept increasing the flood of overcapacity."[13]

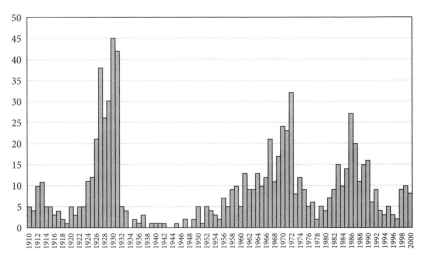

Figure 1.3. New York Skyscrapers (Taller than 70 Meters) Built, 1910–2000

The iconic structures of American skylines form the silhouette of the Great Depression: New York's Chrysler Building, Empire State Building, and RCA Building; Chicago's Merchandise Mart, Wrigley Building, and Tribune Tower; Philadelphia's PSFS Building; Los Angeles's City Hall; Dallas's Cotton Exchange Building; Detroit's Fischer Building; and Houston's Gulf Building. These are enduring architectural feats of the 1920s, vestiges of the real estate eruption that came before the fall. Many were speculative projects, unsupported by actual real estate demand; begun toward the end of the 1920s, when loans were still available; and finished after the crash, when lenders had little choice but to make funds available to complete construction or else see their entire loan go bad. None was financially successful for its original investors. They remained partly or largely empty for a decade or more after completion, as would hundreds of others.

Lenders were caught in the euphoria, too. Real estate was built when—and *because*—a loan was available to finance it, even in the absence of hard-nosed analysis of demand. The construction boom meant more job creation and employment, but since so much construction was based on the availability of financing rather than actual underlying need, more workers were hired than dictated by organic demand. Florida had a famous and fraud-riddled real estate surge that came to an ugly end in the hurricane of 1926, but its equivalent played out in any number of major U.S. cities, especially New York and Chicago.[14]

The lending boom of the 1920s also brought significant growth in business loans for the acquisition of utility companies by larger utility companies. These came to be known as "utility pyramids."

Ever since 1882, when Thomas Edison first lit the homes of Manhattan customers through his Pearl Street Power Station, U.S. utility companies had been racing frantically to capture market share. Edison's most important successor was his former personal secretary, Samuel Insull, who became one of the most powerful executives in the nation. Utilities were the hottest listed stocks—the era's go-go stocks. At the 1929 peak, utilities were 18 percent of the New York Stock Exchange's value, its largest single component. These stocks averaged prices fifty-seven times the earnings per share, with at least one more than ninety times the earnings per share, far above conventional levels, especially for such capital-intensive stocks.[15]

Insull became the powerful chairman of Chicago's Commonwealth Edison utility and was a master at building and buying utilities. The companies he controlled were collectively the largest supplier of power in the country. He built Commonwealth Edison into a company with $500 million in sales, using only $27 million in equity. His companies acquired a network of gas, light, power, and transit companies over thirty-two states, serving ten million people. In the late 1920s, he sought to further consolidate control of these companies using more debt, with the stock of these subsidiaries as collateral.[16]

Across the industry, these highly leveraged utilities were ripe for investment speculation. "Holding company" ownership was increasingly popular: a shell company would buy operating utility companies, often with debt at both levels, sometimes referred to as "double leverage." This was an ominous trend, given lofty stock valuations. Actually, there were holding companies that owned holding companies, creating a third layer of debt. In such a three-story house of cards, if 40 percent leverage were employed at each level, the ultimate owner could control a million-dollar company with only a $64,000 investment. This meant greater upside opportunity and greater downside risk. Acquisition debt was often more than 60 percent and, in some cases, more than 90 percent of the purchase price. This holding company activity was sufficiently widespread to attract a Federal Trade Commission investigation in 1928.[17]

Merger and acquisition activity across the entire private sector reached an all-time high in 1928 and 1929, largely financed with debt and surpassing the 1890s levels that had inspired early 1900s antitrust enforcement. Insull's biographer says of the era's lenders:

> During the expansionist fever of the late twenties, [bankers] began throwing money at everyone who seemed prosperous; . . . At a party, the new president of the Continental Bank sidled up to [Insull's son] and . . . said, "Say, I want you to know that if you fellows ever want to borrow more than the legal limit, all you have to do is organize a new corporation, and we'll be happy to lend you another $21,000,000." . . . Insull's bookkeeper said, "The bankers would call us up . . . [and ask] isn't there something you could use maybe $10,000,000 for?" . . . This situation had the impact of three stiff drinks on an empty stomach.[18]

This passage could just as easily have been applied to the era's real estate lenders.

Hubris and a sense of invincibility among lenders typically run rampant in the years before a financial crisis. In the 1920s, the short-term boost to economic growth was so sweeping that then-presidential nominee Herbert Hoover boasted in 1928 that Americans were "nearer to the final triumph of poverty than ever before in the history of any" country; "the poor-house," he claimed "is vanishing from among us."[19] Automobile executive Myron Forbes said, "There will be no interruption of our permanent prosperity," and famed Yale economist Irving Fisher submitted that "stock prices have reached what looks like a permanently high plateau."[20]

In the legendary stock market spike during the first nine months of 1929, utilities gained 48 percent; industrials, 20 percent; and railroads, 19 percent. The Roaring Twenties had ushered in so much financial gain and optimism that Americans learned to buy stock on margin, and broker loans quadrupled from $1.6 billion in 1923 to $6.4 billion in 1928. These debt-fueled stock purchases helped power the Dow Jones Industrial Average from 94 in 1923 to 362 in 1929.

Broker loans are made to brokers to fund margin accounts for their clients. A significant amount of the stocks purchased by broker customers during the good times were bought with margin loans of 90 percent, meaning that a customer could buy $1,000 of stock with only $100, and owe the remaining $900. However, if that stock went down to $800, the customer would

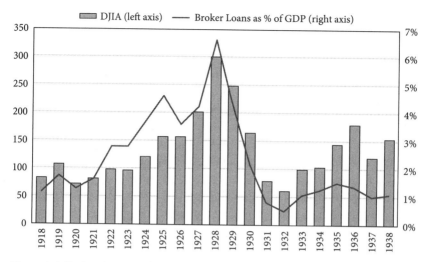

Figure 1.4. Broker Loans and the Dow Jones Industrial Average (DJIA), 1918–1938

immediately have to pay another $180 to get the loan back to 90 percent of the now-diminished value of the stock: this is referred to as a margin call. If, however, that customer did not have that amount of cash—and many did not in those speculative times—the stockbroker would have to sell the entire position since no fraction of that $800 could be sold to reduce the loan to less than the current value of the stock. The math is ruthless, as the world would soon realize.

Margin loans exploded to 5 percent of total stock market value compared with 2 percent in the 2000s. Note in Figure 1.4 that when margin loans went up, so did stocks. Unfortunately, the converse is also true. Congress enacted a regulation to limit margin lending to 50 percent of a stock's value in the aftermath of the Depression.

The key period for overall private debt growth ran from 1923 to 1928, when total private loans skyrocketed by $40 billion—from $116 billion, or 137 percent of GDP, to $156 billion, or 161 percent of GDP—all in a $90 billion economy. U.S. government debt actually declined from $22 billion to $18 billion as the robustness led to temporarily high earnings and higher tax payments. The majority of this $40 billion increase came from just four categories: $13 billion in residential mortgages, an estimated $5 billion in commercial real estate debt, an estimated $5 billion in utility debt, and $5 billion in broker loans.

Households borrowed for a lot more than housing. They borrowed for cars, appliances, land, and farms. The 1920s inaugurated an era of consumer installment debt, especially for automobiles such as the popular Model T, which were beginning to surpass trains as the preferred form of transportation.[21] But even though some commentators have attributed much importance to them in this era, installment loans were still a very small part of the total debt picture, reaching only $2.9 billion.[22] This figure included $1.4 billion in car loans. Overall, nonmortgage consumer debt was flat as a percentage of GDP during the 1920s and declined rapidly after 1932.

Images of failed farmers in the 1930s Dust Bowl are indelibly part of the story of our Great Depression, but farm mortgage debt was not a part of the 1920s credit boom. It actually declined during the decade. But that masked another runaway lending story: farm mortgages had tripled to $10 billion between 1910 and 1920, a greater percentage increase than in any other sector. Farmers had been emboldened by rising agricultural commodity prices in that era, especially during global shortages caused by World War I. Eastern investors, inexperienced in farming, drove farm lending, often purchasing vast swaths of prairie sight unseen. They plowed under millions of acres of native prairie grass and planted corn, soybeans, and mostly wheat, and enjoyed several years of bumper crops. These debt-financed land purchases caused agricultural land prices to rise, as ever. However, after 1919, agricultural commodity prices plunged with restored, postwar European farm production, and the now heavily indebted U.S. farmers wrestled through the 1920s in a trap of high residual debt and low prices.

After the 1929 crash, both farm mortgage totals and agriculture commodity prices collapsed as loans were called, and the farm industry was decimated. The initial impact on GDP was less than from the real estate sector because agriculture made up less than 10 percent of the economy; however, it provided 25 percent of all U.S. employment, and farm unemployment heavily affected overall unemployment numbers. As for the newer farms, absentee investors withdrew, leaving them unplanted. Without native grass, and now without a crop (and before the Civilian Conservation Corps' contouring program), these lands contributed significantly to the Dust Bowl of the 1930s, one of America's worst ecological calamities.

Behind every financial crisis sit bankers and nonbank lenders who made a lot of bad loans. Banks, savings-and-loan associations, life insurance companies, bond houses, and other institutions competed vigorously for new loans, and a colorful array of lending executives grabbed the financial headlines. Prominent among them were S. W. Straus, inventor of the mortgage real estate bond business, and Charles E. ("Sunshine Charley") Mitchell, chairman of National City Bank (now Citibank). Straus moralized against America's wastefulness and overindulgence, even as his bond house dominated its peers when it came to financing new real estate–backed bonds that used lowered lending standards.[23] Mitchell's real estate lenders were among the most aggressive in the banking industry, searching high and low for new opportunities to lend and using generous credit standards. His salesmen buttressed the enterprise by selling millions of shares in his bank, shares that plunged in 1929.[24]

Because lending growth was so extraordinary, banks led the way in the bull market of the 1920s and, though largely over the counter, had an even higher sector market capitalization than utility stocks. The Bank of New York and National City Bank were each worth more than $1 billion and stood among the top ten stocks in the country by market cap—greater than Chrysler, Standard Oil of New York, and Sears.

Lenders relaxed their credit standards, and the more people who qualified for home loans, the higher the ratio of buyers to sellers and the higher home prices went. Rapid lending growth in the 1920s directly affected housing prices. In the mid-1920s, housing prices in Manhattan rose 32 percent.[25] The 1920s was easily one of the greatest real estate booms in American history. Between 1923 and 1929, sale price per square foot for office buildings in Manhattan increased by a sizzling 70 percent. For a while, it was all a jubilant self-fulfilling prophecy.[26]

Construction peaked in 1926 but remained strong through 1928. As early as 1925, however, signs of overbuilding were clear. At their 1926 convention, the president of the National Convention of Building Owners and Managers expressed concern about overproduction, denouncing speculative builders for borrowing "the full cost of construction, regardless of return," and selling the buildings "at a profit" before moving on to erect additional structures.[27]

Until the Federal Reserve raised rates in 1928, two years after the construction peak, it was not acting to curb loan growth. If anything, Anna J. Schwartz states, "The Fed may also have induced more risk taking by providing banks near the brink of failure with loans from the discount window, contravening the rule that a central bank should lend only to illiquid, not insolvent, banks. In

1925, the Federal Reserve estimated that 80% of the 259 national banks that had failed since 1920 were 'habitual borrowers.' These banks were provided with long-term credit. A survey in August 1925 found that 593 member banks had been borrowing for a year or more and 293 had been borrowing since 1920."[28]

With this, banks were both encouraged to lend more *and* to be less than diligent when it came to building their own independent deposit and funding sources. Overbuilding was so pronounced that a correction was inevitable, and overbuilding impairs the success of all projects, even the earliest, originally sound ones.

There was an abundance of fraud in this era, too—advertising worthless land as wonderful, pumping and dumping stocks, committing insider trading, and selling stock in fraudulent companies. Such names as Ivar Kreuger and Charles Ponzi led the way with fraudulent investments and illicit sales.[29] Fraud is an element in many financial crises but not the cause. In the 1920s it was a symptomatic sideshow—rampant because it was harder to detect in the madness and because so many people were easy targets owing to their greed and fear of missing out on the easy wealth they saw around them.

Figure 1.5 provides a sense of the relative size of certain key spending and balance amounts during this lending period. Nominal GDP grew a strong $12 billion in this five-year period, after growing a mere $3 billion in the previous, troubled four-year period. But private debt grew by a staggering $40 billion, including $9 billion of growth in bank loans.

Notice how lopsided those figures are. Private debt does not normally outgrow GDP by this large an amount. It's direct evidence that too many of these loans were not yielding proper economic returns and that they were bad loans that would not get fully repaid. Economists refer to this relationship as the credit intensity ratio, and when private debt growth exceeds GDP by this wide a margin, it's usually a very bad sign.

Bank deposits and broad money, which are close to the same thing, were both growing rapidly. Since loans are one of the key means for creating an increase in deposits (when you get a loan, the bank puts the proceeds into your deposit account), in this case it is reasonable to assume that most of that deposit increase is a function of the loan increase.

Growth in net exports was a minor factor in this period, as was the growth in the holdings of gold. The total gold in the United States during this period was about $3 billion to $4 billion, in an economy with a $90 billion GDP— and $160 billion in loans. The changes in the total U.S. gold stock during

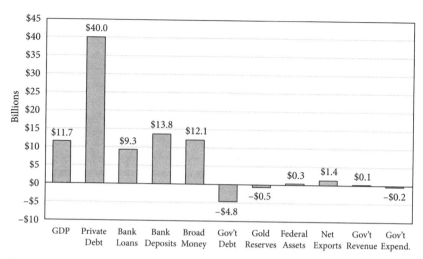

Figure 1.5. Change in Key National Financial Indicators, 1923–1928

this period were only a few hundred million dollars in any year, an amount dwarfed by the changes in private debt. Gold holdings by the Treasury and the Fed barely budged—while private loans, again, grew by $40 billion.

In the same period, government debt declined.

Figure 1.5 vividly illustrates the driver of financial crisis: runaway lending. As noted earlier, in a larger economy, a rough guideline is that when a private debt–to–GDP ratio grows by 15 to 20 percentage points in a five-year window, especially when it reaches or exceeds an overall ratio of roughly 150 percent to GDP, a financial crisis is likely. In the United States, by 1928, both of these thresholds had been met, and the proverbial horse was out of the barn.

As in the other crises examined in this book, *overlending was the necessary and sufficient explanation* for the boom and bust of the 1920s and 1930s.

On to phase two. By the late 1920s, sky-high real estate values had started to fall—in the same way that housing values started to decline in 2006 well in advance of the 2008 crisis. Then, in October of 1929, the stock market collapsed, with stocks eventually dropping by more than 80 percent. The unprecedented reliance on margin debt ensured that the correction was sharp. From the end of September to the end of November, the value of utilities dropped 55 percent; industrials, 48 percent; and railroads, 32 percent. Without private debt and leverage, stocks would not have scaled these heights, and the downside in the fall of 1929 would have been far lower.

A financial crisis often takes time to unfold and is often staggered over a period of several years. The Great Depression didn't begin suddenly on October 29, 1929, when the market crashed. Overall construction activity had started to slow in 1927, and the decline had accelerated in 1929; steel production and automobile sales slowed in 1928; stocks crashed in 1929; and widespread bank failures did not begin until 1931. In December 1929, two months after the crash, industry titan and then U.S. Treasury secretary Andrew Mellon intoned, "I see nothing in the present situation that is either menacing or warrants pessimism. . . . I have every confidence that there will be a revival of activity in the spring."[30]

From 1929 and 1933, GDP contracted by an astonishing $48 billion, from $105 billion to $57 billion. The easiest way to think about GDP is as total spending for final goods and services in an economy. Economists express it as consumption plus investment plus government spending (plus net exports)—or C+I+G. That simply means that consumers and businesses and the government were collectively spending $105 billion in 1929 but only spending $57 billion in 1933. Large GDP drops of varying magnitudes had occurred in the nineteenth century, but nothing remotely comparable has happened to a developed economy since then, which makes it hard for us even to imagine. It would be as if U.S. GDP collapsed from $14.7 trillion to $7.3 trillion in 2009. Instead, U.S. GDP declined only by $300 billion, to $14.4 trillion. There is simply no comparison. Even adjusting for inflation, the differences are profound. But note that adjusting for inflation itself can be misleading because even though prices dropped, the amount of debt owed did not and debtholders had to pay for this high debt with now-diminished incomes.

Figure 1.6 gives a sense of the relative size of declines in certain key spending and balance amounts during this period.

Spending collapsed. Bank runs—customers withdrawing their deposits en masse—depleted those banks, forcing them to call loans, and that would contribute significantly to the spending collapse. Lending and GDP were inviolably lashed together in the boom time—the former feeding the latter—and they were just as inviolably joined in the contraction and decline.

Banks are notorious for having bad loans on their books they either aren't aware of or are slow to acknowledge and disclose, and this was true in the late 1920s. In fact, banks can readily defer the recognition of a given loan

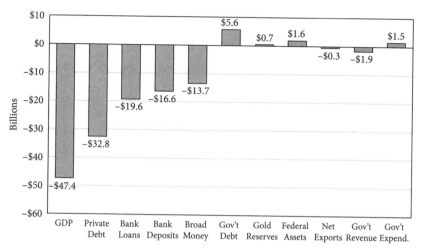

Figure 1.6. Change in Key National Financial Indicators, 1929–1933

problem by a year or two simply by being slow to revise forecast assumptions or deferring reviews—not to mention modifying payment terms. Banks reported little in the way of credit quality problems, even when billions in problem loans already lurked on their books. As in most crises, these credit problems were recognized only well after the point of gross overcapacity had been reached.

Since by 1928 total loans had skyrocketed by 34 percent in just five years, it is reasonable to estimate, based both on analysis of this period and comparison to other crises, that 15 percent to 20 percent of this loan growth, or $6 billion to $8 billion, was composed of problem loans, a large portion of which eventually became losses. That ratio of losses to new loans in an era of rampant loan growth is not unusual. Banks alone, which were responsible for about 25 percent of all private lending during this period, charged off $3.1 billion over the next several years on a capital base of $8 billion. ("Charging off" meant writing the loan off as a loss on the books of the bank.) Real estate bonds issued between 1920 and 1930 totaled $3.9 billion, and 80 percent of them were failing to meet their contracts in 1936—which likely meant that roughly another $2 billion in losses were already present. Other types of lending institutions had losses as well.

That alone explains the failure of thousands of banks and other financial institutions across the country. When bad debt grows to a size that it approaches the total net worth of the lending institutions, a financial crisis is likely.

When losses exceed 2 percent of loans in a commercial bank, it is of significant concern. By 1934, losses had reached 3.5 percent of loans, and cumulatively from 1930 to 1937, losses exceeded 13 percent of loans. More than nine thousand banks failed between 1930 and 1933, equal to some 30 percent of all banks extant at the end of 1929. In just a hundred days after the banking panic of 1930, more than eight hundred banks closed their doors. At the landmark moment when New York's Bank of the United States failed in early 1931, other bank failures began to snowball.[31]

Home prices plummeted, and residential mortgage foreclosures reached a thousand per day in 1933. Building-and-loan associations had funded the largest portion of mortgage growth in the 1920s and had increased in number from some 8,000 in 1919 to 13,000 at the 1927 peak, but they declined by more than 5,000 by 1933 as associations were frozen or closed. Henry Hoaglund of the newly formed Federal Home Loan Bank Board summarized the mortgage lending problem nicely in 1935: "A tremendous surge of residential building in the [last] decade . . . was matched by an ever-increasing supply of homes sold on easy terms. The easy terms plan has a catch. . . . Only a small decline in prices was necessary to wipe out this equity."[32]

A popular misconception was that all banks were equally vulnerable to runs and failure. But the banks that failed were those with the highest concentrations of mortgages and other real estate loans. One problem with these mortgages was their lack of liquidity, but the more fundamental problem was credit risk. In practice it is difficult to separate the two. Nonetheless, the facts are stark. For banks, the higher the concentration of real estate loans, the faster the failure; those with the lowest concentrations of real estate loans were most likely to survive.[33]

Banks and other lenders had funded the expansion. Bad loans were made, and for many banks the total of these bad loans was so large that it approached or exceeded their capital. Rumors started about certain banks, many well-founded stories of troubled borrowers and bad lending practices. Millions of dollars of deposits fled as customers made runs on these banks, lining up outside to withdraw their precious deposits one by one.

It is important to understand those runs on banks, and why those runs led banks to call loans—in other words request early repayment—and how banks calling loans was one of the key causes of the collapse of GDP.

As customers made runs on banks by withdrawing deposits, banks could have survived by getting additional funding from the Federal Reserve or other institutions to cover the shortfall, or by selling stock to raise new funds. But for the most part, the Federal Reserve, other banks, clearinghouses, and other institutions were not willing to lend those banks funds to solve their liquidity problem because they had so much bad debt. And there was not enough time or investor confidence to raise funds by selling new shares of stock.

So those troubled banks resorted to trying to sell loans to other banks to raise cash. But for most banks, there were no buyers for these loans. The loans were illiquid, and there was no well-developed secondary market of potential loan buyers. But even if there had been, these loans would have been sold at such massive discounts that would have left those institutions inadequately capitalized and subject to regulatory closure for the simple reason that the loans were often deeply troubled. The desperate need to sell loans is symptomatic of bank management that did not put in place other forms of funding and liquidity that could have tided that institution over in times of duress. Lack of secondary markets in which to sell loans does not cause financial crisis, it exposes a bank's lack of preparedness for adversity. Most banks and other lenders kept only the thinnest layer of extra liquidity that provided little help in these times. Banks and other lenders, in the 1920s and today, largely neglect this pivotal safeguard.

So troubled banks usually found they had only one option left. They needed to call the loans of their remaining solvent customers, or loans where they could sell the collateral. This is what they did on a massive scale, as their only and last-ditch effort to stay afloat. The evidence of this is that loan paydowns, the amount of loan payments in excess of new loan advances, totaled $33 billion in this period, $20 billion in banks alone, all in an economy that was only $92 billion in 1930. This paydown was accompanied by vast asset sales, forcing down prices. It was a catastrophe. While the calling of loans, the dreaded specter haunting the 1930s, was not the only reason loans declined, it was a forcefully central one.

Quite simply, the contraction of loans and other debt—forced and unforced—was the single most impactful event of this period. It contributed more than anything else to the collapse in spending. It impaired thousands of good businesses, radically curtailing their spending and investment—and thus GDP. For example, otherwise healthy retailers whose inventory loans were reduced by half since their bank was forced to call loans, ended up with their sales reduced by as much as half as a direct consequence. With smaller inventory loans they were forced to carry less inventory, which meant lower sales. Otherwise healthy retailers whose inventory loans were called in full were usually forced to close. It also forced the sale of thousands of homes and other assets, bringing fear to those households and radically changing their spending behavior. And it brought fear even to those who did not have to pay down a loan, causing many to hoard what cash they did have. This view is in essence the invaluable debt deflation theory of Irving Fisher.[34]

For households, many mortgage loans were only five years in maturity in this era, and banks would not renew those loans as they came due, where they had previously renewed them routinely. If the mortgages of otherwise creditworthy borrowers were not renewed, that borrower was damaged. As in most financial crises, thousands upon thousands of inculpable citizens and businesses got hurt along with the offenders.

The calling of loans caused businesses and households to use funds for loan paydown rather than spending, which took a chunk out of GDP. Calling loans affected spending directly because if a person spent $10,000 of income on paying down debt instead of on goods and services, then spending (and thus GDP) was reduced by $10,000. And if businesses and households collectively paid down debt out of earnings by $100 million in a given year, then GDP would have been reduced by up to $100 million. (The other option was for those businesses and individuals to elect to sell assets—often distressed selling—or take money out of their savings to pay down the loans instead.)

The widespread contraction of loans on this scale in a crisis—a decline from $161 billion to $128 billion (a portion of the decline was a result of "charged-off" loans)—is inconceivable today, yet this loan contraction, or curtailment, and the consequent damage had been routine in the nineteenth and early twentieth centuries. Bank loans in that era had shorter maturities, and it was an obvious and expedient way to get cash to meet withdrawals— though it invariably exacerbated the crisis. In the 2008 crisis, because the U.S. government and the Federal Reserve acted in a very different way by providing banks with liquidity, there would be only 5.5 percent net loan paydown at year's end versus 24 percent in the Depression. The impact on GDP would therefore be far less, only a 2 percent decline in the Great Recession versus a 46 percent decline in the Depression.

It goes without saying that these banks were in no position to make new loans, and this further starved the economy. The money supply fell dramatically, as has been widely reported. But the money supply is largely the sum of deposits and currency, which fell because of the runs and loan paydown.

The Fed could have intervened to reverse this but did not. So the decline in the money supply was a result and not a cause. Given that called loans and forced paydowns were part of the massive GDP contraction from 1929 to 1933, the bank runs that caused them were a vital part of the story.

Even though banks called loans, it wasn't enough for many of them. The bank runs still caused thousands of banks to fail. As a general matter, banks failed not because of a lack of capital or earnings, as popularly believed, but because of a lack of "liquidity"—deposits or any other funding source—that resulted from these runs. Banks normally can pay salaries and other expenses out of the cash provided by earnings, but absent earnings (or newly raised capital), a bank can still pay salaries and other expenses out of new customer deposits—if a regulator is not present to prevent this. It's an important, dimly understood, and somewhat frightening truth about banks. As long as a bank can raise new deposits, it can continue to operate. However, if a bank is losing money because of bad loans and the rapid withdrawal of existing deposits, and can garner no new deposits, then it has no source of money for its expenses and can no longer operate.

The Federal Reserve and other government entities could have acted decisively to supply liquidity to the banks in the crucial period from 1929 to 1933 but did not. Though the Fed was very small in comparison to the private lending market, with only $5 billion in assets as compared with a private debt market of $160 billion, the Fed, backed by the government, had ample capacity to help. If it had, the extensive loan calling might have been averted. It did not act partly because of the widespread belief that banks deserved their fate. Americans were outraged at businesses, banks, and the government for the disaster, and some felt that calling the loans of borrowers and letting banks fail was a natural and appropriate consequence for their profligacy, which would "purge the rottenness out of the system." President Hoover later attributed that very quote and attitude, perhaps unfairly, to his Treasury secretary Andrew Mellon. At the very least, many banks had little forbearance for their customers, and the government had little forbearance for those banks.

Fear itself may well have been a large cause of the collapse in spending. Depositors who withdrew their funds from a bank in a panic were motivated to spend less, which also contributed to GDP contraction. Depositors taking these funds out in the form of cash or currency would often simply put as much as they could "under the mattress" and thus out of economic circulation.

A word on rates: After a brief and ill-judged 2 percent increase in interest rates in 1929 (well after overcapacity had been created), interest rates declined, easing pressure on borrowers. Even though they declined, the Fed's gold reserves actually grew slightly, and specie at banks only declined slightly—both in amounts minuscule compared with massive changes in loan and deposits. This cumulative 2 percent interest rate increase may well have added to the woes, but it was not decisive by itself. Interest rates have often increased by 2 percent without causing a stock market crash. Increasing interest rates certainly adversely affected borrowers in the period after the overbuilding occurred, but lower interest rates, even dramatically lower interest rates, would have perhaps softened but not prevented the economic collapse. If a building is empty, the loan is going to go bad no matter the interest rate.

Other factors have also been cited as causes of the GDP collapse. For example, much has been made of the Smoot-Hawley Tariff Act, signed June 17, 1930, with the goal of restricting imports and preserving American jobs. Today, compared with other countries, trade is a small part of the U.S. economy with gross exports at 12 percent of GDP, and it was a much smaller part in the 1920s and 1930s, with gross exports at around 3 percent to 6 percent of GDP. Exports and imports were both only about $4 billion to $5 billion annually during the late 1920s, and while both did decline to $2 billion for a short span, it was an amount inadequate to explain the overall GDP drop. Net exports, which is the way trade is entered into the computation of aggregate demand and thus the measure of the impact on GDP, declined less than $1 billion. Smoot-Hawley may not have helped, but it was a minor factor.

Others point to an effective moratorium on international debtor repayments to the United States as a cause. Two billion dollars' worth of German loans payable to U.S. banks were at risk, primarily because of Germany's reduced ability to obtain enough dollars through trade and in an increasingly bellicose international scene. This hampered liquidity and threatened the capital of certain banks but again was small in the context of the $160 billion of overall U.S. private-sector loans.

The agricultural sector has been blamed as well and did suffer mightily in the period, including a significant volume of called mortgages. But in the late 1920s, the agricultural sector was less than 10 percent of GDP, so even a large agricultural calamity could only have affected overall GDP by a proportionate amount.

Bad loans were at the heart of the Great Depression story. By 1930, since so much real estate sat empty, construction across the country slowed dra-

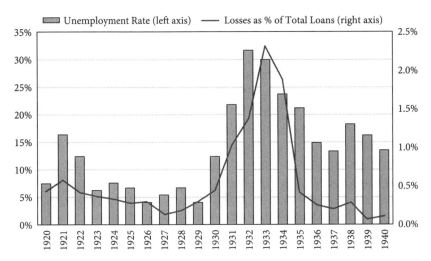

Figure 1.7. United States: Unemployment Rate and Loan Losses as Percentage of Total Loans, 1920–1940

matically. Construction had become such a huge part of the economy, estimated at over 20 percent of GDP, that the resulting layoffs in the construction industry infected other sectors, eventually driving the nation's unemployment rate, which had been near 4 percent in the 1920s, to the tragic levels of 12 percent by the end of 1930 and 32 percent by 1932 (Figure 1.7).

On paper, President Hoover was amply qualified to lead the recovery phase. He had been a star in business and government when he assumed the presidency in 1929, just months before the stock market crash. A globe-trotting titan in the mining industry, he had had two highly lauded government turns, first fighting Europe's famine after World War I and then helping victims of the Great Mississippi Flood of 1927. He had seen economic depression first-hand in the post–World War I depression and had been secretary of commerce under Presidents Harding and Coolidge. Though faulted by some for his arrogance and publicity seeking, he was a man of action, experientially suited for crisis.

Through Hoover's leadership, the U.S. government stepped up its spending from $3 billion to $4.5 billion—almost half as much as the increase under President Franklin Roosevelt. More spending could have increased GDP, but the thought of raising spending from $3 billion to $30 billion to compensate for the entire GDP shortfall was beyond the scope of anyone's imagination, ability, or political creed at that time. By 1936, under Roosevelt, government spending would increase to $8 billion. But the spending shortfall from pre-Depression levels dwarfed even this amount. The amounts were simply much smaller than the problem. Ultimately, it would take World War II for government spending to approach the levels required to fully restore GDP to pre-Depression levels and then some.

Some of the programs Hoover initiated foreshadowed Roosevelt's efforts. Hoover tried to prop up wages, bring more protections to unions, lend funds to banks and corporations, provide unemployment relief, aid farmers, and expand public works. Two initiatives under Hoover are now widely panned as harmful: the restriction of international trade under Smoot-Hawley, discussed earlier, and the increase in taxes in the Revenue Act of 1932. Both had an adverse impact on spending at a time when more spending was the very thing the economy desperately needed—although the amounts involved in both of these erroneous policies were very small, once again, compared with the lending issue.

However, whatever else he did, Hoover did *not* do the single most important thing needed. His administration did not enact policies and programs to stop bank runs or slow the instances of bankers calling loans and not renewing maturing loans. In other words, he did not stop the precipitous decline in loans. And so GDP continued its precipitous decline as well. Under Hoover, the Fed, wed to the constraints of the gold standard, did not act as lender of last resort or help offset the decline in lending (and money supply).

By 1933, when Roosevelt took office to great fanfare, unemployment was 30 percent, and office vacancy rates were in excess of 30 percent. His administration put in place a number of job-creation and spending programs similar to Hoover's, only larger: the Works Progress Administration (WPA), the Tennessee Valley Authority (TVA), the Public Works Administration (PWA), the Civil Works Administration (CWA), and the Civilian Conservation Corp (CCC). It supported increased lending activity through the Federal Housing Administration (FHA) and the Home Owners' Loan Corporation (HOLC), and it put in place a safety net in the form of Social Security, to name just some of his administration's key programs. Roosevelt took spending from the $4.5 billion level of the Hoover administration to as much as $7 billion to $8 billion a year. It was an amount still far short of what would have been needed to restore GDP to its pre-crisis levels—but it was something. Roosevelt's programs meaningfully provided opportunity, restored hope, and saved lives,

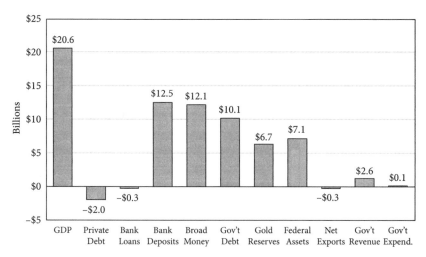

Figure 1.8. Change in Key National Financial Indicators 1934–1938

even if they did set a precedent for government spending and fiscal stimulus that conservatives still decry today.

As FDR took office, a quarter of the nation's mortgage loans were in default, resulting in foreclosures by which nearly 25 percent of America's homeowners lost their homes.[35] To counter this, the FHA was founded in 1934 to provide insurance for mortgages that conformed to certain standards, and Fannie Mae (the Federal National Mortgage Association) was established in 1938, with the purpose of providing local banks with federal money for home mortgages.

But by far the most important thing Roosevelt did through his policies and actions was to stop loans from further contraction. As a result, in the third phase of the crisis, from 1934 to 1938, GDP grew by $21 billion. Figure 1.8 illustrates this and provides a sense of the relative size of certain key spending and balance amounts during this period.

Roosevelt stopped loan contraction with his monumental April 1933 decision to discontinue private ownership of gold. Many have characterized this as Roosevelt "taking the United States off the gold standard," but what he did was somewhat different. His Executive Order 6102 prohibited "the hoarding of gold coin, gold bullion, and gold certificates within the continental United States by individuals, partnerships, associations, and corporations."

Roosevelt's order required that on or before May 1, 1933, all persons de-
liver to a Federal Reserve Bank or member bank all their gold coin, gold bullion, and gold certificates (those more than a hundred dollars per person)
except as may be required for industry. The Federal Reserve would pay $20.67
per ounce in coin or currency. "Two months later, a joint resolution of Congress abrogated the gold clauses in many public and private obligations that
required the debtor to repay the creditor in gold dollars of the same weight
and fineness as those borrowed."[36]

This immediately and dramatically reversed the outflow of the previous
three years. Instead of people withdrawing deposits from banks or using currency to buy and hoard gold, they were required to deposit all their gold.
With this, the contraction of deposits ended—which in turn brought an
end to the contraction of loans, just as changes in gold policy in Germany
and Britain two years earlier had brought an end to the contraction of loans
in those two countries.

The executive order immediately brought hundreds of millions of dollars
of deposits back into the banking system as Americans compliantly deposited their gold, reversing the outflow and contraction that had begun in earnest in 1930. In 1934, in a bold act of fiat, the United States increased the
price of gold from twenty to thirty-five dollars per ounce, which immediately revalued gold upward by billions of dollars—directly increasing the
money supply.[37] (This was a devaluation of the dollar.) In the years following
the increase in price to thirty-five dollars, billions of dollars of additional
gold and accompanying deposits flooded into the system. The contraction
problem had been solved.

In 1932, gold and gold certificates at the Fed had been $3.1 billion ($4.2
billion, if we include all gold held by the Treasury and private citizens). The
revaluation alone took that amount to more than $5 billion, and by 1938 the
total was $11.8 billion ($14.5 billion for the country as a whole). Bank deposits at the Fed, by definition, tracked that closely, increasing from $2.5 billion
in 1932 to $8.7 billion in 1938. Much of that gold came from overseas, pulled
by the favorable price and pushed by the gathering storms of war. The result
was a large amount of new deposits in the United States, some of which would
inevitably be spent here. The largest portion of the world's gold was now in
the United States.

In contemporary banking, the Federal Reserve injects money into the system by buying government securities from banks. In the 1930s, its approach
was different. The Fed increased deposits and thus the money supply by man-

dating that gold out in the economy be deposited to banks and then the Fed, and then it sweetened the equation with a substantially higher price.

Roosevelt also created the Federal Deposit Insurance Corporation (FDIC) in the Banking Act of 1933, and with it, deposit insurance. The government would now guarantee deposits even if a bank failed, which removed the rationale for individuals to withdraw their money from banks. It should be noted, however, that other major countries, such as Britain, France, and Germany, did not enact deposit insurance, and their recoveries did not suffer in comparison. In those countries, the change in gold policy alone was sufficient to reverse the contraction of deposits. (See the relevant month-by-month figures in the Crisis Recovery Worksheet at www.bankingcrisis.org.)

The contraction was stopped, so the recovery could begin. But that did not get banks (or any other private lender) to start growing loan portfolios again. There was simply too much overcapacity and therefore no need for loans. Once an economy is massively overbuilt, only time can bring enough new demand to absorb that overcapacity. By 1929, it was going to take years and even decades for the real estate overcapacity to be fully absorbed. And once lenders had made the ill-advised loans that resulted in overbuilding, it was going to take years to work out those bad loans—and it was going to take billions of Depression-era dollars to recapitalize the banking industry. The fact that bank loan contraction had damaged thousands upon thousands of good businesses made the climb out of the Depression that much harder.

Absent loan growth, the major boost to GDP was the continued increase in government deficit spending, reflected in the $10 billion increase in government debt during this time. Additional growth came as households took savings from "under the mattress" and into a less cautious spending pattern. Unemployment also gradually improved after FDR's arrival, stepping down to 13 percent in 1937 (until an ill-advised pullback in government spending and a tax increase dented the still-fragile recovery, and unemployment rocketed back to 18 percent). Nothing came easily. The Dust Bowl drought that struck farmers intermittently from 1934 to 1940 was just one of many challenges.

In the end, the increased economic activity surrounding World War II boosted the country all the way out of the Depression. This was not an unprecedented salve. The recovery from earlier U.S. depressions had been much aided by such things as the onset of war and its expenditures.

Unnoticed by many, the combination of the Great Depression and World War II also facilitated a great deleveraging in the private sector. The Great

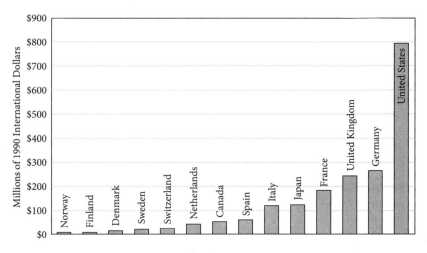

Figure 1.9. 1928 Gross Domestic Product by Country

Depression brought the ratio of private debt to GDP down from 175 percent in 1930 to 126 percent by 1940, then the war took it down again to a century-low level of 37 percent by 1945. We might call this fifteen-year period the Great Deleveraging. The path to achieve it had been brutal, but it ideally positioned the private sector for the high postwar growth that was indispensable for the federal government to deleverage. Resulting private debt levels were so low that a financial crisis was significantly less likely for several decades.

In smaller industrialized economies throughout the world, a similar plotline of leverage boom, bust, and recovery unfolded. From the standpoint of sheer size and impact, the history of the Great Depression outside of the United States is primarily the history of Germany, Britain, and France. The GDP of the United States was larger than the GDP of those three countries combined, and their GDP in turn was collectively larger than that of the rest of Europe combined. Of all the countries outside the United States, Germany was the worst economic offender, with its profligate lending creating a major expansion followed by a major GDP collapse.

Germany, after emerging from the hyperinflation of the early 1920s, saw runaway private lending growth, with aggregate bank loans alone more than *tripling* from 8 percent to 31 percent of GDP in the 1920s (data on bond and other nonbank debt are not available). France had a strong expansion too, with GDP growth averaging 14 percent from 1923 to 1928, and bank loans doubling from 15 percent to 27 percent of GDP; its heady times were called

Table 1.2. Germany Crisis Matrix: 1920s and 1930s

Billions of Deutschmarks	1925	1930	1932	1925–1930 Change
GDP	65.26	75.08	50.91	9.82
Public Debt	n/a	21.77	21.89	n/a
Private Debt	*	*	*	*
Bank Loans	5.37	28.46	27.59	23.09
Mortgages	1.78	15.41	15.92	13.63
As Percentage of GDP				1925–1930 Change
Public Debt	n/a	29%	43%	n/a
Private Debt	n/a	n/a	n/a	n/a
Bank Loans	8%	38%	54%	30%
Mortgages	3%	21%	31%	18%

*Limited data points.

From 1925 to 1930, Germany's bank loans increased over fivefold, and mortgages increased almost ninefold.

années folles, or the crazy years. Britain did not enjoy the fully robust 1920s that its industrial neighbors did, in large part because just as the good times began, Britain administered a self-inflicted wound. In 1925 Winston Churchill, whether owing to false national pride or misguided economic beliefs, put Britain back on the gold standard it had left during World War I. Its lending surge was offset by the contraction of the restored gold standard.

In the bust phase, Germany's GDP fell from 81 billion marks in 1929 to 51 billion in 1932, a drop of 37 percent in nominal terms, nearly as steep a drop as in the United States. The stock market fell by 45 percent. Unemployment rose to an astonishing 29 percent. This new economic calamity was the perfect platform for the great electoral gains of the Nazi party in 1932 and Hitler's appointment as chancellor in 1933. France's GDP dropped by a stunning 42 percent before beginning to recover. Having not climbed as high, Britain did not sink as low, although it did experience 15 percent unemployment.

For Japan, the 1920s were a turbulent decade, with recurring trouble, culminating with a GDP drop in 1927, and a bigger drop in 1930, both following an outsized expansion of lending in the mid-1920s. As in the United States, real estate, both residential and commercial, was the dominant sector that spun into a bubble, including the new urban housing developments that came alongside train stations and electrical plants, as well as heightened investment in rice paddies. This situation quickly evolved into speculation and land fever. During the 1920s, the price of *takuchi* (nonagricultural) land in Osaka "grew at annual rates of over 25 percent," rising to more than 30 percent in the late 1920s.[38] According to Takashi Nanjo, land prices had slumped to 74 percent by 1929.[39]

Private debt was a core cause of the Great Depression and, as the rest of this book will show, of most other major financial crises. Many economists have argued that a combination of several factors caused the Great Depression and other major financial crises. This is not an unreasonable suggestion. For example, the economic historian Charles Kindleberger noted no less than thirteen factors in the crash of 1873.[40] But long lists of reasons hint at explanatory scrambling and belie the fact that in every economic period, even in good times, there are always a number of adverse factors at work. Economists must also be able to make a plausible financial case for causality and the weighting of each item on the list.

And lists of many complex factors introduce causal obfuscation where there is causal elegance to be found: overlending is the necessary and sufficient explanation for a majority of financial crises, whether or not other possible causes are present. While the presence of a large net export position can help mitigate the problems brought by high private debt growth, no other factors—even in combination—yield the same close correlation and powerful result as private debt growth. Nor do they add to or change the power of models used to predict financial crises.

In some key respects, the Great Depression was similar to the 2008 crisis in the United States. In both crises, mortgages and other real estate lending soared as lenders lowered credit standards. In both, overbuilding peaked two to three years before the crisis, and by that point, bad loans associated with the overbuilding had already made widespread lender failures inevitable. And in both, most participants were blithely unaware of the problem until the stock market crash and property value collapse.

The critical difference between these two crises was the willingness of the government to intervene to save certain banks and other financial institutions from failure and thus save at least some of the innocent from calamity. This was a lesson from the Great Depression—that the government should act in a crisis to prevent banks from failing and thus prevent loans from contracting.

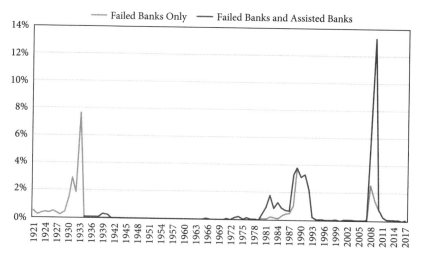

Figure 1.10. Deposits of Failed and Assisted Banks as a Percentage of Total Deposits

Figure 1.10 illustrates this. The number of bank failures in the Depression dwarfed those in the Great Recession. However, if we consider the total deposits of those institutions that were "assisted," or rescued, the bank distress in the Great Recession tops that of the Great Depression. With these rescues, the Fed essentially played its "lender (and investor) of last resort" role. Issues of fairness aside, if those institutions had not been rescued, the period after the Great Recession might have looked more like the 1930s.

With this Great Depression lesson in hand, Japan's crisis of the 1990s and the Global Crisis of 2008, which both had similar relative magnitudes of overbuilding and bad debt creation as the Great Depression, had much less severe aftermaths. This approach had the benefit of preventing the mass unemployment and the Hoovervilles of the Great Depression, but it would have left in place a giant overhang of private debt. In contrast, as terrible as it was, the United States emerged from the Great Depression with very low levels of private debt, which was an advantageous position from which to power renewed growth. Both Japan after its 1990s crisis and the United States after its Great Recession were still carrying very high loads of private debt that burdened their economies and dampened growth for a number of years.

Our next chapters will cover the great crises of the 1980s and 1990s in the United States, Japan, and beyond—the moment when the great global deleveraging that followed World War II turned into a great global releveraging.

CHAPTER 2

The Decade of Greed

The 1980s

Many remember the 1980s as a renaissance in the United States. Newly elected president Ronald Reagan and Federal Reserve chair Paul Volcker were credited with defeating the inflation of the 1970s. Real GDP growth averaged 3.3 percent. Unemployment declined to less than 6 percent, and the stock and bond market ended the decade up 228 percent and 253 percent, respectively.

Yet those memories belie stark realities of calamities and crises. The decade of the 1980s was one of the most economically turbulent and crisis laden in American history. Indeed, it was perhaps the most chaotic in terms of the number of sectors adversely affected. The results of the period led to more than two thousand bank failures, more than eight hundred savings-and-loan failures, the junk-bond crisis, the commercial real estate crisis, the Latin American debt crisis, and an energy-lending crisis triggered by an oil price collapse. There was even an agricultural lending crisis early in the decade. In each one of these, it was a rapid buildup in private debt that brought the overcapacity and crisis. This decade saw the largest wave of bank failures since the 1930s. And it saw the largest percentage one-day stock market drop in U.S. history, on October 19, 1987, a collapse parried only when the Federal Reserve flooded the market with unprecedented levels of liquidity.

Even the achievements of the 1980s should be put in context. The stock market ended up rising 228 percent, but that was less than the gains of the 1960s and 1990s. Real GDP growth was 3.3 percent, but growth in the 1960s, 1970s, and 1990s was just as high, if not higher. Unemployment improved but had been lower in the 1960s and early 1970s, and was again lower in the late 1990s.

Reflections on this period routinely miss what, economically speaking, was its most important characteristic: the 1980s saw an unprecedented ex-

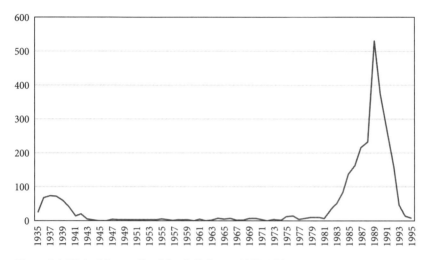

Figure 2.1. United States: Total Bank Failures, 1935–1995

plosion of both government and private debt. This was all the more notable in that it followed thirty years of a significantly improving ratio of federal debt to GDP and flat overall growth in *total* debt to GDP (Figure 2.2).

Indeed, the year 1981 may be the greatest economic dividing line of the post–World War II era, a watershed in U.S. economic history: it was the moment when the era of postwar deleveraging ended and the era of releveraging began—complete with a quickly ensuing financial crisis. This dividing line also marked the point at which, not coincidentally, U.S. rates ceased their long postwar rise and began their equally long decline.

The very low level of U.S. private sector debt in 1945—it was less than half the level in ratio to GDP seen earlier in the century—was a noteworthy exception in twentieth-century economic history. It was not just private debt that was low in the immediate postwar period. The United States had low levels in housing, commercial real estate, infrastructure, and any number of other things, a state of undercapacity made more acute by a population boom. This, coupled with the record low levels of private debt, were key reasons that the United States had no notable nationwide financial crisis from 1950 to 1980.

But, as measured by total debt to GDP, the United States started releveraging in 1981. In fact, in the brief period from 1983 to 1988, private debt to GDP expanded from 103 percent to 124 percent of GDP[1]—one of the largest such increases in the twentieth century. Mortgage loan growth

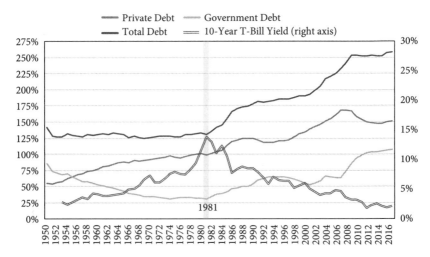

Figure 2.2. United States: Debt as a Percentage of GDP and Long-Term Interest Rates (10-Year T-Bill Yield), 1950–2017
Left axis scale for all but 10-year T-Bill.

was the biggest part of this, almost doubling from $1.1 trillion to $2.1 trillion.[2] Though the impact of this rising total on households was offset somewhat by declining rates (from a high of 18.45 percent in 1981 to 10 percent by 1987), it brought a sharp increase in delinquency and foreclosure rates, along with a pronounced spike in mortgage industry losses in the early 1990s. Commercial real estate loan growth was the next most pronounced, almost doubling from $551 billion to $1 trillion.[3]

The third biggest loan growth contributor was manufacturing, which also nearly doubled its leverage from $543 billion to $1.07 trillion.[4] This era of manufacturing debt growth left industry vulnerable to the imminent onslaught of global manufacturing competition. Junk bonds, the riskiest form of corporate debt, were a major subset of private debt, more than quintupling from $30 billion to $160 billion.[5] There were also large spikes in loans for oil and gas, for agriculture, and to Latin American countries, each of which led to a crisis within its respective sector.

Government debt, which had actually declined slightly as a percentage of GDP in the 1970s, from 34 percent to 31 percent, thundered ahead to 50 percent during the 1980s.[6] Throughout the century, most problematic debt expansions were either composed of private debt or public debt, but not both, and usually one offset the other. Not in the Reagan era. His tenure saw

Table 2.1. U.S. Crisis Matrix: 1980s and 1990s

Billions of Dollars	1983	1988	1990	1991	1983–1988 Change
GDP	$3,634	$5,236	$5,963	$6,158	$1,602
Real GDP (2012 dollars)	$7,118	$8,866	$9,366	$9,355	$1,749
Inflation	3.2%	4.1%	5.4%	4.2%	0.9%
Federal Debt	$1,377	$2,602	$3,233	$3,665	$1,225
Private Debt	$3,750	$6,483	$7,378	$7,495	$2,733
Business Debt	$1,996	$3,408	$3,776	$3,689	$1,412
Manufacturing Sector	$543	$1,077	$1,306	$1,193	$534
Wholesale/Retail Sector	$261	$486	$538	$529	$225
Memo: CRE	$551	$1,038	$1,105	$1,089	$487
Household Debt	$1,754	$3,075	$3,602	$3,806	$1,321
Mortgage	$1,116	$2,055	$2,489	$2,667	$939
Memo: Junk Bonds Outstanding	$27	$148	$181	$184	$121
Savings and Loans Failures	6	32	223	163	26
Commercial Bank Failures	44	200	158	105	156

As Percentage of GDP					1983–1988 Change
Federal Debt	38%	50%	54%	60%	12%
Private Debt	103%	124%	124%	122%	21%
Business Debt	55%	65%	63%	60%	10%
Manufacturing Sector	15%	21%	22%	19%	6%
Wholesale/Retail Sector	7%	9%	9%	9%	2%
Memo: CRE	15%	20%	19%	18%	5%
Household Debt	48%	59%	60%	62%	10%
Mortgage	31%	39%	42%	43%	9%
Memo: Junk Bonds Outstanding	1%	3%	3%	3%	2%

In the five years leading to 1988, U.S. private debt grew by 73 percent. Sectors with the greatest concentration of overlending were mortgage, manufacturing, and commercial real estate, which together comprised 72 percent of the increase.

much of both, simultaneously, as he led record government and military spending. It was stimulus on steroids.

At the end of the 1970s, America faced two major and causally related problems—high oil prices and high interest rates.

The United States had become deeply reliant on oil through decades of cheap and plentiful supply. But by the early 1970s, the preponderance of production had moved overseas and the little-noticed consequence of this had been to cede market and pricing control to the largest overseas producers.

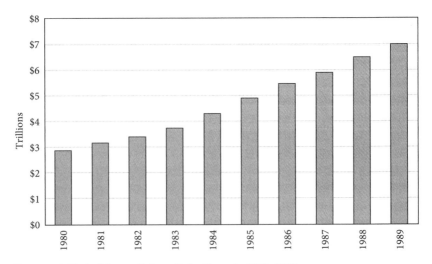

Figure 2.3. United States: Private Debt Growth, 1980–1989
Private debt more than doubled in the 1980s.

They had banded together as the Organization of Petroleum Exporting Countries (OPEC), which itself was modeled on the oil production consortium in early twentieth-century Texas.

Through OPEC's influence, oil prices began to increase dramatically starting in 1973, both to fill OPEC coffers and as a result of Middle East displeasure with the United States in disputes surrounding the 1973 Arab-Israeli War and the 1979 Iranian Revolution.[7] Under President Richard Nixon and then President Jimmy Carter, the United States had unsuccessfully tried to counteract these price increases with domestic price controls, which eventually led to domestic oil shortages and long lines of angry motorists at the gas pumps. So first under a chastened Carter and then under Reagan, domestic prices were deregulated, and soon domestic oil prices and profits rocketed to levels commensurate with those overseas. This resulted in a mad scramble to increase production within the United States as the 1980s began. U.S. exploration immediately exploded, attracting hundreds and then thousands to drill for more oil. The theory and hope, later forgotten, was that over time this increased production would increase supplies and bring down prices.

The high oil prices that came with the 1973 war and the 1979 revolution had been a core driver of the insidious inflation in the 1970s. With Paul Volcker's appointment as chair in 1979, the Federal Reserve resolved to stamp out this inflation with a dramatic increase in interest rates, pushing the Fed funds rate as high as 20 percent and both the ten-year Treasury bond and the three-month Treasury bill to 14 percent.[8]

These ultrahigh interest rates devastated the savings and loan (S&L) industry, the main provider of the nation's home loans. Most of the mortgages carried on the books of these S&Ls (also commonly called "thrifts") were at a fixed rate with a thirty-year term. Many of those loans had been at a rate of roughly 6 percent, and the interest on savings accounts used to fund those loans was roughly 3 percent, giving rise to the pejorative that S&Ls were a 3-6-3 business: thrift executives booked deposits at 3 percent, lent them out at 6 percent, and were on the golf course by 3 p.m.

But with spiking interest rates, thrifts had to pay interest rates to savings depositors that were much higher than this proverbial 3 percent, in fact, often more than the 6 percent they earned on their loans. They had to do this— or else risk losing their depositors to the new money-market mutual funds offered by Merrill Lynch and others that paid high rates. There was no good choice: either lose their deposits and fail—or keep their deposits by paying high interest rates and incur huge operating losses. To make matters worse, these thrifts were effectively stuck with their low-rate mortgages. With low fixed rates, those mortgages could only be sold at a steep discount to their principal value. If they sold them, they would have to take losses so dire that their net worth would have fallen below statutory minimums.

Attempts to save the S&L industry began in earnest in 1980 and 1981 with the Depository Institutions Deregulation and Monetary Control Act of 1980 (DIDMCA), the Economic Recovery Tax Act of 1981 (Kemp-Roth), and certain actions of the Federal Home Loan Bank Board (FHLBB), the S&Ls' chief regulator. DIDMCA allowed S&Ls and banks to pay market rates on their deposits, something they hadn't been able to do since 1933, and thus keep those deposits.[9] The next problem for S&Ls was how to dispose of their low-yielding, long-term mortgages and how to replace them with higher-yielding loans so they could become profitable again. This was addressed in September 1981 with FHLBB actions that allowed S&Ls to sell these underwater mortgages and amortize the loss on sales over ten years rather than take the losses immediately, and further allowing them to take losses against past gains. It was accounting magic.[10]

The new rules ignited the market in the purchase and sale of mortgages, a previously quiet pursuit. Lewis Ranieri of Salomon Brothers, the top securities firm on Wall Street at the time, led the way. Salomon bought these mortgages from troubled thrifts and then resold them to investors or other thrifts. For a time, this was the most profitable activity for Salomon, and then for all of Wall Street, before junk bonds claimed that title. S&Ls had billions of dollars of mortgages to sell and very few buyers, so firms such as Salomon could name their price; S&Ls got only poor financial offers—offers that they took only because they had few alternatives and they could amortize the loss on the transaction. S&Ls then used the proceeds to buy replacement blocks of mortgages with a better yield.

This was so profitable for Salomon Brothers that its appetite got bigger, and it bought increasingly large blocks of mortgages, which gave S&Ls more capacity to increase their lending activity. Mortgages, which had only grown 7.8 percent a year from 1980 to 1983, began to grow by more than 12 percent per year, from $1.1 trillion in 1984 to $2.1 trillion in 1989.

Salomon's innovations in this sector were legendary. They took the mere buying and selling of blocks of mortgages to another level with the 1983 invention of a bond composed of mortgages, called the collateralized mortgage obligation (CMO). If rated, institutions could buy CMOs. Congress soon aided this market by exempting investment banks from having to register these securities in each state.

The FHLBB then reduced the S&L net worth requirement from 5 percent to 4 percent in 1980, and from 4 percent to 3 percent in 1982.[11] In 1980, it also removed the limit on the amounts of brokered depositor, or "hot money," an S&L could hold.[12] Traditionally, S&Ls had raised deposits from customers in their neighborhoods, but that approach didn't result in enough new deposits to fund aggressive loan growth. With brokered deposits, an S&L could hire a firm such as Merrill Lynch to sell its certificates of deposits (CDs) through its vast nationwide networks of stockbrokers, who made commissions on these sales. If S&Ls needed more deposits, they simply raised the rates they were willing to pay on these CDs. The Federal Savings and Loan Insurance Corporation (FSLIC) insured these deposits, so the customer didn't have to worry about the soundness of a particular S&L. Brokered deposits removed a barrier to growth, and fast-growing S&Ls raised billions this way. Ultimately, this allowed for greater lending mischief.

In September 1981, the FHLBB conjured more magic by permitting troubled S&Ls to issue "income capital certificates" to be purchased by FSLIC and included as capital,[13] and in late 1982, it began counting "appraised equity capital" as a part of reserves. This allowed S&Ls to recognize an increase in the market value of their premises and thus build capital on the shaky foundation of current appraisals.

In April 1982, the FHLBB made a momentous change to S&L ownership requirements: it allowed an S&L to be purchased by a single owner. Previously, the FHLBB had placed a premium on diverse, community-based ownership. It had required 400 or more stockholders, of which 125 were to be from the local community. Further, no control group could own more than 25 percent and no individual more than 10 percent.[14]

The government did one more extraordinary thing for the S&Ls. In its eagerness to give them new streams of income to overcome problems in their core mortgage business, it empowered them to make commercial loans; most notably, it gave them more latitude to make commercial real estate loans. And that power would bring a decade of misery. With the Garn–St. Germain Depository Institutions Act of 1982, S&Ls were now permitted to lend up to 40 percent of their assets in commercial mortgages, up to 30 percent in consumer loans, up to 10 percent in commercial loans, and up to 10 percent in commercial leases.[15] This expansion enabled S&Ls to invest in junk bonds, and many became active buyers. The act also eliminated the previous statutory limit on loan-to-value ratios, allowing more lax credit standards.

Most institutions weren't well qualified to manage these new businesses because they had little or no experience with them. The expanded powers and new authority tacitly allowed for conflicts of interest and vulnerabilities—namely, that opportunistic real estate developers could buy S&Ls and then loan money to themselves, as they had in the 1920s. And so they did—in spades. It was a blatant conflict of interest that often shaded into outright fraud.

S&Ls also had fierce competition from banks. Together with the S&Ls need for earnings from commercial real estate, this created a boom in real estate that led to massive overbuilding. Commercial real estate (CRE) construction spending exploded in the mid-1980s. From 1981 to 1987, CRE lending more than doubled from $442 billion to $950 billion,[16] and CRE loans grew from 14 percent of GDP to 20 percent in 1987 (Figure 2.4). Office vacancy during this period went from 4 percent to 16 percent, which soon brought record delinquencies (Figure 2.5).[17]

David and Jean Solomon exemplified U.S. developers who overextended. In the early 1980s, they developed Tower 49, a forty-four-story office building with 600,000 square feet on East 49th Street in New York City, which they sold in 1986 for the then-record price of $301 million. Flush with this success, they immediately began development of three more major office buildings with more than two million square feet of space. But other builders, envious and inspired, followed their lead, and almost simultaneously added

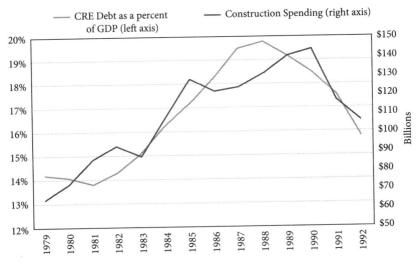

Figure 2.4. United States: Commercial Real Estate, 1979–1992

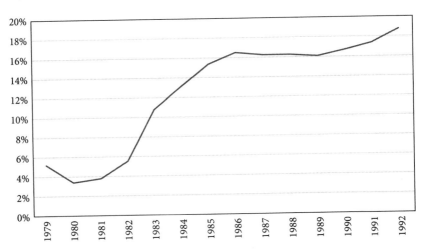

Figure 2.5. United States: Office Vacancy Rate, 1979–1990

another five million square feet.[18] There weren't enough tenants to fill these spaces, especially after the 1987 stock market crash culled investment bank employees. The Solomons and their competitors were soon wiped out. From New England to Texas to California, other U.S. regions saw similar overbuilding with subsequent distress—not just in commercial real estate but also in housing, especially suburban housing.

The overbuilding rampage hit Canada and Britain too. Toronto-based Olympia and York became the world's largest private real estate developer, and by the fall of 1990 was the largest private borrower in the world. Olympia and York had such an outsized reputation that lenders were reluctant to scrutinize company financials in advance of lending decisions or to tightly monitor ongoing performance, lest they be excluded from the lending group. In March, the company told its stunned group of ninety-one lenders that it would have to restructure about $15 billion in debt, and on May 14, 1992, teetering under the weight of its failing Canary Wharf project in London, it filed for bankruptcy protection. At the time, it was the largest restructuring ever for a privately held company, as well as "the largest bankruptcy in Canadian business history—and fourth largest bankruptcy in the United States."[19]

In this same period, another new development was in the making: junk bonds. The stock market had been anemic owing to the inflation and high interest rates of the 1970s. Though the Dow had briefly broken 1,000 in 1972, it had bounced around below that level for the rest of the decade. The trailing twelve-month stock price-to-earnings ratio of the S&P 500 fell below 7 during the 1970s, one of the lowest levels on record, and was still below 12 in 1982.[20] This left company management highly vulnerable to a new breed of investors who wanted higher stock valuations and would use debt, deep cost cutting, and other means to get it.

Volcker's war against inflation using very high interest rates was succeeding, in the view of most economists. But it was proving a costly and painful battle, bringing the bitter recession of the early 1980s in which businesses suffered setbacks, unemployment vaulted to 10.8 percent,[21] and real GDP fell by 2.6 percent in a mere six months. Ronald Reagan, using the campaign slogan "Let's make America great again," took office as president in January 1981. His administration was determined to jump-start the economy, and its preferred path was through tax cuts. Within seven months of Reagan's inauguration, Congress had passed one of the largest tax cuts in U.S. history, the massive Tax Reform Act of 1981, better known as Kemp-Roth. Its provisions, especially those allowing accelerated depreciation for tax loss purposes, gave significant benefits to transactions involving real estate and mergers and acquisitions (M&A).

Soon after its passage, however, government revenues fell as a percentage of GDP, doubling the deficit, and unemployment rates increased further, which sent lawmakers scrambling to lessen these tax benefits. The remainder of Reagan's term brought repeated modifications to the tax laws—in both directions—but the tone had been set with Kemp-Roth, and that tone did not meaningfully change until 1987: the net impact of the tax law changes was to spur a significant increase in real estate and merger transactions.

Private debt financed much of the M&A activity of the 1980s. Interest on debt was tax deductible, and dividends on equity were not. Because of this, from a pure cash-flow standpoint, a company could afford to pay far more interest on, say, $100 million in newly issued debt than it could in dividends on the same amount of newly issued stock.

That fact, coupled with these new tax advantages, meant that the smart way for bold investors to increase the languishing stock price of a company with good cash flow was to buy the outstanding stock with a combination of debt and equity, taking it private in what was referred to as a "leveraged buy-out," or LBO. Company earnings could be used to pay off this acquisition debt over a few years. So by using debt, the investor would own the company for a mere fraction of what was already a lackluster price. Soon enough, the investor could take the company public or sell to another investor at a handsome profit.

Typically, the debt used would be much greater than the equity used, which increased the risk associated with the acquisition transaction, so the interest rate the lender charged on this debt was high to account for this risk. The euphemism for high-risk debt when it came in the form of a bond was "high-yield security," but it was more commonly referred to as a "junk bond." Junk bonds grew from $10 billion outstanding in 1979 to over $189 billion outstanding in 1989. This was not the sole source of private lending growth in the 1980s, but it was a substantial one that illustrated the risk appetite of the decade.

Since stock prices were low, the company could be bought cheaply. Since as inflation came under control market interest rates were declining, the cost of the debt would decline through time. Since the stock market was rising, the company's stock could be taken public at a later date at a higher price. Fortunes were being made on just this simple formula. It was the best possible environment for an LBO, because in this environment an LBO would work even if the fundamentals of the company didn't improve. If company fundamentals did improve through cost reductions or other means, or if non-core assets could be sold at favorable prices, then so much the better.

Michael Milken of the investment bank Drexel Burnham Lambert was the legendary leader and innovator for this type of transaction. He had started in the 1970s by buying and selling junk bonds that had been high-quality bonds before the company became troubled. Since most investors steered clear of them, these bonds were called "fallen angels," and Milken, reasoning that they often had more intrinsic value than the market assumed, profited handsomely.

As the effectiveness and scope of Milken's operation increased, he began underwriting and selling bonds that had a junk rating *at issuance*, especially as part of the financing of an LBO. This was his great innovation. These bonds weren't fallen angels: they had never been angels to begin with. Because of the spectacular returns he obtained for his clients in these transactions, investor appetite for these bonds grew rapidly, and the challenge became finding enough underwriting opportunities to meet the demand. Inevitably, these LBOs started to involve ever-larger companies. But even this growth satisfied neither Milken's ambition nor the growing demand. With his success, Milken had developed a network of loyal high-yield bond buyers that was far larger than any competitor's, so he had a much greater capacity to complete new deals.

It was quite a machine. A CEO who successfully took his company private in an LBO using junk bonds sold by Drexel, or an investor who successfully bought a company using junk bonds sold by Drexel, made their companies available to Drexel to buy the bonds of the next such deal. In fact, Milken sometimes insisted that companies borrow more than they needed so they could use the extra funds to buy future Drexel offerings. Drexel's growing menagerie of clients became buyers for future deals.

This is where the S&L story and the junk-bond story converge. Historically, S&Ls had been prohibited from buying corporate junk bonds, but with their new Garn–St. Germain powers, they now had that ability and many became active buyers. Drexel took full notice of the new S&L powers, took the initiative to help interested CEOs buy S&Ls, and thus added to the network of grateful clients who would buy future bonds underwritten by Drexel.

LBOs weren't the only source of runaway lending growth, but they epitomized the era's aggressive tone. Drexel's machine was so successful that it was running out of deals to keep growing and satisfy Milken's and his clients' ambition. So Milken pursued increasingly larger deals, paid increasingly higher prices, and came up with a new way to use Drexel's now-extraordinary capacity to underwrite and sell very large amounts of this high-yield debt: the hostile takeover. In a hostile takeover, one company attempts to buy another, but the management and board of that "target" company resist being acquired. So the prospective buyer makes its offer so attractive that the

target company's board is forced by its fiduciary obligation to accept the offer, however undesired it may be.

Before the 1980s, hostile takeovers had been rare, but when they did
happen, the prospective buyer was usually larger than the target company
and was often in the same or a closely related industry. This changed in the
Drexel era. Even a small company, or a management team without a company, could buy a large company in a Drexel-backed deal, given the firm's
extraordinary access to large amounts of funding.

Fear descended on the cozy corporate boardrooms of the business world.
Suddenly, anyone backed by Drexel was capable of buying all but the very
largest companies, and when they did, they would often jettison management,
lay off employees, and cut costs ruthlessly.

Many CEOs had little or no stock ownership in their companies, and
Drexel derided them as complacent bureaucrats who hadn't managed these
companies in shareholders' best interests. Often, Drexel had a valid point
since a disconcertingly large number of companies had high expenses, un-
derperforming divisions, and a stock price below the value that could be obtained if the company were broken up and sold in pieces.

Drexel became by far the largest practitioner of this strategy, and because
the result was extraordinary profits, its competitors soon joined the fray. This
is a core dynamic of a financial crisis: other lenders rush to imitate and keep
pace with success.

Many in Congress and the public feared that these hostile takeovers were
not just targeting poorly managed companies but good ones as well, with disruptive and undesirable societal consequences. But Drexel had invested
considerable time wining, dining, and lining the campaign coffers of various politicians, so the junk-bond industry was well protected in 1984 when
congressional concern inspired efforts to curb the use of junk bonds in takeovers and buyouts. Of thirty such bills introduced in 1984 and 1985, none
passed. In fact, under the laissez-faire Reagan administration, both the Securities and Exchange Commission (SEC) and the president's Council of Economic Advisers expressed support for takeovers. The Reagan administration
even effectively blocked the Fed's attempt to apply its margin limitation of
50 percent to LBOs—the very same margin limitation that had been put in
place as protection from overleverage after the crash of 1929.

As the competition for LBOs increased, prices paid for companies rose,
making the resulting junk bonds junkier. The junk-bond market soon reached
Minsky's Ponzi level—financing deals where the loan could never be repaid

from cash flow and could only be repaid if the target company were resold at a higher price. A great example of this excess was Canadian real estate company Campeau Corporation's flawed acquisitions of two large American department-store chains: Allied in 1986 and Federated in 1988. Campeau paid exorbitant prices for these companies, all gladly financed by the LBO lending industry, and then staggered under the weight of its junk debt. It was soon engulfed in bankruptcy, which caused an overall decline of the department-store sector.

Fraud and chicanery multiplied apace with activity in the LBO space. Illegal activities included insider trading, stock parking, preferential investment offers for a given firm's employees than for its customers, bribery for special treatment in transactions, higher than allowable markups, fraud against clients, and more. Fraud doesn't cause the boom or the crisis. It just feeds on unwitting participants.

The long prelude to the 1987 stock market crash had already begun with the decade's runaway private lending. This lending was happening across the economy—in commercial real estate, the mania for LBOs, S&Ls, and two other crises, both predicated on lending: the Latin American debt crisis, which primarily affected large New York banks, and the crisis caused by the drop in oil prices, which primarily affected Texas and Oklahoma banks.

The increase in oil prices had hit many Latin American countries hard. The U.S. money-center banks, primarily based in New York, viewed this as a lending opportunity. They could finance these countries' shortfalls by "recycling" the burgeoning deposits of oil-rich countries. In other words, they would lend the rapidly accumulating deposits of oil-exporting countries to the suddenly cash-starved oil-importing countries. This demonstrated exceptionally poor credit judgment by those banks, but it was rationalized by Citibank chair Walter Wriston's pronouncement in the 1970s that "countries never go bankrupt,"[22] though many had obviously defaulted on debt, and on many occasions.

At the end of 1970, the total outstanding debt of these countries was $29 billion,[23] but it mushroomed to $327 billion by 1982,[24] at which point the nine largest U.S. money-center banks had Latin American debt totaling 176 percent of their capital and total "lesser developed country" debt totaling 290 percent.[25] The Federal Reserve's marked increase in interest rates in 1979 only exacerbated these countries' struggle to remain current on their debts.

The crisis came in the summer of 1982, when "less-developed countries" around the world, including sixteen Latin American countries and eleven elsewhere, were forced to reschedule their debts.[26] Restructuring created its own problems. Banks abruptly and completely cut off new funding to these countries and tried to collect on the debt, which brought instant recessions in many places. In response, the Fed exercised its convening powers, bringing together lenders, central bankers, and the International Monetary Fund (IMF). This resulted in the usual cocktail of austerity, with government layoffs and cuts in health and education, along with a dose of new IMF funding to help countries make "interest-only" payments on their debts.

Notably, the Fed gave these U.S. money-center banks forbearance in recognizing losses from these loans. Most likely, they would have taken the more draconian step of shutting them down if they were much smaller banks, so this was one more approach to the now-familiar "too big to fail" dynamic. Without this forbearance, the net worth of these banks—America's largest and most notable banks—would have been wiped out, and they would have failed.

After five years of this forbearance, these Latin American debtor nations were still not in a position to repay most of the loans, but the forbearance had done its trick. The U.S. banks' earnings in that five-year period had finally put them in position to create reserves against these losses. Citibank led the pack in 1987 by announcing a then-shocking $3.3 billion loss provision, roughly 30 percent of its exposure from loans to less-developed countries, and other U.S. banks quickly followed Citibank's example.[27] Many of these debtor nations were still not in a position to repay their loans in 1989. So Treasury secretary Nicholas Brady took the initiative for widespread debt forgiveness and restructuring in exchange for continued domestic reforms in these countries. In all, eighteen nations signed on to the Brady plan, and roughly a third, or $61 billion, of the debt in question was forgiven.[28]

Next came the energy lending crisis. In the oil drilling that had followed Carter's and then Reagan's deregulation of domestic prices, Texas bankers mistakenly believed that oil prices would stay high. In fact, oilmen and their lenders quickly came to believe that oil was a scarce resource being inexorably depleted, and therefore prices could only climb.

An early, signature energy lending catastrophe was the 1984 FDIC takeover of the insolvent Continental Illinois Bank in Chicago, which would stand as the United States largest such takeover until the Great Recession. This came at a point when the price per barrel of oil had already dropped from its 1980 peak of almost forty dollars to less than thirty dollars, and had stemmed largely from energy loans Continental had purchased from Penn Square Bank of Oklahoma. Penn Square had made wildly excessive and, in some cases, fraudulent loans to the oil industry and itself had failed in 1982. Continental was one of the first banks to be called "too big to fail," as regulators prevented losses on even its uninsured deposits. Critics pointed to this as giving rise to moral hazard and increasing the risk-taking that characterized the rest of the decade.

At a point when oil was still slightly more than thirty dollars per barrel, sober industry analysis forecasted near-term prices rising as high as ninety or a hundred dollars a barrel, though that level was not attained for another twenty years. Instead, in the spring of 1986, because of debt-financed over-drilling and higher production, the price per barrel plunged from thirty to eleven dollars.[29] The major Texas banks had been heavy lenders to the oil industry, and with this fall in prices, every one of them failed, except for Texas Commerce, which had preemptively rescued itself by merging with New York's Chemical Bank in advance of the worst industry news. They had simply made far too many oil-industry loans, along with far too many commercial real estate loans that depended on the demand brought by the oil boom.

With these crises simultaneously weakening the industry, bank failures erupted: 2,304 banks failed or needed assistance from 1986 to 1992. The FDIC had to step in at an ultimate cost of $36.3 billion, which was in addition to the eventual $160.1 billion in losses in the S&L industry.[30]

This was a disproportionately regional failure centered in the Southwest, the site of so many of the nation's oil fields. Of the 2,304 bank failures, 40 percent happened in Texas and Oklahoma alone, even though their combined GDP was only 8 percent of the U.S. total.

As for S&Ls, in 1983, 10 percent were still technically insolvent and 35 percent were still losing money.[31] Nevertheless, newly empowered owners kept the pedal to the metal, with forty Texas thrifts tripling in size over the next few years and California thrifts doing much the same. At the same time, Congress was parsimonious in its funding of regulators, so the FHLBB staff of examiners was actually shrinking at just the point these thrifts were tripling in size: a guaranteed formula for disaster.

Edwin Gray came in as the new FHLBB chair, understandably concerned about lax lending, and began reversing some of the previous regulatory laxity. He raised the net worth requirement for S&Ls to 7 percent.[32] But he was blocked by Congress when he tried to eliminate deposit insurance for brokered deposits[33] and restrict CRE lending. Politicians who were beneficiaries of the S&L industry's campaign contribution largesse were the key agents of this obstruction.

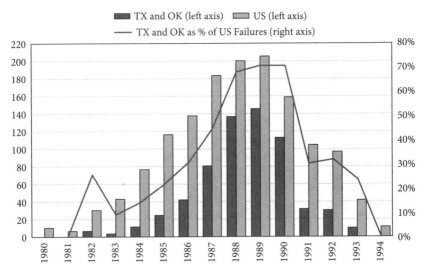

Figure 2.6. Texas and Oklahoma Commercial Bank Failures, 1980–1994

Lending institutions can engage in foot-dragging and obfuscate the deterioration in the credit quality of a loan for months and even years, especially with an inattentive or accommodating regulator. This is especially true in commercial loans, which require subjective judgments about borrowers' prospects. A loan that is troubled may not show up as such in a bank's or an S&L's financial statements for a year or two, or even more.

The tone in Washington began to change with the March 1984 failure of Empire Savings of Mesquite, Texas, which cost taxpayers $300 million.[34] The *New York Times* reported that Empire Savings had grown by $240 million in assets in the first eleven months of 1983. They had used "questionable lending practices" and "artificially inflated" real estate appraisals to achieve this gain. The bank board charged that "the excess of the loan amount over the real value of the property was used to cover all loan fees" paid to Empire "and to pay an incentive bonus to borrowers just for signing the loan papers."[35]

The Empire Savings CEO, Spencer Blain, who later was ordered to forfeit $22 million and serve five years on probation for his role in Empire's practices, had purchased 60 percent of the institution's stock and had a stellar industry pedigree. But Blain was ensnared by the siren song of easy riches, using depositor money to pay himself huge bonuses, not to mention bonuses and fees from Blain-managed real estate projects financed by Empire. It was a conflict of interest replicated on a massive scale at other institutions. It would include such names as Charles Keating, D. L. "Danny" Faulkner, Don R. Dixon, and Edwin T. "Fast Eddie" McBirney III, who were aided by naïve elected officials in resisting intervening regulators.

S&L failures were just beginning. Empire Savings was a harbinger of the decade's crises, not its climax. In January 1985, the FHLBB finally was allowed to cap brokered deposits at 5 percent of deposits at S&Ls with insufficient net worth and put limits on direct investments, such as equities.[36] But with continued failures, such as a new rash in Ohio and Maryland, the FHLBB simply didn't have enough FSLIC funds to cover depositor losses.[37] It had less than $5 billion for losses that it now believed could exceed $20 billion.[38] Eventually, these losses would reach $160 billion.[39]

Unable to fund outright closure of troubled S&Ls, the FHLBB was forced into allowing many to remain open in the hope they could grow their way out of trouble. They couldn't. By January 1987, the FSLIC fund was finally deemed insolvent, but lawmakers were still unable to face up to the sheer dollar size of the problem. This, coupled with pressure from S&L lobbyists critical of "overly harsh" regulators, meant that a sufficiently robust industry recapitalization was not yet in the cards.[40]

In May 1987, the FHLBB began phasing out much of the remaining accounting legerdemain,[41] but that process would take two more years. In August, Congress partially faced up to the overwhelming cost of the problem by passing the Competitive Equality Banking Act of 1987, which added $10.8 billion to the FSLIC, but with only $3.75 billion authorized for any twelve-month period.[42] The act also contained forbearance measures designed to postpone or prevent S&L closures.[43]

Much of the trouble came from Texas S&Ls, reeling after 1986 because of the oil price collapse—which they felt indirectly through their CRE loans. Congress's inability to fund the full cost of the problem at this moment simply meant that it would drag on and snowball, therefore costing even more in the final reckoning. This phase of denial or delusion is typical of many financial crises. Regulators limped along with their limited funds and disposed of 205 S&Ls with $101 billion[44] in assets.[45]

The most dramatic failure of the S&L debacle would come a few years later with Charles Keating's notorious Lincoln Federal Savings and Loan, though hundreds of failures occurred even after this point. Lincoln was seized in April 1989 and cost the government over $3 billion, while leaving about 23,000 customers with worthless Lincoln Federal bonds. Keating had once urged his staff to "remember the weak, meek and ignorant are always good targets."[46] Once he took over Lincoln in 1984, Keating jettisoned existing, conservative management and grew Lincoln from $1.1 billion to $5.5 billion in five short years by lending and by buying land, buying equity in commercial real estate development projects, and buying Drexel-sponsored junk bonds.

Keating, like others in this era, made risky investments and used Lincoln as a personal piggybank. Lincoln exceeded its statutory limits in direct investment—limits that were designed to cap risk—by $600 million, but chafed when the FHLBB began to investigate this and other practices. He enlisted the help of five U.S. senators—Donald Riegle (D-MI), Dennis DeConcini (D-AZ), Alan Cranston (D-CA), John Glenn (D-OH), and John McCain (R-AZ)—along with Speaker of the House Jim Wright (D-TX) to protect him from the FHLBB in 1987. Keating also hired Alan Greenspan as a lobbyist "to help recruit the Keating Five."[47]

Though the beleaguered FHLBB chair Gray did not succumb to that pressure, he soon left the agency, and his successor Danny Wall did succumb, allowing Lincoln to misbehave for almost two more years, thus increasing the cost of that institution's failure. In 1992, Keating was convicted of various crimes related to his management of Lincoln and served four-and-a-half years in prison. Ironically, the government's early 1980s deregulation of the S&L industry, especially in granting that industry new lending powers to help it earn its way out of trouble, led to rampant, ill-advised lending in the mid-1980s. This resulted in the late 1980s and early 1990s in eight hundred S&L failures, almost five thousand insolvent or inadequately capitalized S&Ls, and the need for $160 billion in rescue dollars.

Deregulation—or more accurately, changes in regulation—have figured prominently in many crises beyond this S&L crisis. For example, the British legislation that enabled the creation of joint stock companies in 1824 contributed to the 1825 crisis. Changes in laws and regulation in lending are always occurring in a given country, and business and lending communities are always engaged in an effort to "deregulate" to enable more, different, and expanded types of lending. Growth is the *sine qua non* of business and lending its means.

Enabling legislation does not predestine a crisis, and many crises have happened without it. Furthermore, industry can usually innovate its way around prohibitions. The test is whether, and how much, that deregulation facilitates riskier credit.

After a crisis, laws and regulations about lending often do need to be changed, but it is generally true that much postcrisis legislation, including the 2002 Sarbanes-Oxley Act, which arose after the Worldcom and Enron debacles, and the 2010 Dodd-Frank Act, which came after the Great Recession, looks backward. It is designed to prevent the crisis that just happened and cannot foresee the form that the next crisis will take. These two acts contain items that were helpful and just as much that was burdensome and unnecessary. When regulations such as these are passed, the industry then quickly tries to reverse or evade many of the provisions and often succeeds. This tug-of-war will always be with us and always has been.

It should be noted that the banking industry committed sins similar to those of the S&L industry, at very hefty volumes and without as much deregulation. Further, the United Kingdom experienced a similar banking crisis in this period with different regulatory modifications. Even so, regulatory changes were central to large-scale S&L losses that otherwise would not have occurred.

The October 19, 1987, stock market crash, which became known as Black Monday, came in the wake of these LBO, banking, and S&L trends. For five years, starting in 1982, the stock market took off, responding positively to plummeting interest rates and the higher values implied by the expanding LBO volume. By 1987, the trailing twelve-month price-to-earnings of the S&P 500 had nosed past 20, far higher than the desultory 5 to 10 price-to-earnings level of the mid- to late 1970s (though not inordinately high by either current or historical standards).

But the Dow plunged 23 percent on Black Monday—worse than any one-day loss in the 1929 stock market crash, the September 11 terror attacks, or the 2008 financial crisis. Its own rise had been fed by margin debt, which had increased from $25 billion in 1980 to a record high $57 billion in 1986. This brought an end to a five-year bull market.

Analysts blamed many suspects—turmoil in the Middle East, a higher trade deficit and the resulting fear of higher interest rates, larger amounts of "risk arbitrage" owing to the highly active M&A market, and the more widespread use of computerized trading and portfolio insurance strategies that automatically triggered selling in a declining market. Indeed, some at the time viewed the crash as a technical rather than economic event (a theory belied by the fact that it took almost two years for the market to return to its 1987 highs).

But one factor was more telling than any of these. A few days before the crash, the House Ways and Means Committee had previewed a "takeover-tax" bill that would have taken away many of the tax breaks related to M&A activity. Since the expectation of continued M&A activity was a key ingredient of high valuations, this threat hurt the market.

Once again, high stock market valuations came with an accelerated expansion of lending. When the conditions for that were challenged, the stock market plummeted. As in most financial crises, the stock market crash was first a symptom—albeit a dramatic one—and not the cause itself. Whatever the precipitating event, the high level of margin debt left stocks vulnerable. The sharp decline in prices brought forced selling to meet record margin calls. Futures market margin calls were so high—estimated to have been a tenfold increase—that lenders to members of the Chicago Mercantile Exchange worried that they would exceed their statutory lending limits. It all helped transform a decline into a rout. Citibank, encouraged by a request from the president of the New York Federal Reserve Bank, increased lending to securities firms for this purpose from $400 million to $1.4 billion in a day.[48]

The stock market crash was a stern test for the new chair of the Federal Reserve, Alan Greenspan, who had been on the job only four months. But the Fed had been studying the issue of a stock market drop intently for decades and was well prepared to flood the market with liquidity to counteract the fall. The Fed moved quickly to expand open market operations, which meant buying government securities from banks to infuse them with cash and thus push the federal funds interest rate down from 7.5 percent to 7 percent. It liberalized rules for Treasury securities lending, extended its hours for bank transactions, and increased its supervisory presence. To help reassure market participants, it publicized these efforts and its commitment to providing liquidity.[49]

The decline in stocks came to an end, but stocks truly rebounded only after the early 1990s recession. In the aftermath, the New York Stock Exchange implemented what became known as "circuit breakers," rules that suspended trading for fifteen minutes in the event of a 7 percent decline and suspended trading for the rest of the day in the event of a 20 percent decline, all to give traders time to react in the midst of turmoil.

In early 1989, Reagan's vice president, George H. W. Bush, took office as the new U.S. president, and in an irony he little understood, inherited the soon-to-be-rampant consequence of the 1980s excess. The massive overcapacity and bad loans of the 1980s had led directly to a spate of failures, and a major pullback and recession in the early 1990s. He had won the 1988 presidential election over Michael Dukakis with the mantra "Stay the course," counting on the Reagan aura for victory. But he had not appreciated how fraught and perilous that "course" had been, and as the 1980s came to a close, those 1980s' chickens came home to roost, with a full-on recession and a slew of bad news. When Bush took office, unemployment was 5.2 percent. Two years later it had reached nearly 8 percent. Real GDP growth fell by 1.33 percent from July 1990 to March 1991. Junk bond defaults went from a mere 0.8 percent in 1984 to 10 percent in 1991. In 1990, 325 S&Ls failed, and the number would stay high until 1993. In 1989, 531 banks failed, and they would continue to fail at a high rate until 1993. Mortgage delinquency peaked in 1986, but foreclosures tripled between 1981 and their peak in 1991. While far less onerous than the mortgage credit problems of the Great Recession, this added to the duress. Credit card delinquencies reached 5.5 percent in 1991, and while credit card loans were a small part of the private debt totals, this evidenced consumer stress.

After years of investigation by the Securities and Exchange Commission, Milken himself pled guilty to six counts of securities and tax violations in 1990, served twenty-two months in jail, and paid over $600 million in fines and customer restitution. Drexel filed for bankruptcy in 1991, but junk bonds and LBOs lived on. After a period of relative dormancy, by the 2000s they were growing robustly again. Banks and thrifts were both deeply entwined with the junk bond explosion, and it was no coincidence that the period of greatest 1980s bank and S&L troubles coincided with the heaviest period of junk bond delinquency.

Bush blamed the Fed for the economic woes, claiming that rates were too high—though at 8 percent they were well down from their Volcker-era highs of roughly 14 percent. As the problems worsened, Bush and Congress enacted an S&L bailout plan in 1989 known as the Financial Institutions Reform, Recovery, and Enforcement Act (FIRREA), which replaced the FHLBB with the Office of Thrift Supervision (OTS),[50] provided $50 billion in borrowing authority for the S&L cleanup, melded the FSLIC into the FDIC, and created the Resolution Trust Corporation (RTC) to manage and dispose of troubled thrift loans and assets.[51] The solution and the end of the crisis were now finally in sight.

Other countries misbehaved in the same time frame, including Japan, as we will see in the next chapter, the United Kingdom, France, Italy, and Spain. Margaret Thatcher presided over a massive expansion in private debt from

Table 2.2. U.K. Crisis Matrix: 1980s and 1990s

Billions of British Pounds	1980	1981	1985	1990	1991	1993	1980-1985 Change	1985-1990 Change
GDP	243	269	381	616	648	708	138	234
Real GDP (2010 £'s)	797	791	896	1,063	1,051	1,082	99	167
Inflation	15.2%	11.8%	4.9%	7.0%	7.5%	2.5%	-10%	2%
Public Debt	108	130	171	191	201	292	63	20
Private Debt	151	183	321	773	819	917	170	452
Business Debt	73	91	147	388	407	472	73	242
CRE	2	3	7	39	40	34	5	32
Household Debt	78	91	174	384	412	445	96	210
Mortgage	41	48	103	233	256	291	62	130
Unemployment Rate	6.8%	9.7%	11.4%	7.1%	8.8%	10.4%	4.6%	-4.3%

As Percentage of GDP	1980	1981	1985	1990	1991	1993	1980-1985 Change	1985-1990 Change
Public Debt	44%	48%	45%	31%	31%	41%	0%	-14%
Private Debt	62%	68%	84%	126%	126%	130%	22%	41%
Business Debt	30%	34%	38%	63%	63%	67%	8%	25%
CRE	1%	1%	2%	6%	6%	5%	1%	4%
Household Debt	32%	34%	46%	62%	64%	63%	14%	17%
Mortgage	17%	18%	27%	38%	40%	41%	10%	11%

In the five years leading to 1990, Britain's private debt grew by 141 percent, leading to rising loan losses, a decline in real GDP, and plummeting corporate and financial institution earnings. It reignited rising unemployment after a brief period of relief from early 1980s unemployment.

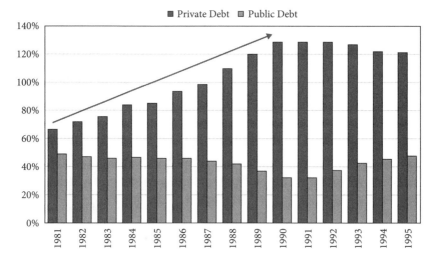

Figure 2.7. United Kingdom: Private and Public Debt as a Percentage of GDP, 1981–1995
In the United Kingdom, private debt increased by £590 billion ($827 billion) from 1981 to 1990.

59 percent to 126 percent of GDP during her tenure, powering an economic expansion and driving up housing prices. But once overcapacity was too great, it brought the paradigmatic recessionary aftermath as unemployment skyrocketed again to more than 10 percent and corporate and financial institution earnings plummeted in the early 1990s. The banking industry of France followed suit, with private debt levels rising from 107 percent of GDP in 1987 to 127 percent of GDP in 1992 with bank failures that followed. Few countries were able to resist the siren song, but Germany was one; although it was buffeted by the economic trauma of its neighbors, it didn't go on a lending binge of its own in this period. Countries are better served not to get caught up in a lending frenzy in the first place.

Why didn't the financial crisis of this era reach the 2008 level of calamity?

The crisis brought plenty of pain, to be sure. But in the United States, several factors were very different in the 1980s than in 2008. For one thing, even though private debt grew almost as rapidly, the overall level of private-sector leverage reached was far lower in 1989 than in 2008. In ratio to GDP it reached only 124 percent versus 169 percent in 2008. With that, the amount of bad debt in the 2000s was greater in relation to GDP than in the 1980s. And since private debt to GDP is effectively the same as the private sector's debt-to-income ratio, the private sector had more capacity to repay in this period than it did after 2008.

Another notable difference was that the industry kept increasing overall loans. Though business debt did contract in 1991 and 1992, overall private debt continued to expand. The pain of a crisis is worst when total private debt contracts. Lending in the early 1990s kept growing partly because the pain was more regionally concentrated and because the household sector was less affected. In contrast to the Great Depression and Great Recession, there were still many regions of the country where banks were less affected and could continue to lend more freely.

Another factor that kept the 1980s crisis from "going to scale" and achieving the grim calamity benchmarks of 2008 was the absence of large totals of derivative contracts to amplify the impact of bad loans. In the 2008 crisis, a huge market in a derivative known as "credit default swaps" (CDSs) had emerged specifically to place bets against the credit quality of mortgage securities. In 1987, the CDS market did not exist. By 2007 that market was $61.2 trillion. In the crisis of the late 2000s, buying CDSs would allow banks and insurance companies, especially AIG, to collectively place trillions of dollars of bets for and against the quality of mortgage-backed securities. That would add hundreds of billions to the cost and destruction wrought in the 2008 crisis. It would cripple and bring down mammoth institutions that had not been directly involved in mortgage lending. With large-scale use of derivatives similar to the credit default swaps of the 2000s, the 1980s crisis would have been far more devastating.

Memory is always selective and sometimes kind. The 1980s, indelibly chronicled in such best sellers as *Liar's Poker, Bonfire of the Vanities*, and *The Predators' Ball*, was a period of rampant, profligate lending that turned into one of the most tumultuous economic periods of the past century. George H. W. Bush shouldered the brunt of these consequences, and in 1992, Bill Clinton reaped the political benefit, besting Bush in the presidential election by characterizing the period as a "decade of greed." His strategist James Carville reminded everyone that the key issue in presidential elections was the financial well-being of voters, proclaiming, "It's the economy, stupid!"

CHAPTER 3

Denial and Forbearance

The 1990s Crisis in Japan

In 2016, as I was beginning to think concertedly about this book, my wife, Laura, and I found ourselves in Hawaii. I had with me *The Bubble Economy*, Christopher Wood's excellent book on Japan's 1990s financial crisis, and was reading it as I looked out over the ocean. I came to a passage about the Japanese luxury hotel craze of that period and realized that a neighboring hotel, the just-opened Four Seasons Resort at Ko Olina, had been part of that building frenzy.[1] Japanese developers had built the building as a high-end luxury hotel and ambitiously created its artificial ocean peninsulas—but the hotel had been shuttered or used for less than its original high-end purpose for almost twenty-five years. Nothing close to the demand for luxury hotels projected by the Japanese had materialized. The hotel was built because banks were making loans hand over fist and not basing their decisions on realistic projections of use.

Vestiges of Japan's 1980s lending frenzy remain in other places: in old American magazine cover stories, such as the February 2, 1987, issue of *Newsweek*, which intoned, "Your next boss may be Japanese";[2] or with adults who grew up in the 1980s and can still remember bits of Japanese because their ambitious parents enrolled them in Japanese-language courses as children to prepare them for the new economic world order. America seemed in the grips of a Japanese corporate takeover. As the Japanese bought more and more high-profile U.S. properties, outraged old-school columnist Paul Harvey warned that Japan's growing financial presence in the United States was "an economic Pearl Harbor."[3]

The hotel in Hawaii, like empty skyscrapers in New York and Chicago in the late 1920s, was a relic of an explosion in private lending that was all but unprecedented in the twentieth century. From 1985 to 1990, Japan's private debt—business and household loans—catapulted from 143 percent to 182 percent, an increase of ¥343 trillion, or $2.4 trillion. That percentage increase was far higher than in the years leading up to the Great Depression or Great Recession.

Japan's runaway lending was concentrated in commercial real estate, the profligate construction of office buildings, hotels, and apartments and the development of tracts of land both in Japan and abroad. From 1985 to 1990, commercial real estate (CRE) loans more than doubled from ¥75 trillion to ¥187 trillion. Japan's loans of this era created building after building that would not be sold or filled for years and even decades. But Japan's use of real estate as collateral went far beyond CRE and conventional household mortgages. It extended to trillions of total yen in household nonmortgage loans and small- and medium-sized business loans.[4] Even bank loans for finance and leasing companies were largely tied to activity in the real estate industry.

Further, Japanese banks were eager, often naive participants in the financing of U.S. leveraged buyout transactions. Japan's lending frenzy drove up real estate prices by an astonishing 300 percent in that compressed period and created a short-term economic surge that Japan and the rest of the world misconstrued as an economic miracle. Its banks, businesses, and households became overleveraged, and the country was fully overbuilt by 1990, as were other markets, such as California and Hawaii, targets of Japan's hyperactive lending.

By the late 1980s, five of the world's ten largest commercial banks by total assets were Japanese. In the 1990s, Japan's economy reached 18 percent of world GDP, yet by 2007, it was a mere 7.9 percent. Japan followed the well-trodden boom trajectory in the 1980s but then distinguished itself by delay, denial, and delusion in the bust in the 1990s. Japan's struggles with its crisis and efforts at bank recapitalization took as long as fifteen years—a distinct inflection from the Great Depression. Japan's financial crisis is a parable of when, and how, policy decisions matter in the postboom phases of financial crisis.

The story of Japan's meteoric 1980s began decades earlier, just after World War II. Japan had become an industrial powerhouse in the early twentieth century, but that war had reduced its industrial centers to piles of bombed-out rubble. Japan's national reputation could be recovered in a robust economic recovery, and the government and its departments, especially the powerful Ministry of International Trade and Industry (MITI) and the

Table 3.1. Japan Crisis Matrix: 1980s and 1990s

Billions of Yen	1985	1990	1998	2004	1985–1990 Change	1990–1998 Change	1998–2004 Change
GDP	330,261	449,392	527,877	520,965	119,131	78,485	(6,912)
Public Debt	220,177	301,288	623,182	905,620	81,111	321,894	282,438
Private Debt	473,498	816,282	968,131	861,193	342,785	151,849	(106,938)
Business Debt	367,846	646,288	711,693	510,225	278,442	65,405	(201,468)
CRE	74,722	187,143	218,041	155,069	112,421	30,898	(62,972)
Wholesale/Retail	92,447	133,505	144,517	97,832	41,057	11,013	(46,685)
Manufacturing	112,311	129,935	142,849	101,776	17,624	12,914	(41,073)
Equipment Leasing	16,692	42,160	33,474	20,420	25,468	(8,686)	(13,054)
Household Debt	105,652	169,994	256,438	256,987	64,343	86,444	549
Mortgages	62,332	99,588	170,404	182,487	37,256	70,817	12,083
Consumer Credit	9,639	32,204	41,617	50,993	22,566	9,413	9,376
Bank Failures	n/a	2[a]	30	0	n/a	n/a	(30)

As Percentage of GDP	1985	1990	1998	2004	1985–1990 Change	1990–1998 Change	1998–2004 Change
Public Debt	67%	67%	118%	174%	0%	51%	56%
Private Debt	143%	182%	183%	165%	38%	2%	–18%
Business Debt	111%	144%	135%	98%	32%	–9%	–37%
CRE	23%	42%	41%	30%	19%	0%	–12%
Wholesale/Retail	28%	30%	27%	19%	2%	–2%	–9%
Manufacturing	34%	29%	27%	20%	–5%	–2%	–8%
Equipment Leasing	5%	9%	6%	4%	4%	–3%	–2%
Household Debt	32%	38%	49%	49%	6%	11%	1%
Mortgages	19%	22%	32%	35%	3%	10%	3%
Consumer Credit	3%	7%	8%	10%	4%	1%	2%

[a]For 1992.

In the five years leading to 1990, Japan's private debt grew by 72 percent. It was primarily business debt with a concentration in commercial real estate, though Japan was also an active participant in the U.S. leverage buyout lending market. There was widespread use of real estate as collateral for household non-mortgage and small- and medium-sized business lending. Note, in the absence of complete sector information, this matrix applies bank sector lending percentages to all private debt.

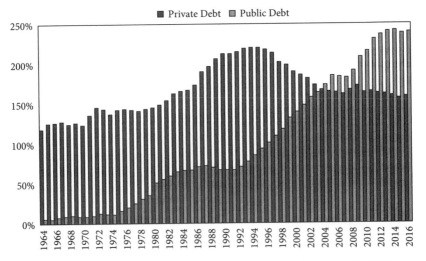

Figure 3.1. Japan: Private and Public Debt as a Percentage of GDP, 1964–2016
From 1985 to 1990, private debt to GDP grew 28 percent. The private debt data for the Bank for International Settlements shown above is nominally greater than Bank of Japan's data cited in the crisis matrix, but both show equally rapid growth, with the latter showing 27 percent growth during these years.

Ministry of Finance, focused almost single-mindedly on abetting growth. The U.S. Dodge Plan of 1949 had fixed the exchange rate at 360 yen to one U.S. dollar to keep Japan's export prices low, helping to power those exports. Japan helped supply the U.S. war efforts in Korea and Vietnam, which critically boosted the Japanese economy, as did the trade benefits granted by the United States in exchange for Japan's support.

The United States encouraged Japan's export-led growth as a means of consolidating and demonstrating the superiority of capitalism in the Cold War era. Japan made a vigorous comeback as an industrial powerhouse, well ahead of other Asian and European countries. Starting with very low postwar levels of private debt, its growth from the late 1940s to the late 1980s was the most sustained high-growth trajectory of any economy in the twentieth century.

In the 1960s and 1970s, rapid loan growth in Japan had generally translated into commensurate GDP growth because Japan was vastly underbuilt as it emerged from the war. Workers were driven to succeed, and "bankers' hours" had extended to the point where employees of lenders were expected to work from 8 a.m. to 9 p.m., if not later. The premium on hard work and success was so pervasive that at Fuji Bank's centenary celebration in 1980, "employees were urged to keep working until they 'urinated blood.'"[5]

There was a palpable sense that Japan had "arrived" in the 1980s: all those decades of extraordinary dedication and hard work had paid off. They had achieved a century-long ambition: to "catch up" to the West and perhaps surpass it. The new ethic was *kokusaika*, which means "internationalization." In the mid-1980s, emboldened and driven Japanese lenders ventured into riskier projects. In 1984, Japan's financial institutions, which had already begun to make loans for projects with less certain returns, began to reach overseas, especially toward acquisition targets in the United States. That year, Fuji Bank bought Heller Finance of Chicago; Sanwa Bank bought the leasing subsidiary of Continental Illinois and later established Sanwa Bank California; and Mitsubishi Bank acquired the Bank of California.

Japan's already high loan growth accelerated in 1985 to compensate for the adverse impact on trade when the United States called on Japan to strengthen its currency in the Plaza Accord. For many years, Japan's currency had been a weak relative to the U.S. dollar, giving it an advantage in the export of cars, textiles, and other goods. Immediately after the accord, the yen rose 50 percent in value, which stunted Japan's trade advantage (the Louvre Accord two years later largely halted the rise in the yen). Traditional exporters instantly reported less revenue in yen terms, making loans to them less profitable. Rather than accept a lower growth rate, Japan compensated by building up other, nonexport-dependent sectors of its economy, namely, and momentously, real estate. This was falsely viewed as a safer category of lending.[6] Japan was ripe for real estate growth. Societies often esteem ownership of land and believe that land values will not decline, but this was particularly true in Japan. Notably, "inheritance tax and corporate income tax favored unrealized capital gains in real estate."[7] And while exporters were hurt because of the Plaza Accord, it increased the buying power of the yen and made others in Japan quite wealthy.

It all became part of a massive Japanese renewal project: down came the gray office blocks where the Japanese had toiled during the tough "catching-up" years, and down came the rickety wooden houses of the nation's "salarymen." In their place were erected contemporary office blocks and stylish homes that expressed the Japanese pride in their wealth. Banks had found a ready market.

Japan's most intense lending growth happened from 1988 to 1990, with nominal loans growing an average of 13.8 percent per year. During this

Japanese economic miracle, CRE lending skyrocketed, and new office buildings, apartments, hotels, and shopping malls soon dominated the landscape.
Japan's largest "blue chip" corporations had gained access to corporate debt
markets and were no longer as dependent on banks. This meant that Japan's
bank lenders were forced to diversify and go downmarket, so they aggressively chased small- to medium-sized businesses and real estate lending.
Banks lent to these smaller domestic businesses and to consumers through
mortgages and a category called "loans for other purposes" that were often
secured by real estate. Japan's city banks made almost 75 percent of their loans
to small businesses, many of which were backed by real estate, though not
categorized or disclosed that way. In addition, a particularly risky form of
bank lending known as corporate overdrafts surged, growing "from 2 percent
to 19 percent (or ¥41.6 trillion) of total outstanding loans between March 1981
and October 1991."[8]

These kinds of loans were riskier than blue-chip corporate loans—and
lending standards were increasingly compromised. The Bank of Japan would
later find that lenders' risk departments, the very places entrusted to inject
caution into lending practices, had instead become dominated by those seeking to promote loans and who overoptimistically valued collateral.

The deregulation of interest rates that banks could pay their customers
began largely in 1985 and was fully implemented by April 1991. Banks could
pay more interest to customers and thus attract more deposits, an important
adjunct to meteoric loan growth. The United States had deregulated its financial system over the course of several decades, from the 1970s to the 1990s.
Post–Plaza Accord, it pressured the Japanese to deregulate in a matter of a
few years. This was another fateful factor. In the ministries, there was no institutional experience or preparation for such swift financial deregulation.
Additionally, lending banks had little understanding of the CRE market. It
all increased the odds of an unfavorable outcome for the lending industry.

Japan's lending frenzy extended down into households. Credit cards accounts tripled from 1983 to 1990, to 166 million. Nonmortgage household
debt increased from 1980 to 1990, from ¥16 trillion to ¥49 trillion. From 1984
to 1990, the average size of a bank mortgage doubled from ¥5.6 million to ¥11
million.[9] By 1991, Japan, a nation that until recently had no significant
consumer-driven debt to speak of, saw its per-capita consumer debt grow to
$3,426, an amount commensurate with that of the United States.

Japan's lending frenzy extended abroad. In highly publicized transactions
that alarmed many Americans, Hiro Real Estate purchased New York's

Socony-Mobil Building in 1987; the next year, the Bank of Tokyo bought Union Bank; in 1989, Mitsubishi Real Estate bought Rockefeller Center; and, in 1990, a Japanese firm called Cosmo World bought the legendary American golf course Pebble Beach. But "trophy" property acquisitions such as these often signal a market at the top and thus herald a tumble. And so it was here. By 1990, Japan's banks owned an astonishing 12.4 percent of all American banking assets. In 1991, Japan's banks accounted for 24 percent of all California banking assets, including 20 percent of all property loans and 35 percent of all commercial and industrial loans.[10]

But the 1980s lending frenzy wasn't just bank based, which is typical of a financial crisis. Leasing companies, consumer-finance companies, mortgage companies, and other nonbank lenders were making significant property-backed loans, and their funding often came from banks. Bank loans to fund nonbank lenders reached some ¥137 trillion by 1991, much of which eventually went bad. During this period, Japan's 30,000 nonbanks were largely unregulated, so the composition of their portfolios was largely unknown. This opacity "made America's savings and loans regulators look almost zealous by comparison."[11]

A 1990 finance ministry study concluded that about 60 percent of all nonbank loans had gone to the property and construction sectors compared with 25 percent at banks. Total nonbank lending would reach ¥130 trillion, or 15 percent of total private debt,[12] with two-thirds of those loans secured by land.[13] Inflated real estate values increased the risk to Japan's unwitting lenders, as they used real estate as collateral for yet more loans—not just for CRE and mortgage loans but also for small- to medium-sized business loans and nonmortgage household loans.

As if this feedback spiral of private lending and valuation wasn't dramatic enough, banks in this period could also own stocks. Lending brought the economic surge, which boosted the overall stock market, and that significantly increased the value of the stocks the banks held. This gave an earnings boost that augmented their lending capacity, which then accelerated private lending.[14] It was a deceptively profitable equation—until the bottom fell out of stocks.

The *jusen* were among the most aggressive lenders during this period. *Jusen* were nonbank institutions formed in the 1970s by consortia of banks to make household mortgage loans since banks had mortgage limitations.[15] During the 1980s, these *jusen* had gone beyond their household mortgage mandate to begin making CRE loans and had done so as aggressively as any other lenders.[16]

Because banks could not legally directly own controlling shares in other financial institutions, the *jusen* were not technically their subsidiaries. Smaller financial institutions, such as credit cooperatives, invested in the *jusen*, while the larger depository firms lent to the *jusen*. Too many of the larger institutions that financed the *jusen* steered them toward loans to risky real estate projects.[17] While the larger financial companies had to adhere to regulations, the *jusen* operated largely in an unfettered market.[18]

A close insiders' network of lenders, business executives, politicians, and bureaucrats fostered Japan's aggressive growth. Japanese securities firms, including its largest, Nomura, would reimburse losses for favored clients—with or without that client's knowledge—because they were offering customers guaranteed investment returns. This practice would not likely to be considered except in the boom-time fever.[19]

The *yakuza*, or crime syndicates, were also in the mix. The Nomura and Nikko securities firms financed the activities of Susumu Ishii, head of the crime syndicate Inagawa-kai, when he tried to corner the shares of the Tokyu Corporation in 1989. These associations were often forged through extortion, and the loans in question were often not repaid, as noted in the 1996 article "Yakuza Settle Bad Debts with a Bullet as Japan Bubble Bursts," from the *Independent* of London. In the "morality tale about Japan's bubble economy," the article notes, "it soon became clear" to banks when they tried, finally, to foreclose on problem loans "that they had not only been rash in the scale of their lending, but foolish in their choice of customers. . . . The yakuza have an advantage over other debtors: everyone is terrified of them."[20]

There were large loans collateralized by fraudulent certificates of deposit, sometimes issued in collusion with bank staff. A customer named Keiko Fujinori notably used forged certificates of deposit to fraudulently obtain hundreds of billions of yen in loans.[21] Property companies forged certificates in collusion with banking officials in an attempt to circumvent lending limitations. And even without collusion, lenders neglected due diligence on fraudulent collateral because of management pressure to meet extremely aggressive loan growth targets.

The financial tipping point was fast approaching: by 1990, total private loans had been growing significantly faster than GDP. Five-year private debt-to-GDP growth was now over 25 percent, and the overall level of private debt to GDP now exceeded 180 percent. As land prices skyrocketed to unsustainable valuations, the land that sat under Japan's Imperial Palace was reputed to be worth as much as the entire state of California. Even if not en-

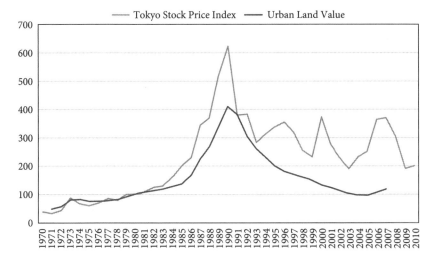

Figure 3.2. Tokyo Stock Price Index (TOPIX) and Urban Land Value Index, 1970–2010 (1980=100)

tirely true, it was a plausible analysis that underscored the preposterous overvaluations and frenzied lending of the time.

Then came the correction. First, in 1990, the Nikkei stock market average dropped by an alarming 39 percent. As in the Great Depression, the stock market crash was a symptom rather than a cause. Behind the story of both market crashes lurked the prequel of overlending and private debt. Stocks had reached unsustainable valuations and a critical mass of bad loans had long since been made. As is often true with financial crises, the rise in the stock market had accompanied the lending boom. Likewise, the stock market's tumble was at first a symptom of peril and a harbinger of the real estate tumble, and then became a catalyst for more financial distress.

The bottom fell out of the real estate market in 1991. Whether office buildings, apartments, hotels, houses, condominiums, or tracts of land, from early 1991 to March of the next year, real estate price declined on average 15.5 percent. The trend continued into 1993, with values falling by another 18 percent by March 1993. Falling real estate prices are often a defining moment that comes pursuant to a lending surge. Prices had risen by some 300 percent, which meant that the return to preboom values would be every bit as dramatic.

The problem of course was that banks had used real estate as collateral based on very high valuations, so the moment those valuations began to decline, the loans were no longer fully collateralized. And the more real estate prices plunged, the bigger the banks' bad debt exposure. The only way to maintain prices was to continue to make real estate loans using those high valuations. It's the crisis trap. Continued lending can prop up real estate values, but as that real estate lending slackens, values decline and impair those loans.

At this point (and probably as early as 1990), a financial crisis in Japan was inevitable. Over ¥340 trillion of loans and debt securities had been extended from 1985 to 1990, or roughly 2.4 trillion of that era's dollars. Time would show that well over ¥90 trillion of these loans would be bad. The banking industry only had ¥35 trillion in capital and reserves. A huge number of buildings and houses sat empty, and the day of reckoning for those loans would come. The government could not prevent the calamity. It could only influence how rapidly the bad news would unfold and how large the eventual damage would be.

With the real estate crash, Japan's economy was in crisis and had reached a crossroads. In financial crises, expansion plotlines are alike, while bust plotlines vary. It's in this second phase that Japan diverged most dramatically from the Great Depression.

In the United States in the early 1930s, the government stood aside and provided almost no support as bank deposits and loans contracted, and so banks failed, bringing down both good and bad businesses in the process. GDP contracted by almost 50 percent, unemployment soared, and cities were filled with Hoovervilles and bread lines. Private debt declined by a staggering 20 percent in four years. Some officials believed that this contraction was a necessary purge.

In the early 1990s, Japan's economy could have taken that same path. It had created as much or more bad debt than in the United States in the 1920s. The level of unemployment, the damage to its banks, and the contraction in its GDP could have been every bit as severe. At this point many of the banks could have and perhaps should have been declared undercapitalized or insolvent. But instead, in stark contrast, bankers and their regulators appeared to look the other way, and Japan's loans and GDP continued to expand, albeit at a slower pace. As part of this, banks took loan losses against their earnings that were astonishingly smaller than their actual problem loans because acknowledging the full extent of the problem would surely have meant the failure of many of the largest institutions.

Japan's banking industry and government remained in denial longer and more deeply than those of the United States in the 1930s. Japan was all too willing to believe that property values would rebound and robustness would return. There were no "runs" since that posture and the government's implicit support kept the industry's funding intact, and the government also boosted deposit insurance strategically through this period. Though the collapse in asset prices occurred in 1990 and 1991, Japan's government did not intervene to provide capital to the industry until 1998 and took until the mid-2000s to complete the process—a period of almost fifteen years.

There were several factors behind this denial. For one thing, the sheer speed and scale of the asset price decline was far beyond anyone's ability to grasp—or, even if they could grasp it, to accept. The scale of the bad lending that brings a financial crisis is almost always too overwhelming to readily absorb. If anyone in Japan's banking or regulatory community had said that the banking industry's losses over the next eight years would be over ¥65 trillion, it would have been dismissed as lunacy, even though any clear-eyed calculations based on the actual property-value decline would have pointed to a loss of that magnitude.

Most participants could not accept that land prices would not recover and favorable growth would not return. Before the collapse of 1991, there had not been a decline in real estate values since World War II, much land was closely held and yielded limited information on sales prices, and the Japanese broadly believed values would never decline. And in a climate where the Japanese expected and required themselves to continue their record of superior achievement, peer pressure spurred them to keep growing. No bank wanted to be the first to show a decline in loans or earnings, and banks learned to postpone the recognition of loan losses through too-optimistic projections and other obfuscations.[22]

Remarkably, banks in Japan at this time had nearly complete discretion in how much they reserved for loan losses and for charging those loans off against earnings, and were not required to disclose problem loans. They were allowed to report income from a loan for a year after they stopped receiving interest payments on that loan. Further, since banks were the biggest taxpayers in Japan, they had to ask permission to reserve for loan losses for each loan because to do so would reduce their tax payments to the government. Banks actually reduced loan loss reserves in fiscal year 1991.[23]

But even this deep level of denial had its limits. Some problems proved impossible to suppress. In 1991, Toho Sogo Bank, despite being covered by the government's deposit insurance system, went bankrupt and became Japan's first bank failure since World War II.[24] The government treated this small bank failure as an aberration.

The finance ministry had introduced a new rule in 1990 to try to moderate what was tacitly recognized as rampant CRE overlending. It required that banks not increase their lending to property companies by more than the percentage increase in their total loans.[25] Beginning in 1991, this contributed to an overall deceleration of CRE lending but brought a shift in lending to other categories, especially household mortgages, which then became the fastest-growing category of lending. This in turn brought overlending and credit problems in the household mortgage sector. And in fact, from 1995 to 1998, when the industry was finally recapitalized, overlending in consumer mortgages and housing loans approached the overlending that had occurred in CRE.

In 1995, Japan finally began to face up to some household mortgage and CRE issues when it intervened to address the *jusen* problem. By 1995, nonperforming loans for the *jusen* had ballooned to 75 percent of all loans outstanding, with 60 percent marked unrecoverable, according to a Ministry of Finance investigation: the findings were that the situation was so bad that the ministry liquidated the *jusen*.[26] Parent firms and creditor banks of *jusen* companies bore the brunt of these losses, writing off all their equity stakes and loans to the companies totaling ¥3.5 trillion.[27] Other banks wrote off ¥1.7 trillion in loans.[28] Ultimately, this cost taxpayers an estimated ¥1.2 trillion.[29]

But total loans outstanding at the *jusen* were below 2 percent of all private loans, so the threat from the *jusen* alone was well short of systemic. The public pointedly decried the use of taxpayer dollars to rescue the *jusen*, which made the government reluctant to rescue any other lenders over the next two years and fed the bias toward denial. So banks, though chock-full of problem loans, kept on lending.[30]

By July 1995, public concern about the condition of all Japan's banks was growing.[31] To quiet these concerns, the Ministry of Finance announced that Japan's provider of deposit insurance, the Deposit Insurance Corporation, would protect *all* deposits for five years, replacing the ¥10 million limit that had previously been in place. In 1996, with concerns unabated, it was further amended to protect all deposits *and other liabilities*—such as bonds—until March 2001. Meanwhile, the business environment continued to be difficult. The 1980s' overbuilding had not been absorbed and in some areas had worsened. The high debt load accumulated in the 1980s and early 1990s stifled businesses and households.

The household lending upturn of the 1980s had resulted in an increase in personal bankruptcies in the early 1990s. Bankruptcies in Japan reached

¥8 trillion in 1991.[32] A growing number of companies began restructuring their debt. Even in the face of this, however, no banks made significant increases to their loan loss reserves. Since selling real estate caused property values to fall even further, and falling property values impaired the loan collateral, banks encouraged debtors not to sell real estate serving as collateral since it would only add to this problem. They simply extended their loans instead.[33] It's a strategy that is sometimes pejoratively referred to as "extend and pretend." Because of this, bank loans didn't contract in the early to mid-1990s, and therefore the majority of businesses had the lending support to continue to muddle through. Unemployment stayed low.

The term used when a government and its regulatory departments show leniency and allow banks to forgo or take extended time to write down impaired loans is *forbearance*, and Japan showed extraordinary levels of this forbearance toward the nation's lenders in the 1990s. And so these "zombie" banks, as they were now sometimes called, marched on.[34]

Concern on the part of the international lending community regarding Japan's banks became such that a "Japan premium" emerged on the offshore borrowings of these banks.[35] This was "particularly galling to major Japanese banks," which were still penalized regardless of their financial strength, and was "intensely embarrassing to the Japanese government and its economic agencies."[36]

Some would suggest that this protracted process and pervasive denial was an intentional strategy rather than an ad hoc process, one that dealt with the financial crisis only to the extent that the government could admit and afford. Could Japan have even planned a fifteen-year process if it had full awareness of the problem in 1991? Perhaps. Paul Volcker pulled off a similar trick in 1982 in the Latin American debt crisis, where a few very large New York money-center banks had losses in excess of their capital. He offered quiet forbearance by letting these banks write off loans against earnings gradually without forcing them to write off the full amount against capital while doing so. But that was just a few banks and one very powerful regulator.

Whatever the case, Japanese actions during these years showed elements of great tolerance and restraint. That would be tested when Japan's Asian neighbors, and the source of much demand for its goods, began to unravel in the Asian financial crisis of 1997.

In the 1990s, a number of the smaller Asian countries—including South Korea, Thailand, Indonesia, Hong Kong, Laos, Malaysia, and the Philippines—were experiencing rapid GDP growth and economic miracles of their own,

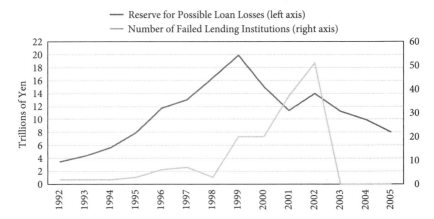

Figure 3.3. Japan: Reserves for Possible Loan Losses and Number of Failed Lending Institutions, 1992–2005
Although stock and real estate prices had dropped by 1991, banks delayed fully providing reserves for those losses for a number of years.

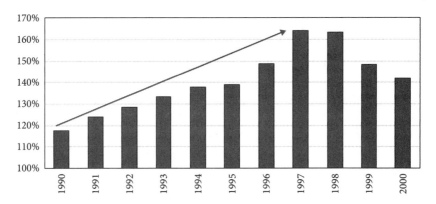

Figure 3.4. South Korea: Private Debt as a Percentage of GDP, 1990–2000

but it all was abruptly interrupted when their currencies and stock markets came tumbling down, beginning in July 1997.

Though it has often been characterized as primarily a currency crisis or even a government debt crisis, the Asian crisis was, like almost all financial crises, foremost a runaway private debt crisis. By 1997, at the start of the crisis, the ratio of South Korea's private debt to GDP had grown 28 percent in five years, and its overall ratio of private debt to GDP had reached 164 percent (see Figure 3.4). Its government debt was a mere 12 percent of GDP. The

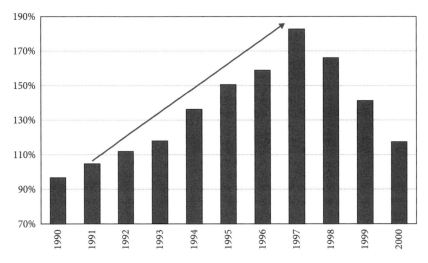

Figure 3.5. Thailand: Private Debt as a Percentage of GDP, 1990–2000

South Korean currency, the won, had been trading in the same general range for several years. Then, after years and years of rampant lending, investors, depositors, and traders were beginning to hear and see fragmented evidence that corporate borrowers were overleveraged and would be unable to pay their debts, putting the banks that lent to them in jeopardy. Foreign investors and lenders withdrew their funds where they could and moved those funds out of the country. As that happened, South Korea's currency collapsed and a fiscal rout began, but only well after years of rampant lending.

The concern that banks had lent too much and corporate borrowers were overleveraged was amply justified. Private debt in South Korea, Thailand, and Indonesia had exploded between 1992 and 1997, creating overcapacity and a bevy of bad loans in all three countries. Corporate debt, as much or more than real estate debt, was the culprit in South Korea. Some of these loans were to corporations that supported Japan's industries and were thus exposed to Japan's slowdown. Figure 3.6 shows the debt buildup in five of South Korea's largest *chaebol,* the large industrial conglomerates in South Korea that were historically family controlled: Samsung, Daewoo, Hyundai, SsangYong, and LG. All became increasingly leveraged and suffered significant reversals. One, Daewoo, was forced into bankruptcy and emerged from that process a much smaller and different company.

Some blamed it on a currency crisis, but the rampage in private lending had fully occurred before the currency drop. Financial crises have occurred

Table 3.2. South Korea Crisis Matrix: 1990s

Billions of Won	1992	1997	1998	1992–1997 Change
GDP	273,267	530,347	524,477	257,080
Public Debt	33,263	63,289	142,793	30,026
Private Debt	350,609	869,949	856,695	519,340
Business Debt	225,368	581,963	584,589	356,595
Household Debt	122,934	270,641	247,773	147,707
As Percentage of GDP				1992–1997 Change
Public Debt	12%	12%	27%	0%
Private Debt	128%	164%	163%	36%
Business Debt	82%	110%	111%	27%
Household Debt	45%	51%	47%	6%

In the five years leading to 1997, South Korea's private debt grew by 148 percent.

in situations when currencies drop, when they rise, and when they are stable. From 1927 to 1930, the U.S. dollar was flat relative to the pound, the German mark, and the French franc. The euro grew 32 percent against the U.S. dollar in the two years leading into the 2008 crisis, before finally dropping midway into 2008. There is limited correlation between currency swings and financial crises.

The currency crisis was a result rather than a cause of the Asian crisis, but that currency drop did indeed exacerbate the problem. In countries where a meaningful percentage of businesses or households borrow in a foreign currency, a currency drop effectively increases the amount they owe. If the currency drops by half relative to that lenders' currency, then the borrower's debt doubles. Koreans had already borrowed too much, many of their loans were already in trouble, and the currency devaluation worsened the situation significantly.

The story was similar in Thailand, Indonesia, and beyond. The financial collapses in these countries affected Japan. The combined 1996 GDP of Thailand, South Korea, and Indonesia was $1 trillion. That was only about 22 percent of Japan's GDP that year, but large enough to worsen the environment for Japan in three key ways. First, it adversely affected Japan's GDP growth since businesses and households in these countries were customers

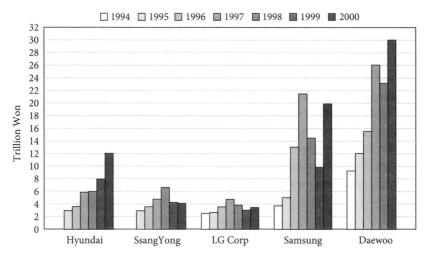

Figure 3.6. South Korea: Chaebol Debt, 1994–2000
Private debt grew rapidly up to 1997 in major chaebol.

Table 3.3. China Crisis Matrix: 1990s and 2000s

Billions of Yuan	1990	1995	2000	2001	1990–1995 Change
GDP	1,887	6,134	10,028	11,086	4,247
Public Debt	129	373	1,631	1,942	244
Private Debt	1,562	4,740	10,910	11,211	3,178
As Percentage of GDP					1990–1995 Change
Public Debt	7%	6%	16%	18%	−1%
Private Debt	83%	77%	109%	101%	−6%

China's private debt grew more than threefold in the five years leading to 1995, which brought loan losses estimated as high as 30 to 40 percent of total loans.

of Japanese companies. Second, it further weakened Japan's lenders because they lent to companies in these countries. Third, it added to general market turbulence, which prodded the Japanese government toward recognition that it needed to intervene with its own domestic banks. After the Asian crisis, it became more difficult for Japan to project an imminent recovery of its stock and real estate markets.

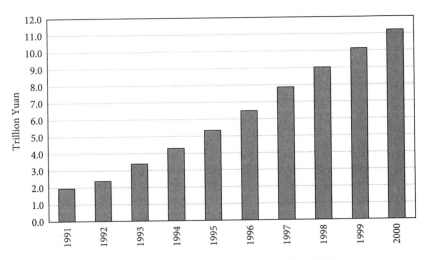

Figure 3.7. China: Private Debt as a Percentage of GDP, 1991–2000

The emerging giant China had a reckoning in this era as well. By 1999, loans in the then-nascent capitalist nation had nearly doubled in a mere four years (Figure 3.7) and had risen from 84 percent to 111 percent of GDP. Problem loans in the banks reportedly reached over 30 percent of total loans, an unfathomable percentage that greatly exceeded the level in Japan.[37] In the China of that era, as occurs in many countries as they first industrialize, it was almost as if lenders didn't yet know how to make a loan and were learning to be lenders as they went along. That certainly seemed true in the United States in the 1830s, given the extraordinary losses lenders incurred as we will see in the next chapter. It appeared that Japan reached those same extraordinary loss levels in 1882, its first financial crisis brought on by its rush to industrialization, though the data is even murkier for Japan in that year than for the United States in 1837.

But as maladroit as it was at lending, China was a wizard at whitewashing its financial crisis. In the early 2000s, China pulled off two astonishing tricks that made credit problems totaling 20 percent of loans (or 16 percent of GDP) effectively disappear from those banks and allowed China's lending and GDP growth to continue. First, China's banks lent ¥270 billion to the government, which promptly injected those same funds back into the banks as equity. It was almost magic. Where did the banks get the money to lend? The government simply lowered their reserve requirement from 13 percent to 9 percent.

In other words, they used funds already on deposit at the People's Bank of China, China's central bank—and with just a few paper entries, the capital of those banks was doubled.[38] The government then set up four asset management companies (AMCs), and the banks transferred roughly ¥1.4 trillion in bad debt (which was "20 percent of the total loan balance at that time") to those AMCs—*at face value.* The banks took back AMC bonds and People's Bank credit in payment.[39]

This was more magic on China's part and a clever way to achieve a government recapitalization and shift the burden to taxpayers.[40] With a large dose of new equity added from overseas, one of the largest bad debt problems in banking history had instantly been dealt with. As circumstance would have it, at this moment, the West started its debt-fueled mid-2000s importing binge, much of which was from China, and China's net exports surged from 2 percent to 8 percent of GDP, supercharging that country's economy. With that, China's banks were soon back. This was supplemented shortly afterward and in the years beyond through additional government capital, additional nonperforming loan transfers, and foreign investment.[41]

China's legerdemain was breathtaking but ruthlessly logical. Unlike the governments of the United States or even Japan, the Chinese government had absolute ownership or control of all the entities involved: banks, borrowers, regulators, and AMCs. China's deftness and creativity in financial problem-solving made Japan in the 1990s and the United States in 1987 and 2009 look positively clumsy in comparison.

Turning back to Japan, for seven years, through a combination of denial and delay, Japan had managed to avoid facing up to its vast bad debt crisis. But with its own mounting problems and a backdrop of the Asian crisis, the day of reckoning was at hand. On November 4, 1997, Japan's Sanyo Securities filed bankruptcy, making it the "first failure of a publicly listed security company since the war." On November 17, Hokkaido Takushoku Bank "asked the Bank of Japan for an emergency loan," likewise another first: the "first failure of a 'city bank' since the war." Then on November 22, 1997, "Yamaichi Securities started voluntary liquidation,"[42] which stunned the markets since, unlike Sanyo, it was one of Japan's four largest securities companies.[43]

Japan then entered phase three of financial crisis, the recapitalization and long climb back. From 1997 to 2003, Japan's government spent huge sums to rescue and recapitalize some of the largest banks and securities firms in Japan. In March 1998 the government finally began a large-scale intervention in the crumbling banking system by injecting ¥1.8 trillion of funds into twenty-one banks.[44] But that amount was far "too small to stabilize the [funding] market,"[45] given that the problem was at that moment perhaps still ¥100 trillion to ¥200 trillion in size even after the banks had already charged off ¥50 trillion of that against earnings. So in October, the Japanese National Diet passed more effective bankruptcy (Financial Revitalization Act) and public capital injection laws (Bank Recapitalization Act), which gave it a more straightforward path to deal with problem banks.[46] It took this path almost immediately, when it nationalized the Nippon Credit Bank in December.[47]

In March 1999, the Japanese government injected another ¥7.7 trillion into fifteen banks, which stabilized the financial and funding market,[48] though some further deterioration of loan quality remained and the problem lingered.[49] With this recapitalization in 1998 and 1999, Japan's banks finally began to take actions to restructure and charge off loans, and they finally began to contract their overall loan totals. Thus began a private debt deleveraging that saw an almost unbroken private debt–to–GDP decline for an incredible twenty years—offset by even greater levels of public debt growth. Private debt deleveraging is difficult. It is hard for an economy to grow if the ratio of private debt to GDP is contracting because private debt growth is a primary engine of economic growth. This protracted deleveraging was the main cause of Japan's stagnant economic performance during this time, sometimes called the Lost Decade, but ultimately so long that it should more appropriately be thought of as the Lost Generation.

In 1999, the Nikkei rallied but quickly fell again, and remained trapped in a desultory trading range for over a decade. Audits in 2001 by the Financial Services Agency showed that banks had still not fully acknowledged the problems in their portfolios. Regulators, who were now more willing to address the problem, assessed bad debt on banks' books to be significantly higher than the banks' estimates of the same.[50] By 2003 bank capital was almost depleted again owing to newly recognized problem loans.[51] Clearly, banks had still not fully acknowledged or addressed the extent of their loan quality problems.

In 2003, "many weakened banks were allowed to operate by showing massive deferred tax asset" gains, and regulators continued to show forbearance since there were simply "too many bad banks for government to nationalize." In May of the same year, the government injected ¥2 trillion into an insolvent Risona Bank, even though it had been represented as sound. In November, Ashikaga Bank, "a big regional bank, was nationalized."[52] The government-led recapitalization continued piecemeal through 2003, and related bank failures dragged on until 2005.

Japan had strung out its massive 1990 overcapacity and bad debt problem for almost fifteen years. Its three years of lending profligacy, from 1987 to 1989, had brought fifteen years of penance. Some mark the long-deferred end of the crisis as 2005, when loan losses for major banks, which had been as high as ¥13.5 trillion in 1998, declined to ¥2 trillion.[53]

Between 1992 and 2004, Japanese banks lost ¥96 trillion. Some observers estimate that the crisis ultimately cost between ¥100 trillion and ¥150 trillion, or 20 percent to 30 percent of Japan's GDP.[54] Estimates of this cost vary. Nomura's esteemed economist Richard Koo calculates certain gains realized by Japan's government and concludes that in the final analysis the cost was far smaller, at ¥11.5 trillion. The European Commission estimates the cost was ¥70 trillion and the IMF estimates that it was ¥21.8 trillion. Estimates vary widely for the cost of every financial crises economists and historians examine.

Yet the most enduring cost was an economy that posted *zero* nominal growth from 1997 to 2016 and remained laden with, and stunted by, one of the world's highest private debt–to–GDP ratios. Japan's businesses were deleveraging but were nevertheless still highly leveraged, and thus found it hard to increase borrowing no matter how attractive the rate and terms. As a result, the factor that could have been pushing Japan's economy forward—growth in private debt to GDP—was absent.

The fact that Japan showed so much forbearance for so long, and then rescued its banks, meant that companies that would have otherwise gone bankrupt continued to operate thereby keeping unemployment comparatively low.[55] The Japanese have always assigned very high value to social cohesion, and this was very much a factor in the 1990s. There was little social disruption. Unemployment at the height of the crisis reached an unusually high figure for Japan but it was still low by the standards of other major crises.

In Japan's slump, the government's tax revenues declined and its expenses increased, and since that time, Japan's postcrisis government debt–to–GDP ratio had climbed to 236 percent, more than double the ratio in the United States. Japan's huge government deficits constituted, in some sense, the greatest Keynesian experiment of all time—which is to say the use of government expenditures to increase demand. And while GDP growth responded, it did not respond at the hoped-for level given the magnitude of the increased government spending.[56]

Some prominent Japanese economists have more recently argued that Japan's approach to rescuing its banking industry was a success compared with the U.S. approach in 2008. The United States dealt with its problem in a much more compressed time frame, yet experienced both more GDP contraction and higher unemployment.

Whether Japan's approach came from default or design is still debated. Though it did result in less disruption and unemployment, it left Japan's economy struggling with very high levels of private debt. The better policy, as always, would have been to have curbed or moderated the runaway lending of the late 1980s to begin with.

The crises described thus far occurred at times when reliable data on private debt were more or less available, albeit neglected. But it is my contention that private debt played the same pivotal role in more distant historical crises and was the core factor in nineteenth-century financial crises. To examine this view, we will take a tour in the next two chapters of major crises that occurred before the Great Depression, with a focus on the same six countries with the largest economies during that time.

In these first Industrial Age financial crises, vast amounts of private debt—incurred to buy land, to build on that land, to grow cotton, and to build railroads and canals—led to overcapacity, troubled loans, and bank failures.

CHAPTER 4

The Dawn of the Industrial Age Banking Crisis

1819–1840

Though financial crises date back to the dawn of lending, the crises in the United States in 1819 and Britain in 1825 can be considered the first major crises of the Industrial Age.

The Crisis of 1819

In 1816, the Second Bank of the United States had been chartered by Congress in large part because the absence of such a bank had made the War of 1812 difficult to finance. It was chartered with a mandate to make conventional loans, and make them it did, with loans skyrocketing from $13.5 million in 1817, its first year of business, to $41.2 million by 1818. By all appearances, the bank did not know how to judge risk, as is often true in a newly industrializing country, and almost immediately had made enough bad and fraudulent loans to bring the nineteenth century its first truly major financial crisis. Its losses spanned all regions of the country, especially the South and West, and "were so enormous that the bank was crippled in its dealings for six or seven years."[1] In just one facet of the aftermath, the property it had been forced to accept in liquidation of its debts resulted in its owning "a large part of Cincinnati: hotels, coffee-houses, warehouses, stores, stables, iron foundries, residences, [and] vacant lots."[2] When Andrew Jackson blamed the Second Bank for this crisis, it was with good reason. The contention between soon-to-be-president Jackson and the Second Bank would figure prominently in a much larger crisis less than two decades later.

The Crisis of 1825

Americans were not the only ones with difficulty in assessing risk. In Britain, during its lending boom in the early 1820s, investors bought dozens of parcels of land and £200,000 worth of government bonds, all from the Latin American country of Poyais. Aspiring settlers filled four ships bound for Poyais. Unfortunately, Poyais never existed. It was a lucrative fiction, conjured by Scottish mercenary Gregor MacGregor, who had set up an office in London to "sell" dozens of parcels of land in a Honduran swamp and fill ships with settlers to Poyais, before he was forced to flee England in 1823.[3] He took the speculation in debt that was at the heart of the United Kingdom's 1825 financial crisis to a remarkable new level—fictitiously conjuring not only investment value but a country as well.

His scheme was part of a British financial crisis in 1825 that brought the nation's entire banking system to the verge of collapse and remains one of history's worst crises. The president of the Board of Trade at the time gravely declared that the country was "within twenty-four hours of a state of barter." About 10 percent of all British banks—73 out of 770—failed within a few months; a "massive wave of bankruptcies" peaked in April 1826; and, in the aftermath, Britain's Parliament was compelled to try and reform the financial system by creating new regulations.[4]

By 1822, British investors had lived through years of economic stagnation and contraction. The economy struggled through its long nineteenth-century deleveraging from government debt amassed during the Napoleonic Wars—debt that had reached 260 percent of GDP. They wanted higher yields than what they could get from traditional British sources. At the same time, the newly independent Spanish colonies in the Americas were turning to London for desperately needed capital for infrastructure, operations, and other purposes. The foreign bond market took off. Between 1822 and 1825 nine Latin American nations floated bonds of over £22 million. These new economies were fragile, investments were ill conceived, and, by 1827, every issuing Latin American nation would default.[5]

Latin American bonds were significant but were overshadowed by a far larger bubble created by newly formed "joint stock" companies. These companies, most unrelated to any Latin American activity, were financed by selling shares to an eager and unsophisticated public as the Latin American debt fever grew. A share with a par or face value of £100 could be purchased for as little as £5 down. The investor agreed to pay an additional sum—usually

Table 4.1. Latin American Debt Sold on the London Market, 1822–1825

Year	Debt Issuer	Capital Created	Coupon Rate	Price as % of Par	Amount Raised in UK	Market Price of Bond High	Market Price of Bond Low	Debt Issued by Nations in: Europe	Debt Issued by Nations in: Latin America	Ratio of LA Debt to Total debt Issued	1824–1825 Only
1822	Colombia	£2,000,000	6.0	84.0	£1,680,000	96.5	38.5	£17,430,800	£3,650,000	17.3%	
	Chile	£1,000,000	6.0	70.0	£700,000	93.0	30.0				
	Poyais	£200,000	6.0	80.0	£160,000	81.0	0.0				
	Peru	£450,000	6.0	88.0	£396,000	89.0	23.5				
1823	None							£6,000,000	£0	0	
1824	Peru	£750,000	6.0	82.0	£615,000	89.0	23.5	£3,300,000	£10,900,000	76.8%	63.2%
	Buenos Aires	£1,000,000	6.0	85.0	£850,000	97.0	69.0				
	Colombia	£4,750,000	6.0	88.5	£4,203,750	96.5	52.5				
	Brazil	£1,200,000	5.0	75.0	£900,000	91.0	51.0				
	Mexico	£3,200,000	5.0	58.0	£1,856,000	88.0	50.0				
1825	Brazil	£2,000,000	5.0	85.0	£1,700,000	91.0	51.0	£7,625,000	£7,844,750	50.7%	
	Mexico	£3,200,000	6.0	89.8	£2,872,000	94.8	60.0				
	Peru	£616,000	6.0	78.0	£480,480	83.0	38.0				
	Guatemala	£1,428,750	6.0	73.0	£1,042,988	74.0	50.0				
	Guadalajara	£600,000	6.0	60.0	£360,000	62.0	50.0				

Table 4.2. U.K. Crisis Matrix: 1820s

Millions of British Pounds	1820	1825	1827	1820–1825 Change
GDP	438	496	452	58
Public Debt	873	860	857	(13)
Private Debt	*	*	*	*
Bills of Exchange	237	284	205	47
Foreign Bonds	8	73	n/a	65
Latin American Bonds	–	22	n/a	22
Joint Stock Companies Formed	n/a	227	n/a	n/a
Number of Banks	1,014	965	855	−49
Bank Failures	32	75	13	43

As Percentage of GDP				1820–1825 Change
Public Debt	199%	173%	190%	−26%
Private Debt	n/a	n/a	n/a	n/a
Bills of Exchange	54%	57%	45%	3%
Foreign Bonds	2%	15%	n/a	13%
Latin American Bonds	0%	4%	n/a	4%

*Limited data points.
Private lending totals are impossible to reconstruct given the absence of data on city banks and other types of debt. However, Bills of Exchange (an indicator of overall trends) increased £47 million from 1820 to 1825, and foreign debt increased twentyfold.

equal to the initial deposit—whenever the company's agent placed a call notice in the London newspapers. In other words, a stock subscription was an ancestor to today's margin loan.

In February 1824, after the success of the Baring and Rothschild banking families with a joint stock venture called the Alliance British and Foreign Life and Fire Insurance Company, these joint stock companies moved from quiet obscurity to center stage.[6] Suddenly investors seemed willing to put money into almost any newly announced joint stock company with a prospectus and a sales agent. The fascination with joint stock companies converged with Latin American investments to create an irresistible overlapping opportunity: twenty-nine companies formed by 1826 to conduct Latin American mining operations.[7]

Besieged by bills seeking authorization for new joint stock companies, Parliament repealed the Bubble Act of 1720—enacted to curb certain joint stock activity in the throes of the notorious South Sea Bubble—that had been limiting the creation of these new companies. An assiduous observer, Henry English, kept track of all the new companies organizing and selling shares by scouring newspapers for announcements and prospectuses. He would find that in 1824 and 1825, some 624 companies had announced their intention to go into business and sell shares. Of these, over half apparently existed only on paper.[8]

In similar fashion to twentieth-century financial crises, growth in private debt and rampant speculation, including through the emergence of new instruments in the "joint stock company," laid the groundwork for financial crisis in the 1820s. Of the £102,781,600 worth of shares sold by the 245 companies that English identified as having actually started business operations, only £17,645,625 had actually been paid in—leaving investors potentially on the hook for £85,135,975, subject to call at any time.[9]

The actions and policies of British banks, ranging from the smallest country bank to the Bank of England itself, ultimately facilitated this unchecked speculation and the ensuing crisis. England's country banks, modest and localized, issued their own notes, which was a means by which they extended loans. As the economy grew after 1822, they flooded loans to district farmers and businessmen. Between 1822 and 1825, the value of country bank notes in circulation more than doubled, even as the number of banks remained relatively constant at around eight hundred.[10] This new infusion of cash from country banks, the continued expansion of city banks, and the Bank of England's own currency expansion, along with a sharp fall in interest rates, stoked the speculative fires.

But the expansion in sectors across the economy had been too great and credit quality became an issue. By the end of the summer of 1825, falling reserves at the country banks and the deflation of the speculative stock bubble were indicators of trouble and worried bankers at small regional banks and London private institutions. Stock prices were down 54 percent from their highs. The Bank of England directors, either unaware of or unconcerned about signs of impending crisis, did not expand credit to support the lending institutions that were beginning to suffer.[11]

In November, there were runs on dozens of country banks, whose bankers now faced a liquidity crunch and turned to their corresponding private banks in London to plead for specie. Private banks, following the financial food chain, turned to the Bank of England for funds, further depleting the bank's already shrinking reserves of coin and bullion. The venerable London bank Pole, Thornton & Company closed its doors five days later, which crippled its thirty-four correspondent country banks.[12] The crisis became a full-on panic the following week, as five more London banks failed.

The Bank of England abruptly reversed its policy in a last-ditch effort to avoid a complete meltdown of the financial markets. Halting the contraction of bank loans is key to forestalling a panic and initiating a recovery. This was as true in the 1800s as the 2000s. The bank raised the discount rate to 5 percent and immediately began making advances to almost any banker who could elbow his way to its discount window. The amount of notes under discount, which had remained fairly steady around £2.5 million since 1823, shot up to £9.6 million by early 1826.[13] All of this activity allowed the Bank of England to increase its notes in circulation by £8 million in just five weeks by the end of December. And on December 17, when the bank's reserves of gold coin were within a few days of running out entirely, a deal with Nathan and James Rothschild brought £300,000 in gold sovereigns from Paris to London.[14] The worst of the crisis was over.

Rampant lending had brought bad debt and failed banks. The key elements that would prefigure two centuries of financial crises were already well in place. France, too, saw an extended financial crisis from 1827 to 1831, culminating in the failure of 252 banks in the years 1830 to 1831.[15] Land, construction, agriculture, and even the silk industry were part of the downturn, and business bankruptcies almost doubled during this period. The Communist philosopher Friedrich Engels described a silk workers' revolt in Lyon in 1831 as the "first working class rising" of the new industrial age.[16]

The Crisis of 1837

Just a few short years later, both Britain and the United States embarked on new and greater runaway lending in the first transatlantic financial crisis. The U.S. expansion of the 1830s played out over several years and featured high-profile characters, such as President Andrew Jackson and Second Bank of the United States president Nicholas Biddle, but it also ensnared hundreds of anonymous bankers, merchants, planters, financiers, investors, and government employees.

During his trip to the United States in 1831, French author and critic Alexis de Tocqueville described Americans as in pursuit of the answer to one question: how much money will it bring in?[17] By the early to mid-1830s, the economy of the United States was in the midst of an enormous credit-fueled frenzy dominated by loans to purchase land, loans for real estate construction, and loans to finance large-scale cotton plantations. This frenzy drove up prices. From 1830 to 1837, U.S. GDP grew by $632 million, or 51 percent, to $1.9 billion, riding on a 22 percent surge in population. Across the Atlantic, the United Kingdom was in a credit boom as well, although it was only half as large, and much of the credit was to finance the burgeoning British textile industry that was a voracious customer for America's cotton.

Upon encountering Chicago for the first time in 1836, British writer and social theorist Harriet Martineau noted, "It seemed as if some prevalent mania infected the whole people. Storekeepers hailed [passersby] from their doors, with offers of farms, and all manner of land-lots, advising them to speculate before the price of land rose higher.... Of course, this rapid money-making is a merely temporary evil. A bursting of the bubble must come soon."[18]

The U.S. population was not only growing fast in the 1830s, through both increased birth rates and large-scale immigration; it was also moving west. From 1830 and 1840, the U.S. population grew from 12.9 to 17.1 million. But the population in the West grew faster. Missouri, including the gateway city of St. Louis, nearly tripled to 383,700. Ohio's population grew by 62 percent.[19] By 1836, observer James Buck noted that building lots in Milwaukee were already selling "for prices that made those who bought or sold them feel like a Vanderbilt."[20]

It spurred a nationwide eruption in construction, funded by loans from wealthy individuals, savings banks, private banks, states, and even insurance companies. It was during this decade that institutions first began to provide a significant portion of real estate loans. The construction frenzy went hand in hand with land sales. Between 1830 and 1836, the federal government alone disposed of 75,505 square miles of land. Most of this—50,999 square miles, *an expanse equal to the whole of England*—was sold between January 1835 and December 1836. Sales peaked at $25,167,833 in 1836 (Figure 4.3).

Prices for acreage in Chicago's Loop rivaled those in New York, rising a dazzling 41,275 percent, from $32 in 1830 to $13,240 in 1836.[21] Writer and attorney Joseph Baldwin later satirized the general chaos of the boom years as "a riotous carnival," unorganized and chaotic, a state "standing on its head with its heels in the air."[22] Meanwhile, in the West, new villages sprang up, existing villages became towns, and towns became cities. Many a young person could make a fortune simply by moving west, buying land on credit in a

Table 4.3. U.S. Crisis Matrix: 1830s

Millions of Dollars	1832	1837	1839	1832–1837 Change
GDP	$1,458	$1,865	$1,877	$407
Federal Debt	$7	$3	$4	$(4)
State Debt	n/a	$117	$198	n/a
Private Debt (est.)	$415	$794	$780	$379
State Bank Loans	$153	$486	n/a	$333
Construction Value	$296	$388	$278	$92
Cotton Production	$47	$68	$71	$21
Canal Investment	$5	$8	$14	$3.6
Public Land Sales	$3	$25[a]	$6	$22
Memo: Construction Debt (est.)	$240	$516	$358	$276
Memo: Cotton Debt (est.)	$41	$62	$16	$21
Memo: Mortgage Debt (est.)	$148	$170	$179	$22
Memo: Canal Debt (est.)	$55	$81	$107	$26
Number of Banks	464	729	840	265
Bank Failures	n/a	19	22	n/a

As Percentage of GDP	1832	1837	1839	1832–1837 Change
Federal Debt	0%	0%	0%	0%
State Debt	n/a	6%	11%	n/a
Private Debt (est.)	28%	43%	42%	14%
State Bank Loans	10%	26%	n/a	16%
Construction Value	20%	21%	15%	1%
Cotton Production	3%	4%	4%	0%
Canal Investment	0%	0%	1%	0%
Public Land Sales	0%	1%[a]	0%	1%
Memo: Construction Debt (est.)	16%	28%	19%	11%
Memo: Cotton Debt (est.)	3%	3%	1%	1%
Memo: Mortgage Debt (est.)	10%	9%	10%	−1%
Memo: Canal Debt (est.)	4%	4%	6%	1%

[a]For 1836.

In the five years leading to 1837, we estimate that U.S. private debt grew by 91 percent—primarily in state banks. Sector debt data is unavailable, but the sector with the greatest increase in spending was construction, which more than doubled. Other sectors with notable increases were cotton, canals, and public land.

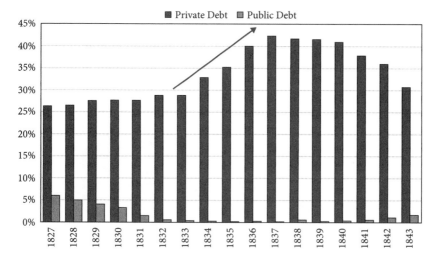

Figure 4.1. United States: Private and Public Debt as a Percentage of GDP, 1827–1843
We estimate that in the United States private debt increased by $379 million (or 91 percent) between 1832 and 1837.

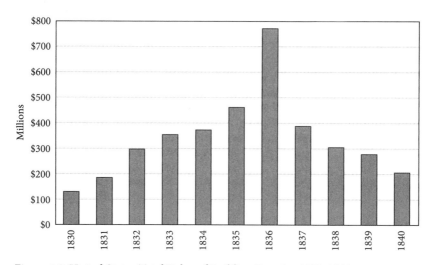

Figure 4.2. United States: Total Value of Building Permits, 1830–1840

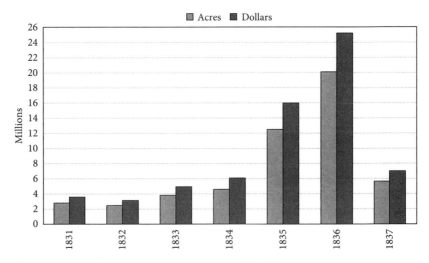

Figure 4.3. United States: Federal Land Sales, 1831–1837

small town, and then waiting for the westward flow of settlers to drive up the price of that land. John Gordon reported on land sales in southern Michigan: "Everyone with whom I converse, talks of 100 percent as the lowest return on investment."[23] No one thought they could lose money on real estate.

The cotton boom developed apace with construction and land sales. In 1830, over two million acres were under cultivation for cotton; by 1840, the number was almost five million.[24] As a tragic corollary, the slave population grew by almost one million between 1820 and 1840, and the price of slaves doubled between 1827 and 1836. Yet more tragically, during the runaway lending period of the 1830s and then again in the 1850s, Southern households and plantation owners engaged in the huge business of buying slaves with debt—and then mortgaging slaves for loans to use for other purposes.[25]

In fact, in the antebellum South, using land and slaves as collateral to acquire a plantation was not *a* way to finance plantation acquisitions but one of the *primary* ways. In one Louisiana county, 88 percent of the mortgages were collateralized by slaves.[26] Of course, slave values went the way of all booms. In the 1830s, the male field-hand price went from $580 to as much as $1,200. Those that lent at that high precrash value saw their loans go bad when values collapsed.

The facts are tragic, appalling, and shameful. According to "Banking on Slavery in the Antebellum South" by Sharon Ann Murphy, "Commercial banks were willing to accept slaves as collateral for loans and as a part of loans assigned over to them from a third party." Many helped finance the "sale of slaves, using them as collateral. They were willing to sell slaves as part of foreclosure proceedings."[27] Murphy continues, "Commercial bank involvement with slave property occurred throughout the antebellum period and across the South. Some of the most prominent southern banks as well as the Second Bank of the United States directly issued loans using" the enslaved as collateral, and the practice was so extensive that over time it implicated other Northern banks as well. Slaves' value could decline over time, but they were valued as collateral because they were easier to sell than land and more mobile. The enslaved were thus often offered as collateral in large groups, as was the case with the Bank of Kentucky, to reduce the risk of any individual slave losing value because of age, illness, poor health, or death.

Given the dearth of lending institutions in the South, slaves were used to capitalize new banks in highly circular and risky transactions to create the so-called property banks and plantation or planters' banks: plantation bank charters required no paid-in capital to begin operations; the reserves of the bank were based entirely on borrowed money whereby investors mortgaged a portion of their land and slaves in return for bank shares.

For example, in 1836 Bernard Marigny and his wife, Anne Mathilde Morales, mortgaged their sugar plantation in Plaquemines Parish—including the house, sugar mill, hospital, kitchens, slave cabins, warehouse, barn, stable, carts, plowing equipment, animals, and seventy enslaved humans—in return for 490 shares of stock in the bank.[28] The entirety of the bank's capital stock was based on these mortgages of plantations and slaves. But this still left the bank with no specie reserves for the issuance of bank notes or loans, so these plantation banks were further financed through the sale of bonds— typically at high yields and guaranteed by the respective state—which was used to gain specie.

American plantations were established and then expanded by owners who borrowed against their slaves, land, and future crops, all without a clear sense of how many other farmers were doing the same. This brought overcapacity to the industry. "Buying a plantation," one grower later told Frederick Law Olmsted, "is essentially a gambling operation."[29]

The high yields on property and plantation bank bonds made them particularly attractive for British investors eager for yields higher than the paltry 3.4 percent or so offered by British government bonds.[30] New York brokerage firms with connections in Britain made sure the debt of these property banks was easily available for purchase on London exchanges.[31] These bond sales contributed to a surge in American foreign debt, which increased from $110 million in 1832 to $220 million by 1836.[32]

British investors tended to overlook the very real fact that Southern plant-ers could mortgage personal property in addition to land, meaning that these bonds often made investors complicit in the African slave trade, even though Britain had abolished slavery in most of its empire in 1833. Imagine the cot-ton boom of the 1830s as the Gold Rush of the South. Any nimble, ambitious soul with a small loan could grab a plot of land and try to spin it into cotton cash. Every cycle like this attracts masses of ordinary people who throw their hats into the ring to get rich, and is a core feature of a financial crisis in its boom phase and not a quirk. It was evident in the 1830s, in the early de-cades of the industrial economy. The rapid growth of the cotton market, a cornerstone export with ostensibly insatiable demand and soaring prices, lured novice farmers, shysters, pros, and mid-nineteenth-century "flippers." Mississippi cotton production increased eightfold between 1819 and 1834, when the state yielded 85 million pounds. Two years later, in 1836, a year before the bust, they had 125 million pounds to sell. Wholesale prices on the commodities market increased from an index level of 84 in 1833 to 131 in 1836.[33]

Cotton and land sales tracked each other. In 1833 the United States sold one million acres of public land in Mississippi. In 1835, it sold three million acres.[34] No other state came close to that bonanza. Joseph Baldwin, the Virginia lawyer, moved to Mississippi in 1836. He muses in his memoir about "the wild spendthriftism, the impetuous rush and the magnificent scale of operations." While the price of cotton kissed the sky and real estate followed suit, "money, or what passed for money was the only cheap thing to be had."[35] In 1830, the United States produced one million bales of cotton, priced at 10 cents per pound. In 1834–35, the price peaked at 17 cents per pound. Pre-crash cotton production peaked at 1.8 million bales.[36]

Great Britain had a colossal stake in this as a trading partner. Between 1820 and 1830, according to early economic historian Leland H. Jenks, "Thirty-six per cent of the domestic exports of the United States went to the British Isles," while "sixteen per cent of the domestic produce and manufac-turers of the United Kingdom . . . were shipped to American ports; and this merchandise formed forty-three per cent in value the total imports into the United States."[37]

Cotton was the raw material for Britain's industrial revolution. It arrived in Liverpool on ships from the American South to be transformed in the mills of Lancashire into textiles and other goods. By the mid-1830s, nearly 90 percent of the cotton imported into Britain came from the United States, and the British market claimed 60 percent of all American cotton production. In 1836, the $50 million of cotton sales to Liverpool brokers represented roughly half the value of all U.S. exports, more than tobacco, manufactured goods, lumber and wood, wheat flour, and rice combined.[38]

The economies of the United Kingdom and the United States would rise and fall together, on cotton. Britain would later rue this concentration and diversify cotton sourcing to Egypt, India, and beyond. Debt fueled all of this—debt in land, construction, and cotton. As in most such expansions, central government debt was a benign factor. In fact, most private debt booms are good news for the government, at least over the short term, and this was true in the 1830s. Revenue from import duties, a primary form of U.S. federal income before the advent of income taxes, grew 133 percent from 1834 to 1836, rising from $21.8 million to $50.8 million. With these revenues and the sale of federal land, the U.S. government was able to fully pay off its debt—an extraordinary development. (The states' debt, as we will see, was another matter.)

In notable contrast to government debt, which disappeared, U.S. private debt skyrocketed. It grew from an estimated $340 million in 1830 to almost $800 million by 1837. Rapid GDP expansion was fueled by the lending boom that came from such lenders as banks, cotton brokers, and bond houses. The Second Bank of the United States was at the heart of the U.S. banking system. Because the currency issued by locally chartered state banks lost value in proportion to the distance it traveled from its home city, the Second Bank—the only bank permitted to have branches across different states—helped to stabilize the values of different bank notes and effectively produce a "nationalized currency."

Yet President Andrew Jackson hated the Second Bank, blaming it for the Panic of 1819, with some justification as we have seen, and believed that banking should be left to individual states. The Second Bank's shareholders included not only the government but wealthy individuals—many of the elite, moneyed eastern interests that as a westerner Jackson loathed. Following Jackson's decisive defeat of Henry Clay in the 1832 election, Jackson vetoed the bill to renew the Second Banks' charter set to expire in 1836. Then he charged his secretary of the Treasury, Roger B. Taney, to create a separate financial apparatus that would remove federal monies from the Second Bank and send it to certain state banks, referred to as "pet banks." In other words, Jackson intended to gut the Second Bank's central role in U.S. banking.[39]

This removal cut the Second Bank's deposits to a meager $2.3 million by 1837. Its loans quickly dropped by almost $13 million and never again reached their 1832 peak. (After it lost its federal charter in 1836, the Second Bank obtained a state charter and tried desperately to stay in business, but closed in 1840.) Freed from any federal responsibility or oversight, states embraced the establishment of new state banks. The number chartered jumped from 381 in 1830 to 703 in 1836. These were often poorly regulated, which is another core element of a financial crisis. These state banks were a prototype for the less regulated lenders who time and again would play an outsized role in precrisis lending mania. Flush with these new deposits and sensing opportunity, these state banks went on a lending spree. Jackson had curbed the Second Bank's power but ironically contributed to the era's profligate lending growth through his support of these state banks. Their loans, fueled by these government deposits, surged from $153 million in 1832 to $511 million in 1836.

Across the Atlantic, British lenders were financing a large portion of the U.S. cotton industry at the same time. Historian John Joseph Wallis relates that around 1836, Southern cotton owners "typically consigned their product to a business that arranged for shipment and finance, in return for which the cotton owner was able to draw on credits for a percentage of the estimated value of the cotton prior to final sale."[40] That was financed through a "bill of exchange" in Liverpool or London markets. The arrangement was typical, and the bills were viewed "good as gold." For American importers of British goods, the same mechanics applied in the other direction. The Bank of England's acceptance and discounting of these bills provided a giddy stream of liquidity for international trade.

By 1836, bill brokerage—the buying and selling of these bills—was a massive transatlantic enterprise in its own right. Given Britain's financial structure, the size and liquidity of this market ultimately depended on this willingness of the Bank of England to buy good bills from brokers.

By 1835, Britain had over 1,200 integrated cotton mill factories, employing a third of a million people. This industry expansion brought a slew of new banks across Britain and Ireland. The 1833 act to renew the Bank of England's charter also allowed for the simplified organization of joint-stock banks and permitted those outside of London to issue bank notes as a means of extending loans. With this, more than 200 new British banks and bank branches had opened for business by 1836, with roughly 75 percent issuing their own currency. These additional issuances made it difficult for the Bank of England to gauge the overall circulation of money in the country and even harder to craft appropriate responses to changing monetary conditions.

By mid-decade, a widespread and troubling excess of real estate development, cotton, and other commodities on both sides of the Atlantic imperiled the loans made to fund those activities. Overcapacity in cotton had been reached and exceeded. There was simply too much of it—more cotton than the British could use for its textile industry and more land and houses being sold than legitimate U.S. demand could support. Cotton had become the equivalent of those vaunted Manhattan skyscrapers of the 1920s or the resort hotels and office towers of 1990s Japan.

U.S. lenders grew concerned about their borrowers' ability to repay months before this would be abundantly verified by unfinished ghost towns hard beside rivers. The *Milwaukee Advertiser* warned presciently in September 1836, "There is a limit to speculating on land. Before three years pass, numbers of speculators will be as anxious to sell out their lands as they have been this year to buy them."[41]

President Jackson was growing more concerned about this widespread and rampant speculation. On July 11, 1836, he signed the executive order called the Specie Circular. It took effect on August 15 and required that government land be purchased with gold or silver instead of paper currency. Like a lightning bolt, it stunned and then deflated the debt frenzy by dramatically curtailing the ability of purchasers to use loans to buy federal land since many loans took the form of paper currency in this era. Land sales collapsed from $25.2 million in 1836 to $7 million in 1837, and secondary market land prices with them.

This collapse reverberated widely. It meant that a significant number of loans made at the higher prices were now inadequately collateralized and at risk. It also meant that loans where the borrowers' only means of repayment was to sell the land were now at risk, an early example of Minsky's Ponzi phase. Most notably, it meant that there were tens of millions of dollars in loan losses for fragile, undersupervised state banks.

The Specie Circular created an enormous demand for gold and silver in the nation's Southern and Western states, since only those forms of currency could be used to purchase land. This further drained reserves in New York and thus curtailed the availability of credit from those institutions. Was

Jackson to blame for the collapse? He faced a classic financial boom dilemma: whether or not to intervene to cool down an overheated market.

The Specie Circular did precipitate the decline in sales and values. But if he had not issued the circular, the real estate loan problems would still have come, only later—at which point the problem would only have been larger and the damage greater. Could there have been a gentler transition than the one brought by the Specie Circular's abrupt prohibition? Certainly—but again, not without allowing the problem to grow larger.

In 1836, we see essentially the same dynamic and false choices evident in 1929 and Japan in the 1990s: once an excess of private debt and overcapacity has occurred, there are no policy solutions to completely avoid damage, only policies to mitigate it after the fact. By 1836, far more land had been sold than could be economically employed. At some point, the overselling needed to stop and the overcapacity given time to be absorbed. It would have been better if some mechanism had been in place all along to moderate the surge in leveraged land sales.

As in the 1830s, so also in the 2000s: it would have been better to prevent runaway private debt growth than to try to fix it later.

Meanwhile, across the Atlantic, the Bank of England reported a decline in its reserves, likely owing to emerging loan problems, to withdrawals to meet loan payments, and to increased imports caused by poor harvests. Since the bank had a requirement to maintain a certain level of reserves, it did what it had to do: it raised rates to attract new reserve funds.

After nine years of rates at 4 percent, the Bank of England raised rates to 4.5 percent on July 21, 1836, and then to 5 percent on September 1, 1836. The rate stayed at 5 percent through the end of 1836 and all of 1837.[42] In the following months, New York banks had to do the same to prevent an outflow of funds to Britain. These higher rates pressured borrowers on both sides of the Atlantic, who were already under strain.

Outside of London, many interpreted the Bank of England's decision to raise rates over a short period as evidence of deeper problems in the city, and economics scholar Geoffrey Fain Williams writes that British financial institutions in the summer of 1836 were "getting very nervous about the credit that was being extended to the United States."[43]

A number of British banks soon faltered. Williams writes of the textile and manufacturing center of Lancashire that "11 banks as failed or disappeared . . . while the directories suggest 19 branches closed in the same period. A number of Lancashire banks failed or endured spectacular losses between 1836

Table 4.4. U.K. Crisis Matrix: 1830s

Millions of British Pounds	1831	1836	1837	1831–1836 Change
GDP	447	525	510	78
Public Debt	838	846	842	8
Private Debt	*	*	*	*
Bills of Exchange	207	280	259	73
Bank Failures	19	61	38	42
As Percentage of GDP				1831–1836 Change
Public Debt	187%	161%	165%	−26%
Private Debt	n/a	n/a	n/a	n/a
Bills of Exchange	46%	53%	51%	7%

*Limited data points.
In the five years leading to 1837, Bills of Exchange increased 35 percent, and bank failures increased markedly.

and 1837, and the Lancashire region's banking system became somewhat infamous." British bank failures tripled from twenty in 1835 to sixty-one in 1836.

A second problem haunted the Bank of England: it had to decide how best to handle the delicate financial condition of the merchant banks that specialized in the financing of trade with the United States. Typically referred to as the "American houses," these were seven large and powerful firms that had become essential and integral to just about every Anglo-American commercial or financial transaction. They were the 1830s version of "too big to fail."

Not all were in bad shape. The relatively staid Baring Brothers had backed away from many of its dealings with the United States earlier in the year. But the Bank of England had worried for months about the three American houses in the most precarious financial situations. These three houses—Wiggin & Company, Wilson & Company, and Wildes & Company—were dubbed the "Three Ws." They had combined liabilities of £2.78 million as of June 1836, but more problematic for the Bank of England was that it held a total of £1.67 million in these companies' acceptances, money it might never see if worrisome trends continued. The Three Ws had been suspect for some time, mostly because of their close ties to the United States. Many believed that U.S. businessmen, abetted by the Three Ws, were rolling over debts to British creditors that they couldn't pay.

By late August, the bank finally decided to stop discounting paper from the American houses altogether. In other words, they stopped lending to these firms against the collateral of their loan contracts. This was terrible news for those firms, who had been seeking assistance from the Bank of England for months, but the decision allowed the bank to try and relieve itself of a problem that had been festering for just as long.

As soon as the policy was announced, though, an American-born director of a large Liverpool bill-broking business, William Brown, told the Bank of England that such a move could be potentially disastrous. The firms involved in the cotton trade, he explained misleadingly, were just temporary victims of the cotton growing calendar and would have the cash to repay their debts once the year's crop was harvested. Without access to bills of exchange during this vulnerable time, he explained correctly, the American houses would surely be ruined and would take down untold numbers of British cotton merchants and American cotton factors with them. So just four days after declaring its hard line on the American houses, the Bank of England reversed its decision.

As summer turned to fall, evidence grew that a crisis might be looming. Bank of England bullion levels gradually shrank, down to a little over £5 million by September. In November a number of Irish banks failed, and the monetary "pressure" was soon felt in Britain's manufacturing districts. Later that month Manchester's Northern and Central Bank of England came to London, hat in hand, asking for an emergency loan of £100,000. It was becoming increasingly apparent to businesspeople and bankers on both sides of the Atlantic that a crisis was all but inevitable by the end of 1836. The only question was when it would start. Over the first few months of 1837, caution and anxiety dominated the money markets of Britain and the United States. In fact, remarkably similar stories were playing out in both nations, without the other knowing about them, since news from one side of the Atlantic to the other traveled only as fast as the packet ships that carried it.

For the American houses in Britain and the major cotton brokerages in New Orleans, the oversupply of cotton had become a matter of life and death. And so all eyes were watching these firms. Prices of the world's biggest crop dropped as the panic and the beginnings of a depression gained hold. Prices had peaked in 1834, but production was continuing to climb and would crest in 1837, putting further downward pressure on prices.

Between January and March 1837, contradictory news from Britain caused wild fluctuations in the U.S. stock market. And the news on cotton became very bad very quickly, with an oversupply sending prices down 30 percent during that same period.[44] On March 4, 1837, New Orleans' largest and most prominent cotton broker, Hermann, Briggs & Company, failed, only hours before Martin Van Buren's presidential inauguration, bringing down with it at least ten other major cotton brokers and dozens of smaller companies. Like so many of the major players in the cotton trade, Hermann, Briggs had been hurt by speculation, overproduction, and depressed cotton prices in Liverpool.[45]

Hermann, Briggs was insolvent by $6 million and had been keeping afloat over the winter by essentially passing bills of exchange back and forth between itself and a Mississippi firm also owned by its partners, using promissory notes from one business to cover the debts of the other, and vice versa.[46] When news of Hermann, Briggs's failure reached New York a week and a half later, the impact was immediate and widespread. Cotton lenders on both sides of the Atlantic were casualties. Within hours, the banking and bill-broking firm Josephs & Company announced its own suspension. Josephs, a large and well-regarded establishment, had extensive correspondent and credit relationships with Hermann, Briggs and had continued lending to the firm despite its own financial troubles. It had even ignored advice from the Rothschilds to cut their ties with the cotton broker. By at least one account, Hermann, Briggs owed Josephs $1.4 million when it suspended.

News of the Josephs failure quickly spread through Wall Street. "Yesterday was the 'beginning of the end,'" the New York Herald declared on March 18. As went the price of cotton, so went the price of land and slaves. A Vicksburg, Mississippi, editor in 1837 wrote that slaves "are selling under execution for a fifth of their real value."[47]

In Britain, rumors swirled all winter about the great difficulties of the American houses, especially the "Three Ws." The entire London business community well understood that these companies, the linchpin of the Anglo-American cotton trade, would take down a cascade of merchants and bankers with them if they failed. People noticed, then, when partners of five of the seven American houses sent a letter to the governor of the Bank of England in late February, explaining that they would collectively require hundreds of thousands of pounds in discounts each week of April and May if they were to survive—and perhaps in June as well.

After two days of negotiation, the Bank of England announced its bailout plan on March 4. The American houses would continue to have access to discounting, half of which would be provided by the bank and half by a group of private banks without any ties to U.S. trade. But a rising chorus of observers criticized the plan.

Back in New York on Tuesday, May 2, the *New York Herald* ran a story exposing a problematic credit scheme involving the Dry Dock Bank, Mechanics' Bank, and the brokerage house Bullock, Lyman & Company. Because of the scandal, Dry Dock president John Flemming resigned his position the following day and was found dead the next morning. Mechanics' Bank survived a run on May 4. Though Dry Dock continued to open for business, other New York City bankers met and announced they would refuse to accept any paper from or offer any assistance to Dry Dock.

New Yorkers appealed to President Van Buren in Washington, noting the growing crisis impact: 250 commercial failures; 20,000 newly unemployed workers; a loss of over $40 million in real estate values.[48] They asked for a reversal of the Specie Circular that Jackson had issued, a postponement of lawsuits against any debtors of the federal government, and an emergency session of Congress to address the issues. Van Buren insisted the problems were best solved at the state level and refused to act.

By the following Monday morning, the panic was "palpable." Angry depositors descended on Dry Dock only to be told it had failed, though an address by Mayor Aaron Clark from the steps of the bank eased tensions by promising that New York's other banks would receive and pay bills drawn on Dry Dock. In New York City, the monetary reserves of the deposit banks fell almost 80 percent between September 1836 and May 1837—leaving very little to insulate the nation's financial system in the event of another external shock.

A general run on all New York City banks followed the news on the Dry Dock Bank. On May 8 and 9, banks' directors reported that they had distributed over $1.3 million in specie to anxious depositors, or roughly half of their total reserves.[49] Realizing that another day or two like that would wipe out their specie reserves entirely, the bankers agreed that as of Wednesday, May 10, all New York City banks would suspend specie payment. Instead of violent mobs, this day of "panic" was surprisingly calm. The stock market even finished the day up 15 percent. Perhaps New Yorkers were relieved that something definitive had been done to combat the anxiety and uneasiness of the preceding months.

But in the next months, 343 of the 850 U.S. banks failed, while British investors were left with losses in excess of $130 million.[50] Bank failures in New York hovered around $100 million, just sixty days into the panic. The Bank of England's directors convened in the spring of 1837 to discuss the fates of the Three Ws, as London waited anxiously. They resolved that the bank should stop making advances to commercial houses that lacked appropriate security. Given the unique position of the American houses in the financial world, however, they would be exempt from this policy. The Bank of England's directors proceeded to bail out Wildes & Company, despite the firm's inability to produce any collateral, and reached similar arrangements by the middle of May with both Wilson & Company and Wiggin & Company.

The bank's actions were again condemned, especially for its preferential treatment of companies that many saw as the source of the crisis in the first place. The *Courier* was especially critical: the American houses, it stated, had "conducted their business with the most reckless improvidence." The bailouts and criticism might well have been grabbed from the headlines of the 2008 financial crisis.

News of the Mechanics'–Dry Dock scandal in New York City finally reached London at the end of May, just as the Bank of England's directors were meeting once again to determine how to address the plight of the Three Ws. When they received this news, they reconsidered their earlier decision and officially ended their support for Wildes, Wiggin, and Wilson on June 2. All three firms suspended payment the next morning. Credit simply ceased.

The once robust cotton trade collapsed, as demand shrank and prices were slashed daily. The *Times* observed that the "more immediate and severe loss will fall upon" the private banks that, along with the Bank of England, had been keeping the companies afloat for the preceding two months. This acknowledgment aside, a certain sense of relief permeated London—as had happened in New York just a few weeks earlier—if for no other reason than longstanding uncertainty, at last, had been removed.

Henry Stephen Fox, British ambassador to the United States, lamented in a speech in London about the economic peril of America: "It would be difficult to describe, or render intelligible in Europe, the stunning effect which this sudden overthrow of commercial credit and honor of the nation has caused."[51]

The year 1837 was the beginning of a long, harrowing, transatlantic meltdown that slid into what some called the First Great Depression. Unemployment was a desperate, de facto state for 500,000 thousand Americans; 39,000 went bankrupt, out of a national population of 16 million. The accumulating bad news created a climate of genuine rage. Agreements seemed meaningless, and the earlier heady optimism—"Go West! Plant

Cotton! Build a Railroad!"—evaporated. President Van Buren, though often blamed for the financial collapse and subsequent misery of millions of Americans, was more the inheritor of the years of profligate lending that had preceded him.

By the end of 1837, concerns had partially receded. This calmer mood pushed the Bank of England's specie reserves up to the highest level in five years. Encouraged, directors lowered its discount rate to 4 percent early in 1838 and again to 3.5 percent in November.[52] But these moves showed the bank to be motivated more by the dazzling glint of its growing treasure than true economic recovery.

Even as it was making credit easier and money cheaper, banking collapses in Belgium and ongoing concerns in the American financial sector had renewed caution; meanwhile, a poor autumn grain harvest forced Britain to import grain. All of this once again led to a rapid drain on bullion, which fell from £10.52 in March 1838 to only £4.12 million less than two years later.[53] Britain soon fell into a familiar spiral, as higher wheat prices forced its citizens to spend more on food, which drained bullion and left less for manufactured goods, which depressed the textile industry, which drove down the price of cotton. By June, with bullion reserves down to just over £3 million, the Bank of England quickly raised its discount rate to 5.5 percent and then 6 percent—its highest ever—and swallowed its pride just enough to accept an emergency loan of £2 million from France. Credit continued to be tight into 1840.[54]

After hitting its low point in 1837, the U.S. stock index rose 15 percent through the end of 1838, though the subsequent depression until 1841 took the index to new lows, before rising again during the mid-1840s. This was part of a brief U.S. recovery in 1838 and 1839 that was fueled in part by a second debt surge—a second wave that sometimes happens in a financial crisis. This one was in large-scale canal construction in nine of the nation's twenty-six states and, to a lesser extent, the earliest establishment of that newfangled investment that would dominate the rest of the century: railroads.

This second, staggered wave, which is sometimes an element of financial crisis, speaks to both denial and opportunism. As we will see, in the mid-2000s, as housing loan problems were first emerging, commercial real estate lenders adamantly insisted that emerging housing problems were a separate issue and would not affect the quality of their loans. And those suffering early housing loan concerns were eager to find earnings growth in another category of lending. They flocked to commercial real estate, using the logic that

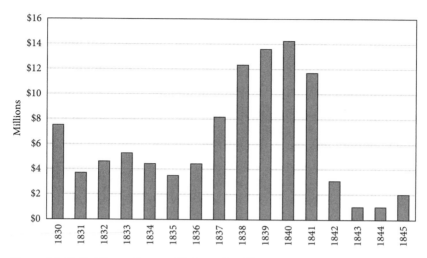

Figure 4.4. United States: State and Private Canal Investment, 1830–1845
Source: H. Jerome Cranmer, table 3, column 1, in the chapter "Canal Investment, 1815–1860," in *Trends in the American Economy in the Nineteenth Century*, Studies in Income and Wealth, volume 24, Conference on Research in Income and Wealth (Princeton, NJ: Princeton University Press, 1960), 555–56.

the only way out of a credit problem is to grow earnings elsewhere. Lenders and investors will try to recoup losses in one sector by lending and investing more in another.

A very similar psychology lay behind the canal expansion in the late 1830s and early 1840s. The phenomenon of second waves underscores the fact that a crisis rarely occurs in a single year but instead often unfolds over several years, in some cases because lenders seek to recoup losses by lending more elsewhere.

The canal expansion was largely financed by state-issued bonds. In the 1830s, state bonds were much more widely employed than U.S. federal bonds, and state governments held more power vis-à-vis the federal government than they would later. In this instance, the state debt for canals functioned much more as a commercial loan—debt to finance construction rather than to finance the governments' operating needs.

The Erie Canal, financed by New York state bonds, opened in 1825, and the investment was a resounding financial success. Entrepreneurs hoping to duplicate that success next proposed thousands of miles of canals, mostly between Atlantic ports and inland waterways, such as the Great Lakes and the Ohio River.

Total investment in canals, which had averaged $4.3 million a year be-
tween 1831 and 1836, shot up to $8.2 million in 1837, before peaking at $14.3
million in 1840. As would be true a few years later with railroads, expenditure
on the canals was met or exceeded by construction spending, with associated debt, on the new towns and farms that sprang up along the canal's path.
A majority of this funding (61.5 percent from 1825 to 1841) came from the
individual states in which they were built and used bonds sold largely to
wealthy citizens of Britain. Economic historian Alfred Chandler writes that
from the start, railroad and canal promotors relied on "Eastern commercial
centers and especially . . . money markets in Europe for funds," and far from
an "afterthought," investors preferred bonds over stock since they seemed
more secure.

In 1835, the total amount of outstanding state debt was $81 million. This
ballooned to $230 million in 1841, with approximately $100 million held
abroad, primarily in Britain.[55] In this same year, for comparison, federal debt
was only $14 million and total private debt was $674 million.

The brief 1838 and 1839 recovery occurred in both the United States and
the United Kingdom. It was a fleeting rebound. During these years, Europe,
and especially Britain, was swept up once more in dizzy enthusiasm for
American bonds and securities. They bought state bonds and financial stocks,
such as that of the Bank of the United States (now simply a Pennsylvania state
bank), and railroads.

But in the wake of the Erie Canal, too many canals were built for demand,
and there were too many cost overruns. By December 1838, increasingly troubled American debt valued at about £6 million "hung over" a nervous London
money market "like a Damoclean sword." When British investors rightly became skeptical, "the new inflow of foreign capital" came to a halt in 1839, "and
the manifold projects of the states were abandoned."[56]

All of the new canals were besieged by cost overruns, delays, and lack of
business, and the bonds to finance them had to be restructured. Investors
"lost fortunes."[57] Pennsylvania's canal bond interest bill was almost as large
as the entire state budget otherwise and quickly fell into default. The Illinois
canal default in 1842 left ghost towns scattered along the banks of the Illinois River.[58]

The enormous canal and railroad projects of state governments were
thrown on the unfinished pile, heavy in debt. A rash of state bankruptcies,
or close calls, followed. In truth, most of the canals were ill conceived, as there

was never enough business to justify them, and canals were soon rendered partially obsolete by railroads. As with real estate booms in the 1920s, debt rather than genuine demand had been the driver of growth.

According to an 1841 estimate, the overall U.S. crisis of this period caused 33,000 business failures and a staggering half a billion dollars in losses.[59] Total capital of American banks dropped 40 percent between 1839 and 1843. Figures from the 1841 U.S. Almanac went further, suggesting that the total extent of U.S. losses on real estate, stocks, and bank deposits between 1837 and 1841 "approached one billion dollars," in an economy that itself was only $1.8 billion. But that loss figure cannot confidently be validated.

Loan data from this period are difficult to obtain and assess, but it appears that loan losses, whether from bank loans, bonds, or other forms, reached as much as an astounding 25 percent to 50 percent of all loans. In a bank, it is a cause of concern if commercial loan losses constitute even 2 percent of the portfolio.

The financial crisis of 1837 inspired financial modernization. President Van Buren ushered in corrective changes in the U.S. monetary policy. Abandoning the Jackson administration's "pet banks" system, a U.S. Treasury system debuted in 1840, principally to distribute government monies. It became a fixture in 1846 and ended the era of public funds held in private banks.

Whigs made bankruptcy legislation a central issue in William Henry Harrison's 1840 presidential campaign, and in 1841 a Whig-controlled Congress passed the first federal law to allow voluntary bankruptcy, extinguishing $450 million of debt from about a million creditors.[60] Although meant to be a curative, this law shocked and confused many holders of this debt, especially British banks and other foreign investors. They were left unsure if their contracts would ever be enforced again. Harrison died after only a month in office, and his vice president and successor John Tyler overturned this law in 1843, much to the Whigs' dismay.

Also in 1841, Lewis Tappan created the very first commercial credit reporting agency, the Mercantile Agency, which was a forerunner of Dun & Bradstreet. With this agency, lenders could check on applicants' solvency. Overborrowing by states and the default of so many state canal bonds led to the prohibition of state bankruptcy and the creation of caps on debt in many states. A number of individual borrowers who were unable to pay—many from Tennessee—fled the United States to the recently established independent country of Texas, slashing the initials GTT ("Gone to Texas") on their doors as they departed. The Constitution they helped write in their newly adopted state went further than that in the United States to restrict the rights of creditors.

The devastating depression lasted until 1843, when U.S. GDP growth returned, boosted further by the Mexican American War and the Gold Rush that began in 1848. U.K. GDP resumed its growth in 1844. Lenders can make bad credit judgments in any era, but it would seem that in the earliest years in the establishment of a newly industrial economy, lenders are especially prone to large-scale lending misjudgments.

But in so many other respects, the underlying dynamic of financial crisis in the 1830s, grounded in overlending and overcapacity, looks very familiar to the series of crises that the next chapter explores. For the next seven decades, a period in which Western economies reached dizzying heights of achievement, it was railroad fever that brought massive waves of speculation. This lending episodically overwhelmed the industrial world, transforming landscapes, filling the countryside with new cities and towns, and driving crisis after crisis.

CHAPTER 5

The Railroad Crises Era

1847–1907

Perhaps no other invention has transformed the world as dramatically as the railroad, accompanied by its indispensable adjunct, the telegraph. Together, they collapsed the human experience of time and space. They completely consumed, disrupted, and transformed the nations that embraced them. Railroad companies quickly became the largest components of the equity and debt markets of the era, issuing a nonstop flood of new stocks and bonds to finance their capital-intensive enterprises. By 1899, railroads had become 60 percent of the market capitalization of the New York Stock Exchange.[1] In 2018, by contrast, no single industry was much more than 20 percent.[2]

Railroads, together with the construction of new depots, towns, and farms along their lines, became the biggest single component of the world's debt, much of it in the form of bonds rather than bank loans. From the Transcontinental Railway to the Orient Express, entrepreneurs and legislators raced to build new railroads. Fortunes were made and lost, and then made and lost again. Railroads involved the biggest names in business and banking, from Cornelius Vanderbilt to J. P. Morgan.[3] The legendary Union Pacific Railroad, part of that first transcontinental line, captivated the attention of the world in the 1860s before falling into financial distress in 1873[4] and then bankruptcy in 1893.[5]

Railroads incurred massive debt to establish and maintain their operations, but the debt required for the land sales and housing and commercial construction in the towns and farms along railroad routes was every bit as large, and often larger. A map of the Illinois Central Railroad, the largest railroad when established in 1851, shows the two main track branches (Figure 5.1). The darker areas alongside them are the land grants provided by the

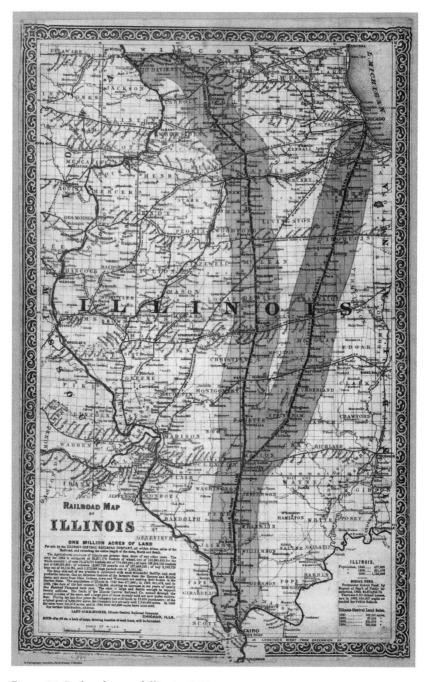

Figure 5.1. Railroad map of Illinois, 1864

government to help finance the company. Two-thirds of the closely spaced towns along these tracks were brand-new, started by the company to provide buyers for its land and thus funds for its operations and to bring in the people and crops that it would transport. From 1851 through 1856, the number of inhabitants in these towns grew from 13,400 to more than 70,000. In 1856 alone, 3,392 farms were purchased within the land grant area, again largely with debt, bringing the total area under cultivation to more than 1.6 million acres.

This sprawling, chaotic, debt-financed expansion of hundreds of railroads throughout the industrial world powered global GDP to miraculous heights. In fact, GDP in the United States grew almost sixfold, Britain's GDP more than tripled, Germany's grew more than fourfold, and France's GDP more than doubled during the last half of the nineteenth century. But devastating financial crises followed railroad expansion from the late 1840s to 1907. The reason was simple. In the race to expand, railroads would inevitably build too much, too fast. They created far more capacity than needed and incurred far more costs than projected. Land prices alongside their tracks would skyrocket and then bust, apace. The townspeople along the way would build far too many homes and buildings, and the farmers would start too many farms. Across these countries, there were few constraints and only rare efforts to curb this pell-mell rush. And when the railroads, farmers, businesspeople, and homeowners then found themselves unable to service their debt, lenders and financial markets would collapse. Those markets would only recover as debts were written off and as enough time passed for demand to grow to absorb the overcapacity. As nineteenth-century observer and sociologist E. V. Grabill wrote in regard to the period leading up to the 1873 crisis, "[Rail]roads were constructed in enormous excess of any possible use that the population of the West, though growing rapidly, could make of them for years to come."[6]

The same pattern would hold in subsequent crises. Substitute "office buildings" or "houses" for "railroads," and the story reads very much the same for the 1980s or 2000s. Borrowers could not pay debts, and ruin followed for railroads, farmers, and banks.

The first steam-powered railroad company made its appearance in England in 1825,[7] and railroads there were at least a minor factor in its crisis of 1837.[8] But only in 1847 did the manic expansion of railroads first become a driving and central factor in financial crises, especially in Britain and Germany. In a very real sense, financial crisis in the mid- to late 1800s followed the tracks—and overcapacity—laid by the railroads themselves.

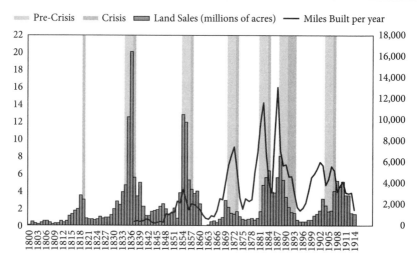

Figure 5.2. United States: Public Land Sales and Miles of Railroad Built, 1800–1914

The pivotal role of railroad overexpansion and debt in the financial crises of this era has been underrecognized. Every history of the crisis of 1873 mentions the failure of Jay Cooke's Northern Pacific Railroad, but most gloss over the massive overexpansion of scores of other railroad companies in the United States, Germany, and Austria above and beyond Cooke.

Figures 5.2 through 5.6 provide a rough sense of the connection between railroad overexpansion and financial crisis that often occurred. Figure 5.2 shows colossal spikes in railroad miles added in the United States in 1854, 1872, 1882, 1887, and 1902 through 1906. These correlate to spikes in federal land sales. Each was followed by a collapse in railroad construction since the resulting capacity had far outstripped demand, and those spikes and collapses played a significant part in the crises of 1857, 1873, 1884, the early 1890s, and 1907, respectively.

Most of these crises saw a delay of a year or more between the point of overcapacity and the onset of the crisis, as is often the case in financial crisis. It was that staggered sequence during which the railroads first realized this trouble but were reluctant to convey this news to their creditors, then inevitably their lenders or bondholders would become aware, and finally the broader financial markets would learn the ugly truth. As we will see, in some crises, in fits of ignorance or optimism, overcapacity actually continued to be created during and even after the moment of crisis.

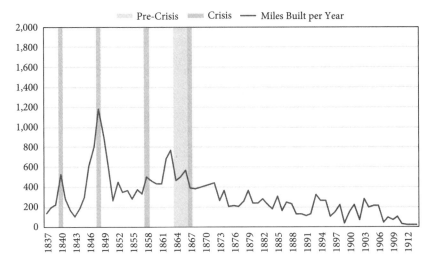

Figure 5.3. United Kingdom: Miles of Railroad Built, 1837–1914

The staggered unfolding of a crisis also happens because it was not just the laying of railroad track that brought the overcapacity but also the manufacturing of railroad locomotives and cars, the building of depots, the purchasing of land, and the constructing of new railroad towns replete with houses and commercial buildings. For example, in the U.S. crisis of the early 1890s, railroad track construction peaked in 1887, but railroad car construction peaked in 1890. The statistic we cite, "railroad track miles added," is thus a rough shorthand for a whole host of associated activities that collectively overwhelmed economies in a connected timeline.

In Britain, major construction spikes in the mid-1840s and mid-1860s correlate to the crises of 1847 and 1866, while smaller bursts of railroad-track miles in the late 1830s and the mid-1850s were at least a minor factor in the crises of 1837 and 1857 (Figure 5.3).

In Germany, major spikes in 1847 and the 1870s were central to its crises in 1847 and 1873. Smaller spikes in the late 1890s were at least a minor part of the overcapacity that led to its crises of the 1900s (Figure 5.4).

France was different. It came somewhat later to the industrialization game, and its railroad development was more constrained by the struggle between those who wanted to nationalize its railroads and those who didn't. Thus, as Figure 5.5 shows, France never had quite the outsized burst of railroad construction as seen in Britain in the late 1840s, Germany in

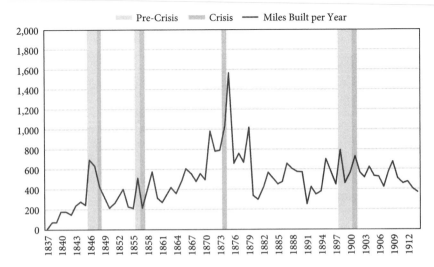

Figure 5.4. Germany: Miles of Railroad Built, 1837–1914

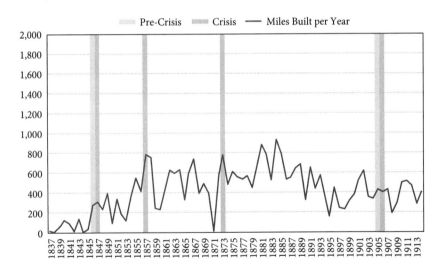

Figure 5.5 France: Miles of Railroad Built, 1837–1914

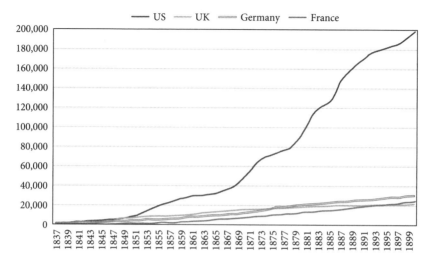

Figure 5.6. Cumulative Railroad Miles Built, 1837–1900

the mid-1870s, and the United States in the late 1880s. And the Bank of France was often more active in intervening when the country's banks were in trouble. France's crises, as we will see, came as much from its agriculture and from its bank's investments in the railroads and industrial development of other countries (especially in Eastern Europe) as from its own railroad overbuilding.

Figure 5.6 compares the miles of track added in the four countries. The importance of this chart is to show that activity in the United States in this period dwarfed that in the rest of the world, as did the U.S. appetite for capital. In fact, the need for capital was so vast that European banks and investors were routinely enticed to invest in the debt of U.S. companies and were thus vulnerable when that debt became troubled. The sheer amount of financial activity in the United States meant that its crisis would resound the most powerfully around the globe.

Worldwide, these cataclysmic crises were intertwined with the most momentous conflagrations of the era. Examples abound: the crises of 1847 helped fuel the Revolutions of 1848; the rise in grain prices that came with the Crimean War fed the creation of overcapacity before the crisis of 1857, which itself exacerbated the tensions that brought the American Civil War; and German exuberance, fueled by reparations after their victory in the Franco-Prussian War, contributed to the crisis of 1873.

Each of these crises could be treated in as much detail as the crises described in the earlier chapters of this book, but each followed a similar pattern, so the scope of this chapter is only to provide highlights. It is a brief tour of the financial crises of 1847, 1857, 1866, 1873, the 1880s, 1893, and 1907.

The Crisis of 1847

The financial crisis of 1847 was brought on by the first major railroad-building expansion in the German Confederation and France and the second such expansion in Britain, which drove up share prices in all three nations. Railroad miles tripled in Britain and France and quadrupled in Germany, though total mileage in France was still comparatively small. Records are sparse, but loans appear to have grown rapidly in all three countries. The potato famine in Ireland, which drove up wheat prices and brought debt-fueled agricultural expansion, compounded the era's turbulence. When the shares of railroads

Table 5.1. U.K. Crisis Matrix: 1840s and 1850s

Millions of British Pounds	1843	1847	1848	1850	1843–1847 Change
GDP	493	628	589	546	135
Public Debt	838	832	831	824	(6)
Private Debt	*	*	*	*	*
Bills of Exchange	231	294	225	242	63
Gross Fixed Capital Formation	27	88	71	47	61
Railroad Miles Built	105	803	1,182	589	698

As Percentage of GDP					1843–1847 Change
Public Debt	170%	132%	141%	151%	−37%
Private Debt	n/a	n/a	n/a	n/a	n/a
Bills of Exchange	47%	47%	38%	44%	0%
Gross Fixed Capital Formation	5%	14%	12%	9%	9%

*Limited data points.
Loan data are incomplete, but railroad miles built grew sevenfold in this period; railroad debt growth was likely commensurate.

and the price of wheat collapsed, lenders failed and economic recession enveloped Europe.

In October 1845, Britain had roughly 1,428 extant or proposed railway companies, which collectively could claim £113,612,018 in capital against liabilities of £590,447,490, for an aggregate net liability of £476,835,472—or about 84 percent of Great Britain's GDP in 1845.[9] Even in December 2008, the *Economist* called the railway mania of the 1840s "the greatest bubble in history."[10]

Beset with "railroad fever," 33,959 individuals subscribed to at least one railway share offering during the 1845–46 parliamentary session. The *Bankers' Magazine* at the time stated that the "real object of the concocters of railway schemes" was "to rob and delude the public by getting their scrip into the market at a premium, and to rob and swindle their subscribers in particular by squandering and embezzling the deposit money."[11] In July 1845 the *Times* reported, in language that foreshadowed the Roaring Twenties, there was not a "man in London, above the condition of a streetsweeper, who had *not* speculated in railways."[12]

Table 5.2. France Crisis Matrix: 1840s

Millions of Old Francs	1842	1847	1848	1842–1847 Change
GDP	11,189	14,506	11,352	3,317
Agriculture GDP	4,380	6,619	4,446	2,239
Non-Agriculture GDP	6,809	7,887	6,906	1,078
Public Debt	4,785	5,715	5,838	930
Private Debt	*	*	*	*
Wheat Production	1,007	2,234	953	1,227
Gross Fixed Capital Formation	1,307	1,912	1,465	605
Railroad Miles Built	17	317	231	300

As Percentage of GDP				1842–1847 Change
Agriculture GDP	39%	46%	39%	6%
Non-Agriculture GDP	61%	54%	61%	−6%
Public Debt	43%	39%	51%	−3%
Private Debt	n/a	n/a	n/a	n/a
Wheat Production	9%	15%	8%	6%
Gross Fixed Capital Formation	12%	13%	13%	1%

In the five years leading up to 1847, railway miles grew briskly, France's wheat production doubled, and capital investment nearly doubled before collapsing in 1848.

Railway stocks rose sharply, with the average railway share price increasing 73 percent from July 1843 to July 1845.[13] Some accounts conclude that £500 million in railway-related securities were trading by the summer of 1845.[14] GDP growth, almost certainly fueled by this loan growth, soared by 8.1 percent in 1844.[15] The Bank of England was part of the lending boom, and after the Banking Charter Act of 1844, the bank reduced its rates and began a policy of aggressive lending—or "discounting" in the vernacular of the time.[16]

But with higher costs and revenue projections that fell short, railroad shares fell into distress, and those railroads called for the additional capital committed by subscribers.[17] As the situation worsened, subscribers facing these calls raised cash the only way they could: by selling railway stocks. This pushed stock prices down, and by October 1848, railway mania had morphed into panic. Investors scrambled to sell railway shares before the bubble burst completely.[18]

Feared shortages and soaring prices had led farms to expand, and many prominent corn (a British term that encompassed wheat) dealers and merchants to speculate. But when news arrived in June of abundant foreign grain supplies, prices immediately plummeted. This caught speculators completely off guard, and many were forced to sell at enormous losses. Wheat and the railroad industry grew together, and interdependently, since railroads enabled western wheat to affordably reach European markets from the eastern United States and to reach more distant markets within Europe.[19]

In July a group of London merchants, traders, and bankers petitioned Parliament to dismantle the 1844 Bank Act to allow it to provide lending support to troubled lenders, which would in turn provide additional lending support to distressed businesses.[20] A growing number of businesses—sent reeling by a combination of losses from corn speculation and the virtual illiquidity of money markets—began suspending payment or failing outright.

At first, most of the affected firms were involved in the "corn" trade and based in either London or Liverpool, the primary entrance point for grain shipments. By the end of August, a total of eighteen such businesses had failed, eight of them prominent London corn houses saddled with liabilities totaling over £1.5 million.[21] Failures peaked in October, with eighty-two suspensions reported by companies as diverse as tea brokers and soap boilers, not only across the United Kingdom (including Manchester and Glasgow) but even in a handful of Continental cities, such as Hamburg, Leghorn (Livorno), and Lisbon.[22] The nadir came after the middle of the month, as both private and joint-stock banks began to fail. The first was Knapp & Company in Abingdon on October 13, but the most significant was the Royal Bank of Liverpool. With an ownership widely considered among the wealthiest in Britain, its suspension sent shock waves across the landscape of British finance and briefly shut down virtually all private discounting (lending) in London.[23]

The Bank of England finally acquiesced and came forward with a commitment to "make advances more freely than it would otherwise have done," providing funding support for banks and thus for their customers. This assurance alone stopped the bank runs and ended Britain's banking panic.[24]

Railways in Prussia and other Germanic provinces—along with associated construction—had grown rapidly too. From Berlin's Silesian station to Frankfurt Oder, to the Berlin-Hamburg Railway and the Frankfurt to Mannheim and Heidelberg service, a loosely connected German railway network had rapidly emerged. Prussian iron and steel production went from 58 million marks to 101 million marks, with presumed commensurate loan growth, and then back down to 57 million marks.[25] In the compressed time from August 1847 to January 1848, 245 businesses and 12 banks failed.[26]

In France, it was agriculture and, to a lesser extent, railroads that brought the turbulence of this period, with the failure of 829 French banks with 207 million francs in liabilities.[27] Agricultural shortages and high prices first brought famine, and France saw food riots, an increased population of beggars, increased urban migration, and heightened levels of hoarding and speculation. To address this shortage, farmers borrowed to expand, bringing an overabundance of crops. Wheat prices collapsed, causing heavily indebted farms to fail and putting thousands out of work. France's GDP tumbled by a stark 22 percent, though there is much uncertainty regarding GDP figures for this era.

Railroads were emerging in France too, but it was a smaller effort, as industry in France lagged behind both Britain and the German Confederation. In France the passage of an 1842 law had provided the general schematics for what eventually became the six great railroad lines, envisioned as privately run but government sponsored and owned.[28] The 1840s nonetheless did witness an expansion of credit, mostly in the form of "speculative investment centered in projects for railway construction." According to one study, the "lapse in confidence occasioned by the agricultural crisis produced a liquidity crunch at just that moment when calls for the unpaid balance on railway shares found French capitalists dangerously overextended,"[29] bringing three railroad failures. Runs on banks resulted in failures in the provinces. Even the Bank of France saw its deposits reduced nearly sixfold between 1845 and 1847.[30]

It should be noted that although France had comparatively less industrial development, this period saw it beginning to invest disproportionately in the industrial opportunities of other countries, a trend that continued through the century. France was thus vulnerable to the financial calamities of those other countries. This financial crisis set a pattern for others in the railroad century. It was the first major railroad-driven crisis and illustrated how this large, debt-fueled sector could topple an economy.

The Crisis of 1857

The next railroad crisis, in 1857, is often thought of as the first truly global financial crisis.[31] In the three short years from 1845 to 1848, under Presidents James Polk and John Taylor, the geographic size of the United States had doubled,[32] and gold had been discovered in the newly acquired territory of California.[33] A "reckless optimism" followed, fueling business expansion in the United States. Just months before the start of the 1857 crisis, the *New York Herald* was proclaiming the "dawning of exceedingly brisk and prosperous times" that would last at least three years before any threat of a downturn.[34]

With reliable long-distance transportation now a necessity to connect the sprawling new nation, U.S. railroads added over 9,536 miles of track from 1853 to 1856, particularly along the nation's western and northwestern frontiers. This more than doubled the total mileage of the national rail network. By 1857 the total debt of U.S. railroads was over $400 million—with much of that owned by British investors.[35]

Table 5.3 shows the rapid growth in debt in this era. However, it is likely that the totals were higher and the trends worse. There was a type of debt not included in the totals shown because of the scarcity of supporting information regarding the *amount* involved. The net worth of all households in the South in 1860 was $6 billion,[36] and $3 billion of that was the value of the slaves they owned.[37] Yet more disturbing, the enslaved themselves were often encumbered with debt. Based on the scarce data available, in total that debt was perhaps $200 million or more.[38] If true, that would make it one of the largest single categories of debt. And if true, and if the slaves were freed, not only would half the Southern household asset value have disappeared, but those borrowers would have been left with a very large amount of debt that they

Table 5.3. U. S. Crisis Matrix: 1850s

Millions of Dollars	1852	1854	1856	1857	1858	1852–1857 Change
GDP	$3,196	$3,564	$4,167	$4,027	$4,263	$831
Federal Debt	$70	$40	$30	$30	$40	$(40)
Private Debt (est.)	$1,211	$1,534	$1,827	$1,896	$1,895	$685
Bank Loans	$430	$557	$634	$684	$583	$254
Railroad Bonds	$137	$261	$360	$411	$535	$274
Memo: Construction (est.)	$634	$778	$730	$721	$602	$87
Memo: Slave Collateral (est.)	n/a	n/a	n/a	n/a	$230	n/a
Railroad Miles Built	2,288	3,442	1,471	2,077	1,966	1,154[a]
Bank Failures	1	25	10	31	14	30

As Percentage of GDP						1852–1857 Change
Federal Debt	2%	1%	1%	1%	1%	−1%
Private Debt (est.)	38%	43%	44%	47%	44%	9%
Bank Loans	13%	16%	15%	17%	14%	4%
Railroad Bonds	4%	7%	9%	10%	13%	6%
Memo: Construction (est.)	20%	22%	18%	18%	14%	−2%
Memo: Slave Collateral (est.)	n/a	n/a	n/a	n/a	5%	n/a

[a]1852–1854 change.

In the five years leading up to 1857, U.S. private debt grew by 57 percent. Sectors with the greatest concentration of overlending were railroad debt and household mortgages, which together comprised 75 percent of the increase.

would have had few resources to repay. This presumably further entrenched the tragic Southern position on slavery.

In 1850, the United States began giving railroads free land to encourage their expansion, and between 1850 and 1857, railroad projects in eleven western and southern states received land grants totaling 22 million acres. Railroads used this land as a source for funding since they could sell it or use it as collateral for debt offerings. Farmers and investors bought land by assuming a five-year mortgage from the railroad, and speculation quickly became rampant.[39] As far west as Nebraska, "lots on the best street in Omaha, which had sold for $500 in the spring of 1856, went for $5,000 a year later," writes Kenneth Stampp.[40]

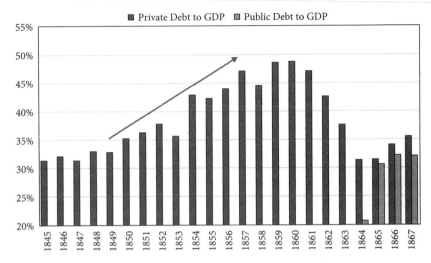

Figure 5.7. United States: Private and Public Debt as a Percentage of GDP, 1845–1867
Private debt in the United States increased by $1.1 billion (or 128 percent) from 1849 to 1857.

One of the more interesting aspects of this crisis is its illustration of a recurrent feature of financial crises: the development of creative lending instruments all but predestined to fail. In this case, clever railroad executives devised a financing method known as the railroad farm mortgage.[41] The La Crosse & Milwaukee Railroad owners invented this deceptively simple scheme. They would approach farmers with land near the planned rail line and entice them to purchase shares of the railroad's stock with debt secured by a mortgage on their farms.

For the farmer the deal seemed like a no-lose proposition. It required not a dime in downpayment and no documentation other than an appraisal by a railroad agent. It foreshadowed the no-down-payment subprime loans of the Great Recession. Dividends on the railroad's stock the farmers bought covered the interest on the loan. The farmer could expect increased land values once the railroad was built and an appreciation in the value of his railroad shares as the company accelerated its operations. But railroads that marketed these schemes were not profitable, and the dividends they paid were unsustainable.[42] It was a catastrophe waiting to happen.

Meanwhile the British economy had soared, fueled by high demand for British manufactured goods in both Europe and America.[43] Then came the discovery of significant gold deposits in Australia in May 1851, only three years after the California gold rush.[44] The shipbuilding industry responded by tripling the total tonnage of ships built, and gold began "heaping up in the Bank [of England's] vault." This allowed the bank to drop its discount rate to just 2 percent in April 1852, the lowest ever, which facilitated a lending boom.[45] The aggregate total of deposits held in London joint-stock banks grew nearly fivefold between 1847 and 1857.[46]

From an abundance of easy credit invariably followed all manner of financial abuses, fraud, and speculation. One writer later described the abuses during this time as "the worst kind of commercial gambling," Borough Bank of Liverpool was among "the most notorious of the reckless re-discounters" (rediscounting was the selling of loans to another lender). The bank rediscounted bills having "no negotiable validity" beyond its own endorsement and without any attempt to evaluate their quality.[47] These practices created a mountain of debt with almost no solid financial ground beneath it.

London discounters found it difficult to turn away potential customers. Financial journalist David M. Evans later described London's financial atmosphere: "In the lenders there was utter recklessness in making advances; in the borrowers unparalleled avidity in profiting by the occasion; and thus an unwieldy edifice of borrowed capital was erected ready to topple down on the first shock given to that confidence which was, in fact, its sole foundation."[48] That shock would arrive soon enough. Much of Britain's lending was in short-term "call loans": in the event of a bank run, that bank would have to call (demand immediate repayment) loans, the immediate calling in of loans would ripple quickly through the economy.[49]

In March 1857, railroad cost overruns and overcapacity in the United States had accumulated to the extent that U.S. railroads were teetering financially.[50] Then two events further destabilized them. The 1850 Swamp Land Act had provided states the opportunity to reclaim any land deemed swampland that had been granted by the federal government to railroads. An 1857 amendment strengthened the states' claims. Historian Scott Reynolds Nelson sees the 1857 amendment as a direct threat, not only to railroad expansion but to the credit standing of bonds railroads had issued that were backed by property.[51] Note that Abraham Lincoln's burgeoning law practice included the defense of railroads in Swamp Act matters.[52] Second, the Dred Scott court decision deepened America's slave-state quagmire and called into question westward economic expansion.

As an aside, Nelson reports that it was railroad interests that helped finance the "free soil" side of the conflict known as "Bloody Kansas," that stemmed from 1854's momentous Kansas-Nebraska Act. Bostonians John Murray Forbes and Nathaniel Thayer had investments in the area threatened by the Swamp Act, which gave them the incentive to defend federal over state rights and was at least part of their motive to come up with the term "free soil," support abolitionist activity, and form the New England Emigrant Aid Society that would help send New Englanders to Kansas. They were also leaders within the new Republican Party, and it would be their preferred candidate and railroad industry lawyer Abraham Lincoln who would get their party's presidential nomination in 1860.[53]

One historian noted that "by June 1857, the amount of indebtedness incurred by railways, manufactures, and promoters of all kinds to the banks of the country and to each other had . . . overreached the saturation point." Catastrophe was imminent.[54]

Farmers now came under duress too. Wheat prices peaked in 1855 and collapsed after the Crimean War ended in February 1856, then kept falling through 1858.[55]

Back in New York, on August 24, 1857, the Ohio Life Insurance and Trust Company failed. This came as "a clap of thunder in a clear sky" and was the event that ignited the 1857 Panic.[56] Despite its name, Ohio Life never dealt in insurance, nor did it issue its own currency in the form of banknotes. It had a home office in Cincinnati, but most of its large-scale financial and investment activity took place in its large branch in New York City, which served as a vital link between flush eastern investors and the rapidly expanding but cash-poor economy of western states, such as Ohio, Indiana, Illinois, Wisconsin, and Michigan.[57]

Ohio Life's investment portfolio was weighted heavily toward securities issued by western railroads, which had generally performed poorly since 1854. It needed to find a way to overcome this problem, so it began making large amounts of call loans to major Ohio railroad companies. Of the roughly $1 million worth of railroad bonds in Ohio Life's portfolio at the time of its failure, some $800,000 in bonds were issued by the three railroads with which company management had personal ties. Credit problems with those bonds helped bring about Ohio Life's failure.[58]

After Ohio Life failed, railroad shares plummeted. "Accompanying the unwelcome reports of falling stock prices were the melancholy announcements of bankrupt companies," wrote James L. Huston.[59] Michael A. Ross writes that "farm prices crashed," and in Keokuk, Iowa, "lots that brought $1,000 before the crash now could not be sold for $10." The chaos unleashed crime on the streets.[60]

The La Crosse & Milwaukee and Milwaukee & Mississippi Railroads failed later in the summer, the effects reverberating through the financial networks, starting with New York banks that had invested in them. The impact then expanded outward until it reached those unfortunate Wisconsin farmers who had taken out loans collateralized by their farms to buy La Crosse stock at the urging of its agents, and now suddenly found themselves with neither a farm, because it would now be repossessed by the lender, nor railroad stock, since it was worth no more than a few pennies on the dollar.[61]

Recent research has demonstrated that a majority of securitized railroad farm mortgages had loan-to-value ratios well in excess of accepted norms and thus were especially risky.[62] It was ultimately Ohio Life's overexposure to railroad investments rather than individual malfeasance that proved to be its undoing.[63]

The repercussions of Ohio Life's collapse were felt far and wide. To meet escalating withdrawals, by mid-September the New York bankers reduced their outstanding loans by roughly $10 million by demanding early payment from other customers, thereby adding to the mounting financial turmoil. When the Clearing House Association decided in mid-September to conduct its daily settlements in specie only, it forced the smaller and less powerful New York banks to call in loans from their own brokers and dealers, which in turn forced many of them into failure and insolvency.[64]

To add to the distress, on September 18, the steamship *Central America* sank en route to New York, with 425 passengers and almost $2 million worth of California gold that might have provided a much-needed boost.[65] On September 25, the presidents of all Philadelphia's banks met and unanimously agreed to suspend payment. With the suspension in Philadelphia, one historian later wrote, "all hope disappeared." Failures and suspensions rippled across the country.[66]

By late October the New York banks alone had reduced their loans a total of 20 percent since early August and announced they would suspend specie payment indefinitely.[67] Between five thousand and six thousand individual American businesses failed during 1857, with total liabilities in the neighborhood of $280 million to $290 million.[68] A newspaper moralized, "If our own word is to be taken for our national character in October 1857, we are the most blundering, headlong, silly and incompetent generation of speculators, not to say swindlers, that ever trifled with magnificent materials, and threw away golden opportunities."[69]

This was to unfold as our first global financial crisis, however, and not just

Table 5.4. France Crisis Matrix: 1850s

Millions of Old Francs	1851	1856	1859	1851–1856 Change
GDP	11,754	18,261	16,493	6,507
Non-Agriculture GDP	7,752	10,602	10,298	2,850
Agriculture GDP	4,002	7,659	6,195	3,657
Public Debt	5,012	7,558	8,593	2,546
Private Debt	*	*	*	*
Credit Mobilier Loans	52	835	684	783
Wheat Production	942	1,872	1,044	930
Building Gross Fixed Capital Formation	164	490	440	326
Railroad Miles Built	338	785[a]	244	447

As Percentage of GDP				1851–1856 Change
Non-Agriculture GDP	66%	58%	62%	−8%
Agriculture GDP	34%	42%	38%	8%
Public Debt	43%	41%	52%	−1%
Private Debt	n/a	n/a	n/a	n/a
Credit Mobilier Loans	0%	5%	4%	4%
Wheat Production	8%	10%	6%	2%
Building Gross Fixed Capital Formation	1%	3%	3%	1%

[a]For 1857.
*Limited data points.
In the five years leading up to 1857, France's wheat production doubled, and railroad expenditures increased tenfold, while miles built more than doubled before plummeting. Crédit Mobilier loans increased fifteenfold.

a calamity for guileless Wisconsin farmers, because banks and investors from overseas had invested in U.S. railroads as well. British firms had been extending extraordinary amounts of credit to the United States for years. This included credit for highly speculative ventures, such as the extension of railroads beyond the frontier and into the mostly unsettled Great Plains.[70] On September 7, the news of the Ohio Life failure reached Liverpool and quickly ricocheted through the streets of London, accompanied by news that discount rates in New York had climbed as high as 12 percent.[71] It became clear that Britain's extensive financial exposure to the United States meant that a crisis at home was inevitable. On October 27, these fears seemed to be confirmed when the Liverpool Borough Bank suspended payment.[72] The iron industry, from the United States to Wales, Scotland, and England, all but shut down owing to a lack of demand largely caused by an abrupt halt to railroad construction.[73]

In France, the speculative rail story was the same, albeit less extreme. Crédit Mobilier and Crédit Foncier had been established in France during the early 1850s, announcing a new era in lending.[74] Crédit Mobilier's directors borrowed and speculated on a grand scale, and for a while the company paid remarkable dividends on paid-up capital—47 percent in 1855 and 24 percent the following year.[75] But by 1857, it was holding large amounts of dubious paper and had incurred debt on speculative ventures that weren't performing well. In the understated words of one contemporary British critic, the firm was forced to admit that "these Railways, these Gas Companies and Omnibus Companies, these lines of Postal Communication, these Steam Packets, these obligations in Switzerland, Spain, Austria, and Russia—had not turned out quite so successful as was expected."[76]

Of all the European cities and nations affected by the 1857 crisis, Hamburg—one of the key ports of northern Europe[77]—probably suffered the most. The liabilities of Hamburg merchants doubled during the four years before the crisis, from 1853 to 1857.[78] Between November 1857 and May 1858 more than two hundred Hamburg businesses suspended payment—a quarter of which were later declared bankrupt.[79]

In a postmortem of its crisis, New York's Mercantile Agency found fault on both sides of the transatlantic trade, especially pointing to American mercantile firms that imported foreign goods far in excess of demand simply because "European letters of credit have been so easily obtained."[80] Finally, the report cited the cycle of indebtedness that seemed to be developing as a normal feature of the financial landscape, in which retailers were constantly indebted to jobbers, who were indebted to wholesalers, who always owed money to importers, and so on, through the whole chain of commerce.[81]

In America, the crisis brought financial pain that contributed to the dark national mood that would soon lead to its Civil War.[82]

"The distress . . . was caused by an enemy more formidable than hostile armies; by a pestilence more deadly than fever or plague. I believe that it was caused by a mountain load of DEBT," concluded the American statesman Edward Everett, the multihyphenate statesman (senator, congressman, governor, Harvard University president), writing in *The Mount Vernon Papers*. The *Albany Argus* editorialized, "The dangerous facility of debt has tempted us into speculations beyond our depth."[83]

In London, a *New York Daily Tribune* journalist watched the economic carnage toppling markets and wrote, "It happens that, among all modern industrial nations, people are caught, as it were, by a periodical fit of parting with their property upon the most transparent delusions. . . . What are the social circumstances reproducing, almost regularly, these seasons of general self-delusion, of over-speculation and fictitious credit? If they were once traced out, we should arrive at a very plain alternative. Either they may be controlled by society, or they are inherent in the present system of production." Two years before, he had observed that crises came from the "industrial system which leads to over-production."[84]

His name was Karl Marx.

The Crisis of 1866

The 1860s saw the last great railroad expansion period in the United Kingdom, with miles of new railroad track laid all but doubling between 1860 and 1863. Trouble once again followed along the tracks of railroads, in the financial crisis of 1866. In May of that year, Overend, Gurney & Company, the oldest and most successful discount (lending) house in London, was forced to close its doors for good, which triggered the crisis.[85]

Overend had transformed itself into a newly authorized[86] type of company, the limited liability company, which as the title suggests, limited the liability of shareholders to the amount of their investment. This was a key new protection for stock investors.[87] Overend issued new company shares in this new form in the fall of 1865, and by October they had risen 100 percent. It had grown rapidly, in part through railway loans.[88] Nonetheless, to anyone paying attention, the Bank of England's actions during that same period indicated that it foresaw trouble: it increased its gold reserves, while also raising the discount rate from 3 percent to 7 percent, with three percentage points added within one nine-day span.[89]

Stories had been circulating since 1860 that some discounting companies had been recklessly extending credit by discounting worthless bills. *Bankers' Magazine* had noted that some "minor discount establishments" had "adventured out of their depth in paper they should not have touched."[90] Concerns about the creditworthiness, stability, and profitability of the new limited liability firms were revived in 1865. Discount houses were suspected of loaning money at high interest rates to other limited liability companies and taking low-quality securities as collateral. The worst offenders may have been a type of lender known as a finance company, since finance companies'

Table 5.5. U.K. Crisis Matrix: 1860s

Millions of British Pounds	1860	1865	1866	1867	1860–1865 Change
GDP	782	951	982	969	169
Public Debt	822	803	801	798	(19)
Private Debt	*	*	*	*	*
Commercial Bills	581	742	729	665	161
Gross Fixed Capital Formation	59	91	89	80	32
Railways	9	23	20	14	14
Manufacturing	13	18	17	14	5
Dwellings	8	11	12	14	3
Railroad Miles Built	431	500	565	393	69
Bank Failures	10	25	43	14	15

As Percentage of GDP					1860–1865 Change
Public Debt	105%	84%	82%	82%	−21%
Private Debt	n/a	n/a	n/a	n/a	n/a
Commercial Bills	74%	78%	74%	69%	4%
Gross Fixed Capital Formation	8%	10%	9%	8%	2%
Railways	1%	2%	2%	1%	1%
Manufacturing	2%	2%	2%	1%	0%
Dwellings	1%	1%	1%	1%	0%

*Limited data points.

From 1861 to 1866, U.K. railroad miles grew briskly, and limited commercial bill data suggest private debt grew briskly as well.

whole business model was "to deal in securities which were beyond the legitimate scope of the banks and the discount market."[91]

The first cracks began to appear in January 1866, with the collapse of a smaller firm named the Joint Stock Discount Company. Then rumors began to spread that partners of Overend in its former structure were hurriedly cashing in their shares and that current partners were selling off their personal estates to try to raise money.[92] A few weeks later, public disclosures during the liquidation of Joint Stock Discount revealed a "rottenness" pervading its financials as well as those of its partners. Nervous individual account holders began to withdraw their money. The apprehension spread. Within two months, deposits at Overend fell by roughly £2.5 million, with another £2 million withdrawn by May.[93]

In April, Spanish merchant firm Pinto, Perez & Company failed, and everyone knew that a substantial amount of its liabilities was owed to Overend.

The revelation a few weeks later that the company's officials were guilty of serious fraud hurt the situation. On May 9, a court ruled that Overend did not have the legal power to collect substantial debts owed to it by the Mid-Wales Railway.[94] "Bears," those pessimistic about markets at the London Stock Exchange, soon picked up the scent of failure and began shorting Overend shares, beating down the already sagging price. Most everyone knew Overend's end was near.[95]

It finally arrived on Thursday, May 10, with a short notice posted on the main entrance to Overend: severe runs had compelled them to stop payment.[96] Bank of England governor Henry Holland sent a small committee to investigate Overend's books, and committee member Robert Bevan reported that "the firm was so rotten" it effectively sealed its own fate.[97] The company had liabilities over £5 million, though it was difficult to be certain since its books were in such disarray.[98]

Holland raised the Bank of England's rate to 10 percent.[99] Three London banks were among the casualties. Scores of bill brokers, discount houses, and finance companies that had thrived in the shadows of the legitimate banking world were similarly wiped out. By August 10, 1866, more than 180 companies had entered bankruptcy proceedings—casualties from the Overend collapse.[100]

Runs on banks continued and rumors swirled, and Holland and the Bank of England acted vigorously to provide short-term funding to banks deemed sound enough for support. Holland sent a letter to Chancellor of the Exchequer William Gladstone, assuring him that things were essentially under control on "Threadneedle Street"—the Bank of England. He explained that the bank had advanced over £4 million to "Bankers, Bill Brokers and Merchants in London—an unprecedented sum to lend in one day and which, therefore, we suppose would be sufficient to meet all their requirements." He told Gladstone, "We have not refused any legitimate application for assistance."[101]

Despite the lingering fallout, the Bank of England was able to maintain gold reserves at a relatively constant level throughout the crisis.[102] This was due partly to the 10 percent bank rate, of course, but also to shipments of gold arriving regularly from Australian mines. The reserves were more than enough to cover any drains, and the bank never did need to invoke an indemnity guarantee.[103]

The 1866 British crisis was seen by many as a validation of *Economist* editor Walter Bagehot's newly articulated rules for what he termed the "Lender of Last Resort," a duty he expected of the Bank of England: lend freely but only to those institutions solid enough to weather the crisis, and only then at an interest rate that could be considered punitive.[104]

After a doubling of railroad miles built, France saw economic turmoil and a spate of failures in the same year, though not at the magnitude of Britain's crisis. Crédit Mobilier and Société Immobilière reached the brink of failure and had to seek assistance from the Bank of France, though only limited assistance was forthcoming. Mobilier had to be dissolved, and Société de Crédit Mobilier Français formed in its place.[105]

Conventional wisdom among many economists holds that after 1866, the United Kingdom experienced fewer financial crises because of the good stewardship of the Bank of England, especially in its "lender of last resort" duties. This stewardship contrasted dramatically, they argue, with the absence of any such central bank in the United States during the period.[106]

Yet the difference in number of financial crises is not primarily attributable to the presence or absence of a central bank since they do not exercise their "lender of last resort" powers until after the lending misbehavior has occurred. Thus they do not prevent the crisis by using these powers but instead ameliorate the resulting damage. The smaller number of crises in Britain after 1866 is attributable to the basic fact that by that year, the majority of Britain's railroad track had already been laid. Hence, the speculative outbursts of construction sufficient to provoke a crisis had largely ended. At that same moment in the United States, only a small portion of the track that would ultimately be built had yet been laid, and there were many massive railroad construction bursts yet to come. In England, new railroad mileage built between 1870 and 1900 was less than that built before 1870. In contrast, the United States built triple the miles between 1870 and 1900 than it did before that time—and it did so in these enormous bursts.

Bagehot described the 1866 panic at the time as "a credit panic." It was not the result of excessive drains on bullion reserves, he argued, or of national expenditures that exceeded savings. It was rather "a failure of credit by intrinsic defect"—the misuse and overextension of credit by even "the most celebrated of old houses." And he was right. Bagehot had aptly and succinctly described the essence of all major financial crises.[107]

The Crisis of 1873

The 1870s boom that led to the global crisis of 1873 came from the renewed expansion of railroads. Railroad expansion this time was tied closely to the expansion of wheat production because agricultural transport was as big or

Table 5.6. U.S. Crisis Matrix: 1860s and 1870s

Billions of Dollars	1868	1869	1873	1874	1875	1876	1868–1873 Change	1869–1874 Change
GDP	$8.41	$8.31	$9.30	$8.98	$9.05	$8.81	$0.89	$0.67
Federal Debt	$2.61	$2.59	$2.23	$2.25	$2.23	$2.18	$(0.38)	$(0.34)
Private Debt (est.)	$3.18	$3.26	$5.04	$5.50	$5.92	$5.55	$1.86	$2.24
Bank Loans	$0.77	$0.80	$1.44	$1.56	$1.75	$1.73	$0.67	$0.76
Railroad Bonds	$0.79	$0.86	$1.84	$2.23	$2.46	$2.17	$1.05	$1.37
Memo: Construction (est.)	$1.09	$1.28	$1.30	$1.15	$1.03	$0.89	$0.21	$(0.13)
Railroad Miles Built	2,468	4,103	5,217	2,584	1,606	2,575	2,749	(1,519)
Bank Failures	10	8	44	43	19	46	34	35

As Percentage of GDP							1868–1873 Change	1869–1874 Change
Federal Debt	31%	31%	24%	25%	25%	25%	-7%	-6%
Private Debt (est.)	38%	39%	54%	61%	65%	63%	16%	22%
Bank Loans	9%	10%	15%	17%	19%	20%	6%	8%
Railroad Bonds	9%	10%	20%	25%	27%	25%	10%	14%
Memo: Construction (est.)	13%	15%	14%	13%	11%	10%	1%	-3%

In the five years leading up to 1873, U.S. private debt grew by 58 percent. Sectors with the greatest concentration of overlending were railroads and mortgages, which together comprised 69 percent of the total.

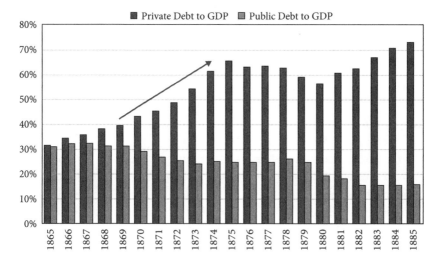

Figure 5.8. United States: Private and Public Debt as a Percentage of GDP, 1865–1885
Private debt in the United States increased by $1.8 billion (or 54.6 percent) from 1868 to 1873.

Table 5.7. Germany Crisis Matrix: 1860s and 1870s

Millions of Marks	1870	1874	1876	1870–1874 Change
GDP	12,876	21,186	19,475	8,310
Public Debt	4,051	3,412	4,203	(639)
Private Debt	*	*	*	*
Bank Loans	3,052	5,808	5,267	2,756
Wheat Production	507	1,136	585	630
Railroad Miles Built	495	1,042	657	547

As Percentage of GDP				1870–1874 Change
Public Debt	31%	16%	22%	−15%
Private Debt	n/a	n/a	n/a	n/a
Bank Loans	24%	27%	27%	4%
Wheat Production	4%	5%	3%	1%

*Limited data points.
In the five years leading up to 1874, bank loans grew by 90 percent; the value of wheat production and the number of railroad miles built both more than doubled.

a bigger source of revenue than passengers.[108] Wheat production increased 89 percent between 1866 and 1873, and railroads expanded apace.[109] In the United States between 1865 and 1873, the total mileage of the railroad network more than doubled, from 31,919 miles to 67,409. During that same period, the amount of bonded debt outstanding of American railroad companies more than tripled, from $539 million to $1.836 billion.[110] In the same period, railroad mileage grew by 70 percent in Germany and more than doubled in Austria and Hungary.

The problem that should have been familiar by then was that this debt-enabled expansion had gone too far, and when the inevitable tumble occurred, those that financed it—lenders making too many bad loans—tumbled too, with colossal bank failures in the United States, Germany, Russia, and Austria.

The American Civil War had led to high wheat prices, and with that, far across the ocean, Russian nobles had bought more land and vastly expanded their production.[111] Joint-stock company formation had exploded in the newly consolidated Austro-Hungarian (1867) and German (1871) Empires. The indemnity paid by France to Germany after its defeat in the Franco-Prussian War of 1871 left Germany flush with new money, and debt-financed speculation had accelerated markedly. In Prussia, 763 new businesses with a total worth of about 6 billion marks were launched in 1871 and 1872.[112] The German stock exchange was 73 percent higher in 1872 than it had been two years earlier.[113]

In Germany, real estate investment companies called *Baugesellschaften* (building societies) emerged in the 1870s, more interested in "real estate speculation than in actual construction," according to historian John Lyon.[114] This foreshadows events with U.S. savings banks and real estate securities in the 1920s and 1980s. A special law in Prussian-dominated German states allowed for home purchases without down payments and, contrary to other mortgage bonds, usually went along with interest-only payments.[115] Germans could thus acquire houses without equity, paying interest instead of rent, which led to excess mortgage lending and then "foreclosure rates of about one third of all housing units in the 1870s economic crisis and an ensuing 15-year interruption of building activity."[116]

In France, by 1872, struggling to rebuild its battered cities, its national pride, and its economic momentum after that same Franco-Prussian War, bank loans had almost tripled in just three years, and railroad miles built had more than doubled in four years. Over the next two years, both tumbled.

In Austria-Hungary, 70 new banks formed between 1868 and 1873 in Vienna, and 928 joint-stock companies with market capital of 2.8 billion marks were formed between 1871 and 1873. In all, between 1867 and 1873, a total of 1,005 new companies were chartered. By 1874, half would fail.[117]

Mortgage loans in Austria-Hungary ballooned from 166 million Gulden in 1868 to 427 million Gulden in 1878,[118] with speculation financed by a new genus of banks, as in Germany, called *Baubanken* (construction banks). Charles Kindleberger describes how the *Baubanken* stimulated "a class of peasants . . . that sold their farm land in the periphery of cities, especially Berlin."[119] The wealthy landowners, the *Junkers*, made a large profit, and expelled their tenant farmers. David C. Goodman and Colin Chant note that earlier, land prices typically correlated to agricultural use, "but as farmers came to realize the value of their land for housing, prices began to escalate."[120] This created a wandering population of displaced people. Families in search of affordable housing, wheeling carts of their belongings, clogged the city streets. A group of *Schlafburschen*, or "sleepers," would rent "a patch of floor in someone's apartment for a night or two." Packing-carton manufacturers advertised "good and cheap boxes for habitation."[121] Beyond this, a consortium of princes and aristocratic families throughout Europe eagerly rode the coattails of the "railroad king" Bethel Henry Strousberg, legendary for his railway development in Romania.[122]

Given the greater railroad capital demands in the United States, Germans and Austrians bought U.S. railroad bonds as well. Traces of this transatlantic bubble can still be seen today: railroad promoters in North Dakota named a town Bismarck to "attract German capital."[123]

Back in the United States, Philadelphia banker Jay Cooke, who is so central to most versions of the 1873 crisis story, typified the railroad finance excesses of the day. He made his fortune as a young man and then gained a national reputation selling U.S. war bonds during the Civil War.[124] After the war, wanting to invest in a railroad but having determined that most of the important lines were already controlled by syndicates of wealthy investment banks and businessmen, he shifted his focus to the frontier and took control of 60 percent of the Northern Pacific Railroad. It had an enormous land grant but was on a sparsely populated and rugged route, so it had suffered chronic delays.[125]

Its losses and ongoing need for new capital were large, and so Cooke needed to quickly increase funds by selling both land and $100 million in Northern Pacific bonds. He spared neither effort nor hyperbole. Typical was one ten-column-inch ad that ran in the *Times* of London early in 1872, extolling the "excellent lands" available for purchase as well as the "salubrity of the climate, and diversity of natural resources."[126]

The Northern Pacific turned out to be a hard sell, though, and was burning through capital far more quickly than Cooke could raise it. Almost from the start he resorted to making up the difference with funds from his Jay Cooke & Company banking firm.[127] Things were dire enough that in 1871 and 1872, Cooke's brother Henry, then the president of the recently created Freedman's Saving and Trust Company, transferred between $500,000 and $600,000 out of the small deposit accounts of freed slaves to Jay Cooke & Company, which resulted in the loss of the meager savings of thousands of newly freed slaves.[128]

Wheat fortunes were lashed to railroad fortunes in the 1870s. Rapid expansion of production and technological advances in agriculture drove the price of wheat down by 56 percent, and North American farmers began to undercut the pricing of European wheat. This left Ukrainian and Russian grain producers with a glut, and they soon found themselves unable to make payments on their new mortgages, with the bitter result that Russian banks foreclosed on nearly six thousand estates in the winter of 1872–73.[129]

This brings us to Vienna in early May 1873. In the euphoria, Viennese stocks had risen to unsustainable levels, and on the afternoon of May 9, stocks crashed. The *Maklerbanken* (agency banks), with their large investments in Austro-Hungarian exports, collapsed first. Many of the building and loan societies that had financed overvalued land purchases followed.[130] The collapse bruised every business sector.[131]

What began in Austria made its way to U.S. lenders in September 1873. Most of the early casualties, including the New York Security & Warehouse Company and the stock brokerage Kenyon, Cox, & Company, were brought down directly or indirectly by their exposure to railroad companies, which were in worse shape than imagined.[132] As we saw with the Great Depression, the first bank failures do not happen randomly. In 1873, they happened to those with exposure to railroads and its associated construction.

When Jay Cooke & Company failed on September 18, the country was uniformly shocked, though rumors had been circulating for some time.[133] The failure brought on a full crisis. Soon dozens more banks, brokers, and other railroads failed.[134] Mercantile failures exploded. The 5,183 failures in 1873 grew to 5,830 in 1874 and 7,740 in 1875.[135] Banks called in loans as fast as they could, damaging good businesses and further damaging the bad, and loans fell from $940.2 million to just $853.4 million in a mere two months.[136]

When Jay Cooke and Company filed for bankruptcy, Berlin could no longer hold and collapsed the same month. That year, one-third of all Prussian banks failed,[137] and 61 banks, 4 railroads, and 115 industrial companies went bankrupt.[138] The Prussian Office of Statistics reported that 444 public Prussian companies lost 2 billion marks.[139] Many stocks were soon worthless. In France, a number of savings banks were suspended and notaries (issuers of long term credit) failed.[140]

Overcapacity meant that the United States—and much of Europe—descended into a half-decade of economic depression and stagnation. From 1873 to 1875, 121 U.S. railroad companies defaulted, with a total of $552 million in outstanding debt.[141] Earnings from passenger service would not fully recover until 1879. Freight traffic fell off by up to 50 percent. It took seven years to regain the 1873 level.[142]

With the collapse in demand from railroads, by the end of 1874, half of all U.S. foundries had closed down.[143] Other firms tried to stay afloat by cutting back on the labor side, using layoffs, reduced hours, pay cuts, and the payment of wages with company IOUs to mitigate the lack of liquidity. Indeed, this crisis is also notable because it was the first financial crisis in which a large number of Americans had become wage earners, no longer able to retreat easily into subsistence life on farms. From this point onward, the prevalent condition of wage labor would fundamentally change how financial crises were experienced. Unemployment was punishing, and at one point roughly 25 percent of all workers in New York City were jobless, leading to protests, demonstrations, and violence as workers gathered to demand jobs in such places as Chicago, New York, and Boston.

The 1873 crisis also contributed to post–Civil War racism, as many whites blamed former slaves rather than railroads for their economic woes. This not only bolstered the cause of "redemption" (the return of white Democrats to political power) but also increased physical violence against African Americans. This scapegoating of minorities for economic trouble occurred in Europe, too.[144]

The 1873 crisis took a devastating toll, and across all of these countries, it was notable for the length, unevenness, and turbulence of the recovery. The United States did not truly regain its momentum until 1879, France not till 1880, and Germany not till the mid-1880s.

Table 5.8. France Crisis Matrix: 1870s and 1880s

Millions of Old Francs	1877	1881	1885	1877–1881 Change
GDP	21,105	22,567	20,791	1,462
Non-Agricultural GDP	12,375	13,981	13,001	1,606
Agricultural GDP	8,730	8,586	7,790	(144)
Public Debt	19,985	20,366	23,754	381
Private Debt	*	*	*	*
Bank Loans	1,600	2,400	1,500	800
Gross Fixed Capital Formation	1,292	2,088	1,373	796
Railroad Miles Built	533	885	789	352

As Percentage of GDP				1877–1881 Change
Non-Agricultural GDP	59%	62%	63%	3%
Agricultural GDP	41%	38%	37%	−3%
Public Debt	95%	90%	114%	−4%
Private Debt	n/a	n/a	n/a	n/a
Bank Loans	8%	11%	7%	3%
Gross Fixed Capital Formation	6%	9%	7%	3%

*Limited data points.
In the five years leading up to 1882, France's bank loans grew by 50 percent. Railroad miles built increased by 66 percent.

The Crises of the 1880s

In 1882, France once again touched the hot flame of financial crisis. From very low levels in the late 1870s, railroad miles built had exploded by 1881, and in the three years leading to 1882, banks loans had grown by a startling 85 percent. The period saw the spectacular rise of the banking industry, with such notable events as the doubling of the capital of Crédit Lyonnais, the 1881 founding of the Bank of Lyon, and especially the 1878 founding by Paul Eugène Bontoux of the Société de l'Union Générale.[145] Bontoux's bank lent aggressively to all sectors but especially to railroads both in France and abroad. Collectively, the industry was making an excess of ill-judged loans that would come back to haunt them.

The Paris Bourse reflected the surge in activity, with a burst of listings of construction, trade, and transport companies.[146] In 1881 alone, 163 new companies entered the market to raise capital.[147] It all came tumbling down in January 1882, and with it, Bontoux, whose bank among other missteps had fraudulently misrepresented its capital position. He was tried and sentenced to five years in prison but fled to Spain.[148] A number of other, mainly industrial banks failed. The painter Paul Gauguin, a stockbroker at the time, had his earnings crushed in the crisis. He decided to take his brushes and devote himself to painting.[149]

On the other side of the globe, Japan had aggressively industrialized after the Meiji restoration of 1868, in a determined quest to catch up to the industrial powers of the West. This included the establishment of factories and banks. But Japan quickly took this to a level of overcapacity and saw resulting bank failures by 1882. China, too, suffered a banking crisis in 1883 centered in Shanghai.

In the United States, the 1884 crisis came as annual railroad miles built grew from 2,280 (1877) to 11,599 (1882)—far too much capacity at that moment—before plunging to 3,131 (1885). An adjunct was the rapidly expanding western cattle and meatpacking industry, extending from Texas cattle drives, to Chicago's meatpacking plants, to the rail transport of the meat to the East Coast. It had its own bout with overcapacity and collapse at this time. Private debt grew by 52 percent between 1879 and 1884. U.S. GDP fell by 4.3 percent in the two-year period culminating in 1885. The crisis is best known for bankrupting former president Ulysses S. Grant and Grant & Ward, the firm he had established with his son and his son's close friend. The crisis took down several other lending institutions and thousands of small firms.

Émile Zola's novel L'Argent [Money], penned in serial form beginning in 1890, reflected on the decade with a searing indictment of "the evils of 'speculation'" and showed that the path to financial crisis or, in his words, "the ways of the speculator, the promoter, the wrecker, the defaulter, the reptile journalist, and the victim, are much the same all the world over."[150]

The Crisis of 1893

The U.S. financial crisis of the early 1890s came with the 1887 spike in railroad construction, the largest in U.S. history.[151] With it, railroad miles built quadrupled. The associated upturn in locomotive and freight car production peaked in 1890, and steel production peaked in 1892. This period saw another avalanche of largely debt-financed federal land sales from 1883 to 1890, also the most in U.S. history. It was an indicator of the accompanying surge in residential and commercial construction, which peaked in 1889 and 1890, respectively, creating another layer of overcapacity.[152] Production of rails,

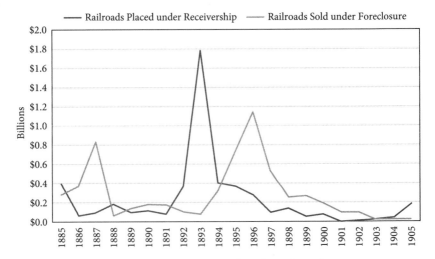

Figure 5.9. Distressed U.S. Railroads: Value of Stocks and Bonds, 1885–1905

Table 5.9. U.S. Crisis Matrix: 1880s and 1890s

Billions of Dollars	1886	1887	1891	1893	1894	1886–1891 Change
GDP	$12.20	$12.76	$14.04	$14.56	$13.37	$1.84
Federal Debt	$1.78	$1.66	$1.55	$1.55	$1.63	$(0.23)
Private Debt (est.)	$9.07	$10.10	$12.91	$13.85	$13.43	$3.84
Bank Loans	$2.85	$3.40	$4.72	$5.13	$4.86	$1.87
Mortgages	$1.03	$1.12	$1.69	$1.87	$1.91	$0.66
Railroad Bonds	$3.88	$4.19	$4.84	$5.23	$5.36	$0.96
Memo: Construction (est.)	$1.45	$1.65	$2.01	$1.82	$1.60	$0.57
Railroad Miles Built	8,400	13,081	4,620	3,024	1,760	4,681[a]
Bank Failures	21	27	69	326	92	299[b]

As Percentage of GDP						1886–1891 Change
Federal Debt	15%	13%	11%	11%	12%	−4%
Private Debt (est.)	74%	79%	92%	95%	100%	18%
Bank Loans	23%	27%	34%	35%	36%	10%
Mortgages	8%	9%	12%	13%	14%	4%
Railroad Bonds	32%	33%	34%	36%	40%	3%
Memo: Construction (est.)	12%	13%	14%	13%	12%	2%

[a]1886–1887 change.
[b]1887–1893 change.
In the five years leading up to 1891, U.S. private debt grew by 42 percent. Railroads and mortgages comprised 58 percent of that total.

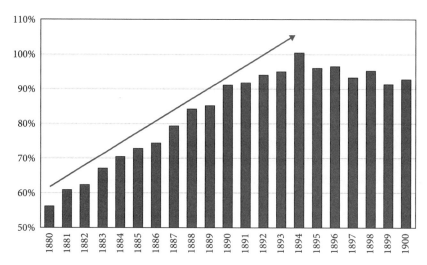

Figure 5.10. United States: Private Debt as a Percentage of GDP, 1880–1900
Private debt in the United States increased by $7.6 billion (or 121 percent) from 1880 to 1893.

steel, locomotives, and freight cars collapsed and would not fully recover for half a decade.[153] This timeline illustrates a common element of financial crises: the staggered overcapacity peaks and the protracted agony of the bust.

Railroad companies started to collapse in 1892, with a huge number placed under receivership and sold under foreclosure over the next five years, as shown in Figure 5.9. The stocks and bonds of railroads placed under receivership had been less than $200 million from 1888 to 1891, grew to $358 million in 1892, and then tripled to $1.8 billion in 1893—an amount equaling 12 percent of GDP. Bank failures rose from 17 in 1889, to 69 in 1891, to a cruel 326 in 1893. The stock market echoed the pain, with sharp reversals in 1890[154] and then again in 1893.[155]

Fatally overextended, the Philadelphia and Reading Railroad collapsed on February 23, 1893, just days before President Grover Cleveland's inauguration for his second term.[156] Rumors of financial problems at the National Cordage Company also drove it to receivership on May 4,[157] as banks called in its loans, and the New York stock market crashed the following day. Other railroads fell in succession, including the Erie Railroad in July, the Northern Pacific again in August, the Union Pacific in October, and the Atchison, Topeka, and Santa Fe Railroad in December.[158] The bill for railroad overcapacity was coming due—again.

Businesses were overextended as well. The number of commercial failures grew each year, starting in 1887 with 9,634, but reaching 15,242 companies, with liabilities of $346 million, in 1893. The companies that failed in that year were on average double the size of those that failed the previous year.[159] The agriculture sector had expanded in the upturn, but farmers suffered when wheat prices crashed in the crisis.[160]

Europe saw some but much less distress, primarily because a relatively larger part of their railroad expansion was behind them. None of their railroad expansion was even a fraction as dramatic as that of the United States in this period. Yet there were still some international problems. Firms such as Baring Brothers had profited extensively by encouraging their clients to purchase risky Argentine bonds during the 1870s and 1880s. But in 1890, "a bloody revolution, crop failures, and rampant inflation" in that nation drastically reduced interest in this debt. Afraid that the instability in Argentina might spread to other financial markets, many European investors rushed to cash in their bonds in favor of hard currency. This, in turn, led to both the decline of Baring as "the Goldman Sachs of its day" and the beginning of a run on gold in the United States.[161]

U.S. unemployment reached levels that brought labor unrest, the destruction of property, and in some cases, the loss of life in places across the country. The effects of a crisis on the wage labor market, labor unrest, and misery, so evident in the 1873 crisis, were even more pronounced in this one. U.S. unemployment climbed.[162] In the 1890s, Jacob Coxey—formerly a member of Grover Cleveland's Democratic Party—would become involved in the Populist Party and challenge capitalism, even though he was a prosperous business owner. When the panic of 1893 hit, he was forced to lay off workers from his mining and manufacturing businesses. Facing that misery, he devised a plan of public works to improve the infrastructure of the United States while giving jobs to the unemployed masses. He spearheaded a protest with a band of the unemployed known as "Coxey's Army," which started with a hundred men in Ohio and grew to five hundred by the time it reached Washington. This march inspired thousands of others to organize protests around the country. Coxey would be arrested on the lawn of the Capitol—for trespassing on the grass—with his revolutionary ideas ignored.[163]

Conventional wisdom holds that this crisis had a great deal to do with silver and hard currency, in particular the enactment of the Sherman Silver Act in the summer of 1890 and its subsequent repeal in the summer of 1893 after the banking crisis began. Both have received much attention as well as blame for the crisis. However, what actually transpired in 1893 does lend much support to this perception.

The act increased the amount of silver the government was mandated to purchase to 4.5 million ounces monthly. It was passed largely because of a deepening agricultural depression brought on by years of drought, storms, and overproduction. Midwest and southern farmers were hit especially hard, and farmers "seethed with discontent" as "debt payments and low prices restricted agrarian purchasing power and demand for goods and services."[164] The Free Silver movement arose, gaining support from farmers, who sought to invigorate the economy and bring about inflation, thus allowing them to repay their debt with cheaper dollars, and mining interests, who sought the right to turn silver directly into money.

Yet the volumes and price of silver were such that it appeared to play little role in the creation of overcapacity during the crucial years of 1885 to 1890. After the Treasury silver purchases began in late 1890, when the act took effect, it did so at an overvalued price, which gave investors a silver-to-gold arbitrage, and the amount of gold at the Treasury dropped rapidly from $150 million to $80 million. This concerned the Treasury, but other than a brief, minor drop in GDP in 1890, both GDP and private debt moved ahead at a pre–Silver Act pace.

The Sherman Silver Act was quickly repealed in August 1893 after that year's banking and stock market crash. But this was only after the crash had already happened. Gold and silver totals were stable, though specie declined by $139 million in two years—but, again, only *after* 1894. Inflation was low or negative, and long-term rates for the most part were stable during the period. The actual trends, flows, and aggregate value of silver would suggest its role was minor—especially when set against much larger GDP and private debt totals.

Historians have also made much of J. P. Morgan's 1895 rescue of the U.S. Treasury. This is another factor that happened well after the crisis, so it was not causal but is worth comment. The depression that followed the crisis had reduced government revenues, and it ran a deficit in 1894 and 1895. Consequently, its gold reserves were rapidly declining. They were approaching a level at which the United States would not be able to redeem notes in specie, a potential disaster and profound international embarrassment in a gold standard world.

Morgan offered his services to President Cleveland to replenish the Treasury's gold by underwriting a $65 million U.S. debt offering. The Treasury's negligence was the issue since this rescue could have been avoided had it forecasted the deficiency properly and planned for it. Under those circumstances, it could have executed a debt offering and used the proceeds to buy an adequate supply of gold well in advance of that need. Cleveland was loath to accept Morgan's offer because he correctly feared a populist backlash, but he had no choice. Morgan's firm profited handsomely on the transaction, which fueled the negative perception among voters of Cleveland's obeisance to Wall Street.

This crisis harmed attitudes toward industrialization, government intervention, and basic tenets of capitalism. The era's business distress led to the first huge wave of U.S. mergers and acquisitions, which began in 1895 and peaked in 1899. In turn, this brought a wave of antitrust activity.

The Crisis of 1907

The year 1907 saw the last financial crisis in which railroad overcapacity played a major role. The impact of railroads was joined by the impact of the emerging electric utility industry. This crisis is in some respects a bridge between the railroad century, which we might also call the age of steam, and the coming age of electricity. Edison had invented the first practical lightbulb in 1878, and by 1882 his Pearl Street power station—financially backed by the omnipresent J. P. Morgan—was providing lighting to homes and businesses in lower Manhattan.[165] The 1907 crisis even foreshadowed the Great Depression, as New York saw its first, fledgling skyscraper boom.

With this dawning age of electricity, the world developed an insatiable appetite for copper. It was needed in the power-generating plants themselves, for the wires that brought electricity to houses, and in industry and transportation. A race was on to string copper wires across the United States, Britain, Germany, France, Japan, and beyond, a race that accelerated in the 1890s and 1900s. Copper mining surged, and many of the era's fortunes came from it. As with railroads, the indirect construction activity that expanded alongside electricity industry–related expansion was as great as or even greater than the direct activity—and just as perilous.

The burgeoning electricity industry had a major impact on copper prices from almost the very beginning, with copper price spikes in 1888, 1899, and 1906–7 (Figure 5.11). These three price spikes reflected periods of rapid expan-

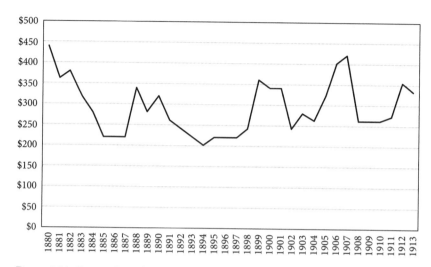

Figure 5.11. Copper Price (per Ton), 1880–1913

Table 5.10. Germany Crisis Matrix: 1890s and 1900s

Millions of Marks	1895	1900	1901	1902	1895–1900 Change
GDP	25,254	32,448	31,617	31,928	7,194
Public Debt	12,627	14,926	15,492	15,964	2,299
Private Debt	*	*	*	*	*
Bank Loans	9,433	14,272	14,202	14,946	4,839
Mortgages	5,198	6,758	6,956	7,271	1,560
Gross Domestic Capital Formation	2,830	5,100	3,890	3,520	2,270
Railroad Miles Built	704	563	726	569	163[a]

As Percentage of GDP					1895–1900 Change
Public Debt	50%	46%	49%	50%	−4%
Private Debt	n/a	n/a	n/a	n/a	n/a
Bank Loans	37%	44%	45%	47%	7%
Mortgages	21%	21%	22%	23%	0%
Gross Domestic Capital Formation	11%	16%	12%	11%	5%

[a]1900–1901 change.
*Limited data points.
In the five years leading to 1900, Germany's bank loans grew by 51 percent.

sion and overcapacity, and the associated debt-financed copper speculation played a role in three calamities: the spectacular demise of Paris's Comptoir d'Escompte in 1889,[166] Germany's crises of 1901, and the broader global crises of 1907.

Germany's rapid industrialization in the second half of the nineteenth century transformed it into one of the world's leading industrial powers, including in electricity.[167] Large banks played *the* major role in this industrialization.[168] Germany's growth required large mobilizations of capital and funding, and electric companies first obtained funds through issuing shares, then moved to loans,[169] with bank loans peaking in 1900.

The signs of excess came in December 1900, when the director of the Allgemeine Elektricitäts-Gesellschaft (Germany's General Electric Company) said "the electrical industry now has a productive capacity in excess of the demand for electrical manufactures."[170] Electricity company shares fell.

In July, the *Economist* reported that "the manufacturers of structural iron, owing to the dullness in the building trades, are accumulating stocks of finished material, which cannot be disposed of,"[171] and in September reported that "all mills in Western Germany that produce pig-iron and rolled goods are now accumulating supplies of these materials far beyond their immediate wants, since . . . they placed orders far ahead, and for quantities that could be consumed only under the continuance of demand as it then existed. But now demand has slackened remarkably."[172] Cement producers met in November and decided to halve production, given "very evident overproduction."[173] Even the coal industry, which had for most of the year been unable to meet heavy demand, eventually had to cut production "in the face of decreasing consumption."[174] Soon, "factories had trouble disposing of their products, stocks rose, orders became rare, [and] it became impossible to find new capital."[175]

But, as a harbinger of other twentieth-century crises, it was the trail of real estate excess that accompanied the expansion of electricity that in October 1900, triggered the first stage of the financial crisis. In its October 27 issue, the *Economist* described a "sensational event." Two mortgage banks—Prussian Hypotheken-Aktienbank and Deutsche Grundschuld Bank—had failed on certain financial commitments; consequently, their shares fell by about 20 percent each. Other mortgage banks convened to help them out, likely fearing that these banks' troubles might affect them as well.[176]

But the two mortgage banks' shares continued to fall, each declining 60 percent to 70 percent, and the *Economist* reported that they had been engaging in questionable lending practices. Grundschuld had replaced £2 million in first-class mortgages with "worthless" mortgages.[177] The *Economist* also reported that £3 million of the Grundschuld Bank's obligations were secured by "second-class mortgages," which had only paid out less than a third of the interest they were obligated to pay that year. Eventually, both mortgage banks failed, along with two others, the Pomeranian Bank and the Mortgage Bank of Mecklenburg-Strelitz, which had also announced they too would be unable to meet certain financial commitments.[178] Two large banks in Saxony, the Dresdner Creditanstalt and the Bank of Leipzig, failed in 1901: they had loaned too much money to industrial concerns.[179] A run on Saxon banks followed.

Scientific American, in a scathing report on the German crisis of 1901, chided German capitalists for getting ahead of themselves and overlending to industry. "The banks were only too ready to lend money for industrial purposes," the magazine wrote. "The censors who taunted the English manufacturer for his conservativeness," the magazine wrote, "are silenced for the moment."[180]

In 1901, Germany saw a drop in stocks, GDP, and loans, with reverberations felt across Europe. While Germany's day of reckoning came early, it would take until 1907 for this copper and electricity frenzy to fully catch up to other countries.

In the global trading boom that began in 1904, stock prices in the mining sector outpaced manufacturing, railroads, and other industries. The price of copper had been 14 cents per pound in 1903 and soared to 25 cents per pound in 1906, but when production almost doubled to 1.6 billion pounds by 1907, prices dropped to 17 cents, affecting lenders to that industry. Lenders found themselves overleveraged on railroad lines, construction, and copper mines, and now faced the global crises of 1907 and 1908. Many view the October 1907 failure of New York's Knickerbocker Trust as the onset of the global crisis. But this crisis erupted first in Alexandria, Egypt; then, Tokyo, Japan; Genoa, Italy; and Hamburg, Germany—and beyond.[181]

Japan, an exporter of copper, had emerged out of economic doldrums and into what the governor of the Bank of Japan called "a fever of enterprise,"[182] with the number of its new businesses and the prices of its stocks rapidly increasing. But those stock prices declined steeply in early 1907, with the collapse of the Tokyo stock market. A fall in commodity prices, especially copper, and other financial difficulties resulted in a 12 percent decline in Japan's exports between 1907 and 1908. Bank failures and bankruptcies would continue until 1908. By October 1907, twenty-four banks had already closed and fifty-eight were under pressure.

Table 5.11. France Crisis Matrix: 1900s

Millions of Old Francs	1901	1906	1907	1908	1901–1906 Change
GDP	25,612	28,468	30,724	30,866	2,856
Non-Agriculture GDP	17,388	19,323	20,646	20,372	1,935
Agriculture GDP	8,224	9,145	10,079	9,609	921
Public Debt	25,120	24,258	23,919	24,399	(862)
Private Debt	*	*	*	*	*
Bank Loans	4,600	7,200	6,400	7,400	2,600

As Percentage of GDP					1901–1906 Change
Non-Agriculture GDP	68%	68%	67%	66%	0%
Agriculture GDP	32%	32%	33%	31%	0%
Public Debt	98%	85%	78%	79%	−13%
Private Debt	n/a	n/a	n/a	n/a	n/a
Bank Loans	18%	25%	21%	24%	7%

*Limited data points.
In the five years leading up to 1906, France's bank loans grew by 57 percent.

The collapse in copper prices led to the Ashio riots, in which workers at the Ashio copper mine—Japan's largest mining concern and one of the largest in the world—rioted for three days against the Furukawa Company in February 1907.[183] The *Japan Times* luridly described the scene: "Towards evening the mob assembled at Motoyama, set warehouses on fire, and the whole mountain side was enveloped in smoke."[184]

France saw rapid lending growth in the early 1900s that led to financial turbulence as well. France's bank loans grew by 57 percent from 1901 to 1906. Its investment in Russian enterprise between 1900 and World War I hovered between 20 percent and 25 percent of GDP, increasing its credit risk and vulnerability. Domestically, France saw a collapse in the Lyon silk market.[185] Two French banks suspended payments, Maurice Gallet and Company in Paris (with liabilities of £400,000) and the Société Lyonnaise de Crédit, as a result of its silk speculation.[186]

After Germany's 1901 troubles, the country's bank loans again grew rapidly in the five years leading up to 1907. In the wake of this growth, twenty-nine private banking establishments, eleven registered cooperative credit societies with limited liabilities, one industrial bank, one savings and credit bank, two loan and credit societies, one people's bank, and two credit banks

Table 5.12. U.S. Crisis Matrix: 1900s

Billions of Dollars	1902	1907	1908	1902–1907 Change
GDP	$21.8	$29.1	$26.9	$7.3
Federal Debt	$2.2	$2.5	$2.6	$0.3
Private Debt (est.)	$20.3	$28.8	$28.5	$8.5
Total Corporate Bonds	$7.8	$11.8	$12.6	$4.0
Utility Bonds	$1.4	$2.9	$3.2	$1.5
Industrial Bonds	$0.9	$1.6	$1.7	$0.7
Railroad Bonds	$5.5	$7.0	$8.0	$1.5
Bank Loans	$7.2	$10.8	$10.4	$3.6
Mortgages	$2.6	$3.8	$3.9	$1.2
Memo: Construction (est.)	$1.8	$3.1	$3.0	$1.2
Copper Production	$0.08	$0.17	$0.12	$0.09
Railroad Miles Built	6,026	5,212	3,214	(814)
Number of Banks[a]	13,684	21,346	22,524	7,662
Bank Failures[a]	38	156	69	118

As Percentage of GDP				1902–1907 Change
Federal Debt	10%	9%	10%	−2%
Private Debt (est.)	93%	99%	106%	6%
Total Corporate Bonds	36%	41%	47%	5%
Utility Bonds	6%	10%	12%	4%
Industrial Bonds	4%	5%	6%	1%
Railroad Bonds	25%	24%	30%	−1%
Bank Loans	33%	37%	39%	4%
Mortgages	12%	13%	14%	1%
Memo: Construction (est.)	8%	11%	11%	2%
Copper Production	0%	1%	0%	0%

[a]One-year lag.

In the five years leading up to 1907, U.S. private debt grew by 42 percent. Railroad bonds, utility bonds, and mortgages showed strong growth.

(the Solingen Bank in Solingen and the Bonner Bank für Handel und Gewerbe in Bonn) all failed.[187]

Yet the signature moment of the 1907 crisis was the demise of New York's Knickerbocker Trust Company, with its loans to speculators in copper. Historian Alexander Noyes notes that the United States was already heading toward its financial nadir in 1906. The American money market could not absorb "new stock and bond issues ... and railroads and industrial companies alike were borrowing enormous sums on two- and three-year notes, paying high rates of interest."

"In the two years of 1905 and 1906, $872,000,000 in new bonds, were listed on the New York Stock Exchange," Noyes writes, "whereas, even in the extravagant promotion period of 1900 and 1901, the total was only $367,000,000."[188] It was an ominous sign of a fulminating credit crisis. In the vulnerable commodities sector, high prices, a decrease in exports, and overcapacity also portended trouble.

Overcapacity brought an aggressive downward spiral: "Average prices of commodities on the world's markets lost, in the fourteen months between June, 1907, and September, 1908, nearly all 21 per cent." Before 1908 came to a close, trade had fallen to 26 percent of the 1907 value.[189]

Frank Fayant, an acerbic wit, pilloried stock market fraudsters with his "Fools and Their Money" column of 1907. He noted that copper-mining fever attracted investors ready to risk their fortunes on ludicrous promises. A common thread in every crisis was the volume of bad stock—often bought on loans. Fayant analyzed over 150 companies that sold millions of dollars of stock to the hungry public. He found that of all the offerings broadcast and issued during the 1901–2 period, 104 were "dead and gone" when the panic began, and only *one* company—just one—was paying dividends. And that one company's stock was "selling in the market at less than half what investors paid for it five years ago."[190]

In the 1907 panic, it was "trust companies," a secondary type of lending institution, that loomed large, including the Knickerbocker Trust Company. Knickerbocker was connected to Otto and Augustus Heinze, who had unsuccessfully tried to corner the copper market in October 1907, and the company had been one of the lenders supporting their copper scheme.

On October 17, the 18,000 depositors of Knickerbocker, hearing rumors of troubles and fearing the worst, began a run on the bank. They withdrew $8 million in under three hours.[191] The banking panic that followed engulfed twenty-five banks and seventeen trust companies in October and November 1907.[192] On October 24, according to Noyes, credit was almost entirely suspended on major financial markets.[193] U.S. listings on the stock market declined by 37 percent.[194] As in 1837, stock exchanges closed. Pittsburgh's stock exchange was dark for three months.[195] For three horrible weeks in October, the bottom fell out for banks, trusts, and for the stock market, with the New York Stock Exchange careening to a 50 percent fall.

Most vulnerable were the trust companies, which, in New York, suffered total deposit withdrawals of over 36 percent between August 22 and December 19, 1907. The effect on the trusts was deep and corrosive. They fell like dominos—with the Lincoln Trust Company and the International Trust Company of New York among them.

J. P. Morgan corralled New York's bankers. He told them bluntly that they needed to raise $25 million immediately or risk at least fifty stock exchange houses[196] utterly failing. They were able—barely—to keep the day's trading afloat. The following Monday, $100 million in loan certificates were issued for trading and to fortify cash reserves. Morgan also agreed to purchase $30 million in bonds to rescue New York City from bankruptcy. Though the economic damage was extensive, Morgan's money and status were arguably instrumental in keeping the worst of the financial demons at bay—at least for a time.

The National Monetary Commission opened an investigation, chaired by Senator Nelson W. Aldrich, who was associated with the Rockefeller family, to understand the panic and propose new regulations for banking. This investigation was the first in a series of events that finally led Congress, in December 1913, to pass the Federal Reserve Act and establish the Federal Reserve System. This was designed in some measure to fill the lender-of-last-resort role in times of crisis that Morgan had played and provided the first glimmer of what would become a robust, activist involvement of the Federal Reserve and the U.S. Treasury over the next century.

The railroad crisis era in the United States and Europe had ended, but financial crises would continue. China would see financial crises in 1911 and both the 1920s and 1930s as it struggled through wars, revolutions, and economic turmoil to establish a succession to the imperial government overthrown in 1911.[197]

The United States and Britain would see financial crisis again in July 1914—in the United States by way of overlending and in Britain by having lent too much in countries that were suddenly its enemies. But World War I quickly overshadowed and subsumed those crises.

Next came the Great Depression, the U.S. crisis of the 1980s, and Japan's crisis of 1990, each of which we have already examined. Having now also seen the pattern of crises through the 1800s and early 1900s, we can turn to one of the most recent and calamitous crises of them all: the Global Crisis of 2008. With the perspective of history, and an understanding of the core private debt–fueled overcapacity in financial crisis, one thing is chillingly clear. The Great Recession might have been foreseen as early as 2005.

CHAPTER 6

The 2008 Global Mortgage and Derivatives Crisis

In the summer of 2007, the unemployment rate was at a five-year low,[1] both the stock market and overall household wealth were nearing all-time highs, consumer and business confidence were solidly positive, and banks—the institutions best positioned to know trends in credit—had such confidence in loan quality that they were setting aside only small reserves for future loan losses. Most economists, politicians, businesspeople, investors, and government officials were sanguine about the future.

Yet only a few weeks later, the largest financial crisis to hit the United States since the Great Depression rocked the foundations of the country, and soon the stock market fell nearly 50 percent, banks and corporations began to implode, and unemployment soon doubled to 10 percent.[2] Though the summer of 2007 was calm, almost two years earlier, in late 2005, so many high-risk mortgage loans had already been made that a financial crisis was virtually certain. Almost $1 trillion in soon-to-be-problematic loans—many to borrowers with no jobs or income—had already been made in a lending industry with less than $2 trillion in capital.

The Global Crisis of 2008, which led to what is now called the Great Recession, was inevitable before it was obvious, although few had noticed. Few, that is, except for a small number of the savviest contrarian investors, who began making huge bets in 2006 on what they were certain was an extraordinary and epic problem.[3]

The 2008 economic crisis in the United States was the direct result of the runaway growth in private debt from 2001 to 2007, especially growth in mortgages. Mortgages doubled from $5.3 trillion to an astonishing $10.6 trillion in a mere six years.[4] Subprime loans—the general designation for loans approved under loosened credit criteria—accounted for $1.7 trillion of these loans.[5] The bulk of this subprime lending happened in a short

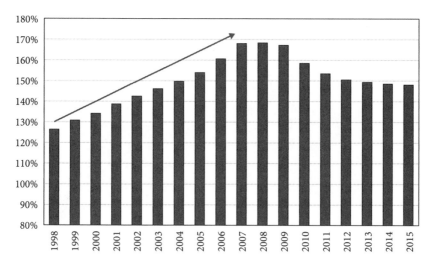

Figure 6.1. United States: Private Debt as a Percentage of GDP, 1998–2015
From 2002 to 2007, private debt to GDP grew 18 percent and reached an absolute level of nearly 170 percent.

four-year span between 2002 and 2006. But, in sheer volume, the bigger problem was the group of ostensibly better loans, the "prime" loans, where loan terms and credit standards had also been compromised. Indeed, "cash-out" refinancings for prime borrowers—where a new mortgage was made at a higher valuation and the owner pocketed the difference—were among the worst-performing loans of all. Far too many loans were made to improperly qualified buyers than should have been, and far more houses were built to take advantage of this lending spree than were needed.

The other category of runaway debt growth was commercial real estate, which shot up by 90 percent to $3.4 trillion, and would cause less but still extensive damage. In addition, and typical of a boom, margin loans for stocks skyrocketed. They grew 120 percent in five years, helping power stocks to record highs.

Together, the story of this runaway mortgage and CRE debt, along with a stock market fueled in part by margin debt, is the story of the Global Crisis and Great Recession. It is the indelible pattern of rampant lending that yields prodigious excess and then widespread failure. And the story of the Great Recession is also the story of things that might have been foretold but were not. Economists, examiners, and policymakers at the Federal Reserve Bank missed predicting the crisis. They missed it because they largely ignored the most

Figure 6.2. A Century of Real Estate Debt as a Percentage of GDP, 1916–2016

relevant and telling data required for predicting financial crises: trends in the nation's loan volumes. The Federal Reserve's model for economic forecasting gave little importance to loans as a factor. Fed thinking had long been that for every borrower there was an offsetting lender, and it did not properly consider that if the volume of ill-advised loans became too large, borrowers would not be able to repay those lenders, which could cripple the banking system.

Not only had residential mortgage loans doubled, but the overall ratio of private loans to GDP was increasing by as much as 4 percent per year, had increased by 18 percent in the previous five years, and now exceeded 167 percent of GDP. Thresholds of 15 percent to 20 percent for the increase and 150 percent for the overall ratio level signal a high likelihood of a financial crisis.

Soon enough, this runaway lending brought the Great Recession, which took its place alongside the Great Depression as bookends to a real-estate crisis era (Figure 6.2).

After a stock market crash in 2000 and the terrorist attack of September 11, 2001, the economy was looking for good news and welcomed the renewed mortgage loan growth of 2002. Some have attributed the lending boom to a decline in interest rates, and rates were certainly a part of the story. In early 2001, thirty-year mortgage rates were 7 percent and dropped by roughly one percentage point in the second half of 2002. They then decreased by another

Table 6.1. U.S. Crisis Matrix: 2000s

Billions of Dollars	2002	2007	2008	2009	2002–2007 Change
GDP	$10,980	$14,480	$14,719	$14,419	$3,500
Federal Debt	$6,079	$9,267	$10,720	$12,405	$3,188
Private Debt	$15,662	$24,354	$24,821	$24,131	$8,692
Business Debt	$7,038	$10,100	$10,680	$10,154	$3,062
CRE	$1,922	$3,354	$3,537	$3,479	$1,432
All Other	$5,116	$6,746	$7,143	$6,675	$1,630
Household Debt	$8,625	$14,254	$14,141	$13,978	$5,629
Mortgage	$6,028	$10,638	$10,608	$10,468	$4,610
Subprime	$475	$1,781	$1,520	$1,258	$1,306
Memo: HELOC	$220	$647	$705	$706	$427
Margin Loans	$148	$326	$165	$203	$178
All Other	$2,229	$2,643	$2,663	$2,601	$414
Bank Failures	10	2	19	133	−8

As Percentage of GDP					2002–2007 Change
Federal Debt	55%	64%	73%	86%	9%
Private Debt	143%	168%	169%	167%	26%
Business Debt	64%	70%	73%	70%	6%
CRE	18%	23%	24%	24%	6%
All Other	47%	47%	49%	46%	0%
Household Debt	79%	98%	96%	97%	20%
Mortgage	55%	73%	72%	73%	19%
Subprime	4%	12%	10%	9%	8%
Memo: HELOC	2%	4%	5%	5%	2%
Margin Loans	1%	2%	1%	1%	1%
All Other	20%	18%	18%	18%	−2%

HELOC = home equity line of credit; RMBS = residential mortgage-backed security.

In the five years leading to 2007, U.S. private debt grew by 55 percent. Sectors with the greatest concentration of overlending were mortgage and commercial real estate, which together comprised 70 percent of the increase.

half point in mid-2003—even though they quickly went back up to between 6.5 percent and 7 percent by mid-2006.[6] "Real" rates (rates minus inflation) declined slightly more.[7] But there have been many interest rate declines not followed by lending accelerations—or by busts. Furthermore, rapid loan growth has also happened in moderate, stable interest-rate environments. This mortgage lending growth came more from the same ferocity of ambition that we have seen in every crisis.

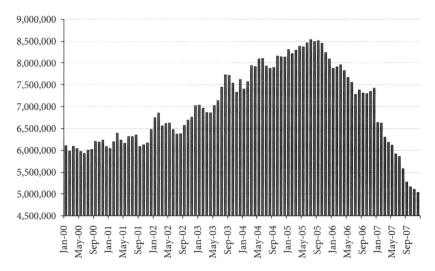

Figure 6.3. United States: Total Homes Sold, 2000–2007

Aggressive lenders dramatically increased the volume of mortgage loans in this period. Home sales jumped. This accelerated lending brought more buyers and higher home prices. House prices rose from an index of 117.2 in 2001 to 204.8 in 2006.[8] Home sales were 6.4 million in 2002, picked up further to 7.7 million in 2003, and then rampaged to 8.5 million by 2005.[9] The higher home prices went, the more incentive there was to build more and lend more. Loan growth itself was driving demand.

Through the key period of this drama, from 2002 to mid-2006, lenders increasingly dispensed with the task of checking on jobs or income, instead making more of the now-famous "no income, no job, no assets," or NINJA, loans. This dramatically enlarged the universe that qualified for a loan and helped enable the huge lending increase. The subprime industry, led by a new, more aggressive breed of lenders, made loans packaged into $1.78 trillion in residential mortgage backed securities, which pushed up home sales and prices.[10]

While it was happening, this burst of lending brought enhanced economic growth. It created jobs and wealth, lifting home prices to dizzying—unsustainable—levels. Unnoticed by many, the national ratio of home price–to–income, which had been 3.5 to 1 in 2000, had reached a troubling 4.7 to 1 by 2005. Miami and Las Vegas, sites of the most aggressive lending, had ratios considerably higher than that.[11]

As in the Roaring Twenties, a CRE expansion followed close on the heels of the residential mortgage expansion, as commercial builders watched the housing boom and escalated their activity accordingly. CRE loans grew by $1 trillion, or 42 percent, during the peak CRE lending growth period from 2004 to 2007, thus both starting and ending later than the housing boom.[12] This emerging CRE lending problem was a third the size of the residential mortgage problem but still huge by any measure.

Like the mortgage lenders before them, CRE lenders began to loosen terms and reduce loan pricing. By 2007, 53 percent were interest-only loans; the allowable loan-to-value ratios had increased, with many made on a ten-year, nonrecourse basis; and underwriting covenants became less stringent.[13] Traditional lenders in this space—banks, life insurance companies, and pension funds—found themselves competing with a growing commercial mortgage-backed security market for deals, which further pressured the industry toward leniency in loan terms.

Lenders enticed borrowers through *artificially* low initial interest rates that automatically ratcheted to much higher rates after one or two years. They also enticed borrowers by reducing down payments to little or nothing—and by 2006, the number of borrowers making zero down payment had increased markedly to 43 percent of all new loans.[14] Practically, this allowed borrowers with good incomes but no savings *and* borrowers of limited means to get a mortgage. They would face much higher payments after one or two years, but homes were appreciating in value by 10 percent to 15 percent annually, so borrowers weren't worried. They reasoned that in a worst-case scenario, if cash-squeezed, they could simply refinance and gain cash access to the additional equity or sell the house at a profit—or so the theory went.

New and newly aggressive mortgage companies spearheaded the explosion in mortgages. Bethany McLean and Joe Nocera characterize these men and women as "worlds apart from the local businessmen who ran the nation's S&Ls and banks. They were hard-charging, entrepreneurial, and intensely ambitious. . . . Some of them may have genuinely cared about putting people in homes. All of them cared about getting rich."[15]

Angelo Mozilo, the CEO of the mortgage lender Countrywide Financial, had a relentlessness drive to "be No. 1" that rocketed his company to the top of the business. The priority at Countrywide was to push "affordable products," the euphemism for artificially low introductory rates and low or zero down payments. In fact, adjustable rate mortgages (ARMs) with artificially low introductory interest rates were 49 percent of its business in 2004, up from 18 percent in 2003, and Mozilo was advocating a policy of ending down payments entirely. Countrywide grew from $363 billion in originations in 2004 to $495 billion in 2005, the largest amount in the business.[16]

Lenders made these loans on more lenient terms because they were getting rich doing it. Until credit problems overwhelmed the lenders, they were engaged in the most lucrative game in town. They charged big fees, sold off (most) of the loans, and reported huge profits. Their employees were getting rich, too. Thousands of newly recruited loan originators and salespeople, who had been earning more conventional salaries, began making hundreds of thousands and even millions of dollars annually in commissions for selling new mortgages, often through telemarketing to the most vulnerable borrowers.

Like Charles Keating before him, Mozilo courted friends in Washington, in a program internally referred to as "FOAs"—"Friends of Angelo." He extended preferential mortgages to elected officials, including the chair of the Senate Banking Committee, Christopher Dodd (D-CT), and the chair of the Senate Budget Committee, Kent Conrad (D-ND).[17]

Subprime loans grew from 7.51 percent of total mortgage loans in 2001 to 17.34 percent of total mortgage loans in 2006.[18] By 2005, 30 percent of the mortgage loans made by New Century, another leading subprime mortgage lender, were interest only.[19] They were among a number of lenders who created ARMs with interest rates that would adjust to a much higher rate in mid-2007, making that date one of particular interest and concern to those few who were paying attention. Stories abound of the unemployed and underemployed getting mortgages during this period, sometimes for more than one home. Home sales were so hot that in some markets frantic buyers would enter bids moments after listings appeared.

In postmortems of the 2008 crisis, much was made of the use of "credit scores," especially an industry standard known as the FICO score. Generally, a mortgage borrower with a FICO score of 670 or above was referred to as a "prime" borrower and those with lower scores as "subprime." Many lenders mistakenly interpreted the FICO score as an absolute assessment of borrower risk. It was not and is not. Actual risk varies based on a number of factors.

As just one example, mortgage borrowers with a FICO score of 700 who make no down payment differ in risk from those with a score of 700 who make a 30 percent down payment, a difference not noticed or understood by most lenders. If a high down payment is required and only a low debt-to-income ratio is tolerated, then the lender can feel comfortable that it has two sources of repayment: first, the borrower's income should be adequate to make monthly payments; second, the sale of the house will more than cover the amount of the loan. The FICO score further reassures that this borrower has been reliable in the past.

However, if no down payment is required, then the sale of the house might actually result in a loss since there are significant costs to administer the foreclosure and sale, and if no documentation of job or income is required, then the lender has no reassurance that the borrower's income will allow for repayment either. A further complication was that younger, newer borrowers with scant activity recorded in the credit bureau files—the "thin files"—were assigned a fairly high score to start, which then changed apace with their actual credit behavior. The initial thin-file score therefore gave false assurance of good credit behavior. For these reasons, any number of loans labeled "prime" could instead reasonably be characterized riskwise as less than prime. By relying so blindly on credit scores, the mortgage market had made a fundamental mistake—a mistake that eventually would lead to billions of dollars in losses.

Traditional banks and S&Ls get funds by getting customers to open checking accounts and buy CDs. They can increase funding by raising the rates they are willing to pay depositors. Smaller depositors don't have to worry about the risk those banks or S&Ls are taking because they're protected by FDIC insurance. In 2008 deposits were insured up to $100,000.[20] However, mortgage lenders such as Countrywide that led this lending boom needed different sources of funds. And that source was largely mortgage-backed securities (MBSs), a technique pioneered in the 1980s.[21] Through this process, known as securitization, mortgage banks bundled mortgages into marketable securities and sold them to investors, such as life insurance companies, pension funds, mutual funds, hedge funds, and banks.

The key sources for purchasing the securitizations of these mortgage banks were the Federal National Mortgage Association (FNMA, or Fannie Mae) and the Federal Home Loan Mortgage Corporation (FHLMC, or Freddie Mac), which together accounted for 55 percent of activity in this area.[22] Both institutions were quasigovernmental, authorized by government but not explicitly guaranteed by government, though many assumed that they implicitly were. They were formed to provide institutional buyers for mortgages made by banks, savings institutions, and mortgage bankers. In turn, they were funded by issuing bonds backed by the mortgages they held. The mortgage market became heavily reliant on these institutions. In 2004 alone, they bought $169.4 billion in subprime bonds.[23]

Investment banks, such as Goldman Sachs and Morgan Stanley, were also a source of securitization for mortgage banks. Fannie Mae, Freddie Mac, or the investment banks would take a group of mortgages originated by Country-wide, bundle them into a bond, and either sell them to investors or hold them on their own balance sheets. Fully 80 percent of mortgage loans made in the era were packaged and sold to Fannie, Freddie, Wall Street firms, and other large institutions rather than kept on the originating lenders' books. An astonishing $3.6 trillion in MBSs were sold from 2002 to 2007.[24]

Even though lenders were using loose credit criteria, investors bought the MBSs backed by those mortgages, largely because debt rating agencies—primarily Moody's and Standard & Poor's—assigned most of them their highest ratings—Aaa for Moody's and AAA for Standard & Poor's. These two private companies were filled with credit analysts whose business it was to evaluate debt securities such as these securitizations and assign ratings from the highest down to their default and near-default ratings of C and D.

Although these debt securities included some portion of substandard mortgages, they got the highest ratings because Fannie, Freddie, and investment banks structured them in a way that rating agencies believed mitigated or solved any substandard risk problem. In a growing number of cases, this was accomplished by slicing the securities into a stack of "tranches," or portions, with the top tranche being the most senior, with a priority claim on the mortgage collateral in the event of default.[25] The last or most junior tranche had the last claim on the collateral. In other words, the last tranche took the brunt of any credit problems, and the top tranche took the least. The tranches were all rated and priced accordingly and then packaged and sold separately.

This meant that the bottom tranches in the bonds, referred to as "mezzanine" tranches, would have terrible ratings and therefore could not be sold—right? Wrong. Many of them received higher ratings, too, because of a clever trick. Bankers would pool a number of these mezzanine tranches into a new security called a collateralized debt obligation (CDO).[26] They argued that grouping different mortgages from different originators and different regions provided sufficient additional diversification to merit high ratings. There were even more obtuse CDO variations for securities with even worse credit.

Ratings agencies themselves were intrinsically compromised. They were for-profit companies that got paid for each security they rated, and each competed with the other for business. Whoever rated the most securities made the most money, and a sure way to get repeat business from issuers was to be lenient with ratings. These agencies got and deserved significant blame for abetting this runaway lending period, yet in its aftermath the ratings system has remained largely unchanged. But it should be noted that it doesn't take a rating agency fiasco or exotic securities to allow for runaway lending and a crisis. There have been plenty of crises without them. Over the last two hundred years, purveyors of credit have used many different ways to minimize or obfuscate concerns about risk. In this book we've reviewed many of them over a period of two centuries. And assuredly, there will be new techniques, now unimagined, in the future.

Many other countries were experiencing their own bout of runaway private lending in the 2000s, so the financial crisis was by no means confined to the United States or, by inference, attributable solely to idiosyncrasies in U.S. regulations, laws, or other factors. By 2008, in the United Kingdom, for example, loans had skyrocketed from 160 percent to 194 percent of GDP in just five years.[27] The United Kingdom was more profligate than the United States on a percentage basis, yet Spain was even worse. The acceleration in Spain's private debt, which was also mainly an increase in mortgage debt, began in 1999, with loans almost quadrupling to 216 percent of GDP by 2010,[28] a far greater increase than any of the other of the world's top twenty GDP countries. Real estate prices rose 200 percent during this period as a direct result of the accelerated lending. Spain's lenders offered every imaginable incentive, including forty- and fifty-year mortgages. Home ownership in Spain reached 80 percent, belying the notion that increased home ownership is always a virtue.[29]

At the peak, over 700,000 new Spanish homes[30] were being built each year, which yielded almost 4 million empty houses in a country with only 24 million total houses. Reports in late 2008 put the housing vacancy rate at 28 percent.[31] As is typical in a lending-led expansion, at first the tax revenues from the construction industry mushroomed, and the government debt-to-GDP profile improved.

The financial crisis of 2008 affected many more European countries. Some economists suggest that this simultaneous global outburst is evidence that the culprit was a technical economic factor, namely, a global savings surplus. This theory is also referred to as a "global savings glut," a phrase coined by Ben Bernanke in his February 20, 2004, speech that anointed the era as the financial "great moderation" (a mordantly ironic speech since at that moment the country was moving irrevocably toward crisis).[32]

A kindred theory is referred to as imbalances, or "increases in cross-border investment flows," as one of its proponents, Robert Aliber, describes in the introduction to a highly esteemed textbook that he helped author on

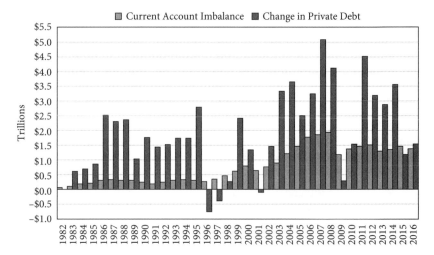

Figure 6.4. Global Current Account Imbalance and Change in Private Debt, 1982–2016
The countries included in this chart are United States, China, Japan, United Kingdom, Germany, France, Iran, Kuwait, Russia, Saudi Arabia, and United Arab Emirates. Current Account Imbalance equals the sum of the absolute value of each country's current account surplus or deficit.

financial crises, *Manias, Panics, and Crashes.* Aliber espouses the view that "the source of banking crises are the surges in cross-border investments." In elegant terms, he argues that the surge in real estate prices in the 2000s followed from the rapid increase in the United States' capital account surplus (the inverse of its current account deficit). It was this surge in cross-border investment that caused lenders to overlend and led to the financial crisis, not the "wayward behavior of Countrywide Financial, Lehman Brothers," and others. Those who look to the lenders, he asserts, mistake "the symptoms of the crisis for the cause."[33]

In other words, lenders had too much money and almost no choice but to lend it. They were victims of this circumstance rather than perpetrators. Others, taking up Bernanke's and Aliber's cause, have clarified or refined the argument—that it is not the imbalance of a single country but the overall *global* imbalance in accounts that creates booms, regardless of which countries experience changes in current account surplus and deficit.[34]

But lending booms are often domestically funded, as in Japan in the 1980s and 1990s. In fact, as Figure 6.4 shows, while there might have been such a correlation in the 2000s, there was no correlation in cross-border investments and rapid lending increases in the pivotal 1980s and early 1990s, when we had major crises not only in Japan but in the United States and elsewhere.

In fact, as the figure shows, changes in private debt are generally much larger than changes in the current account balance. So even in instances where they are correlated, is the small change in the current account balance causing the large change in private debt, or is the large change in private debt bringing about the smaller change in the current account balance? I believe it is the latter. Further, the so-called savings or current account surplus did not occur in advance of the rapid lending growth; it happened contemporaneously and was more likely the *result* than the cause. This is because an increase in the current account surplus would take time to translate into new loans: as a lender, I know it takes months or years to cultivate new lending opportunities. However, a new loan would likely instantly translate into a change in the current account balance: the purchase of a new building or the order of retail goods from overseas usually does happen at the same time as the extension of the loan. In fact, my view is that the *rising trade imbalances of the 2000s would not have been possible if not "financed" by concurrent runaway growth in the United States' and other countries' private debt.* The dramatic increase in Chinese exports in 2003 to 2008 (which economists interestingly refer to as its saving exceeding its investment), which we noted in Chapter 3, could not have occurred if there had not been a debt binge in the West, the very debt binge that brought the crisis (Figure 6.5).

Others cite "contagion" as the reason multiple countries were affected in a similar time frame, as if crises have biological properties.[35] But tellingly, countries that had no runaway lending, did not lend much internationally, and were not overly dependent on exports to countries engaged in runaway lending were largely immune to the contagion. Many countries in Asia and Latin America, for example, suffered little damage from the 2008 crisis.

Like a lending surge within a country, the simultaneous emergence of several lending surges globally is most persuasively explained by cross-border lender links and as a function of human nature itself. Lenders see the rapid growth of their cross-border peers and want to keep up. The world of financial institutions is in some respects quite small and transcends national boundaries. Lending itself reaches across borders, and lending success is often a global game of one-upmanship.

Much of Germany's lending that led to the damage of its own financial institutions was to borrowers outside of the country. In fact, toward the end of the boom, Germany's lenders were viewed as the hapless latecomers who did

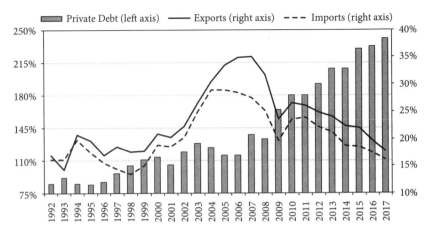

Figure 6.5. China: Private Debt, Imports, and Exports as a Percentage of GDP, 1992–2017

the least homework and, suffering from the fear of missing out, came to the lending and derivative party just as U.S. lenders were wising up.[36] As the explosion in lending in the United States rampaged forward, some of the most astute analysts in this space noticed that a large number of these securities had terrible credit quality and that a large proportion of loans had been made in 2005 with an artificially low interest that would revert to a fairly high rate in 2007.

These analysts reasoned that when this occurred, a very high percentage of loans would quickly become delinquent and the securities with these loans would quickly lose value. As vividly described in Michael Lewis's *The Big Short*, one of these investors, Mike Burry, worked with investment bankers to create a mechanism to use to bet on this calamity, the credit default swap on mortgage-backed securities. CDSs were a type of derivative, which is a synthetic financial instrument that is usually based on an actual underlying stock, bond, or commodity contract and is a way to bet on the movement—up or down—in the price of those underlying stocks, bonds, or commodities. It therefore has the effect of amplifying the risk of their price movement.

Starting in May 2005, Burry deployed his strategy. He paid an insurance company a relatively small premium for a CDS. If the underlying MBS remained good, then Burry would lose only the premium he'd paid. However, if the MBS went bad, then Burry would get paid in proportion to the loss. The worse the problem, the more Burry made. All Burry needed was an insurance company that was as certain that these securities would perform

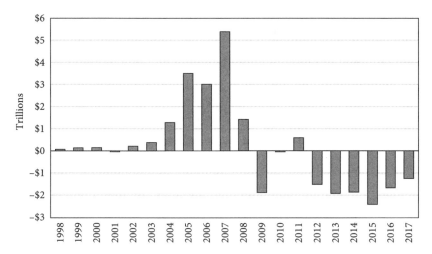

Figure 6.6. Net New Credit Default Swaps for Mortgage-Backed Securities,
1998–2017
*Derivatives amplified loss but didn't cause overcapacity. Buyers in 2005 and 2006
were savvy contrarians. Those institutions that sold swaps in 2008 were in many
cases late to the game and lacked insight on recent trends.*

well as he was certain that they would go bad. Early on for many buyers of
these CDSs, that insurance company was AIG, which had been lured into its
optimism about MBSs by their high ratings.[37]

Other skeptical analysts began to seek CDSs, and other institutions began selling them. In 2007, over $61 trillion in CDSs were sold.[38] Notably,
however, enough bad mortgage loans had been made *before these CDSs were
created that there would have been a financial crisis anyway,* albeit smaller.
In fact, a substantial portion of these CDSs were written on mortgages made
before or during 2005. The creation of the CDS simply made the crisis much
larger and longer than it would have been otherwise and lured some institutions such as AIG to participate, and thus get hurt, that wouldn't have otherwise. Investor John Paulson placed a similarly notable and even larger bet
against the mortgage market.[39]

Derivatives, in this case CDSs, amplified the damage because with them
more institutions could get hurt on the same underlying loan volume. As
early as 1998, Brooksley Born, head of the Commodity Futures Trading
Commission, had advocated regulating derivatives. But President Bill Clinton's Treasury secretary Robert Rubin (and later Treasury secretary Larry

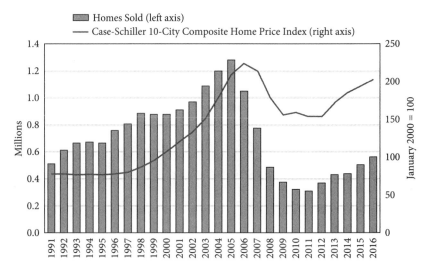

Figure 6.7. Sales and Prices of New U.S. Single-Family Homes, 1991–2016
Note: Homes sold are in millions. For Case-Schiller Index, January 2000=100.

Summers), Securities and Exchange Commission chair Arthur Levitt, Fed chair Alan Greenspan, and various senators derailed Born's efforts, not wanting to constrain activity in derivatives.[40]

In the meantime, with their ears to the ground, institutions that provided funding and bought securities from mortgage lenders, especially from mortgage brokers and subprime lenders, began to hear of problems, get wary, and curtail that funding. As a result, new loans declined with the predictable result that house prices began to fall. New home sales, existing home sales, and new home construction began to decelerate. (Overall loans continued to grow somewhat for a short period even as new loans declined owing to the nature of amortization.) Just as things had spiraled up, they now spiraled down.

The moment that the key asset associated with a boom begins to decline in price is pivotal in most crises; in this case, it was the decline in housing prices. Overcapacity was rampant, and a point of no return had been reached. As we've seen with all financial crises, lenders fail when their funders (and if a bank, depositors) lose confidence in them and pull their funding. This soon happened to the aggressive subprime lender New Century Financial. On April 2, 2007, the company filed for bankruptcy.[41] Funders of mortgage banks and subprime lenders became decidedly more cautious, and thus those institutions had to curtail lending, and home sales and lending growth plummeted further. With funding drying up, things went from bad to worse for most mortgage banks.

The broader market might have taken notice but didn't. Wall Street was still viewing this as a potential problem that would be confined largely to the mortgage industry. Analysts did not recognize its sheer size and magnitude. Real estate and mortgages had become by far the biggest component of the country's private debt and one of the biggest components of the economy. Trillions of dollars were at stake.

Banks, those institutions whose presumed competency was credit risk, were oblivious. Though they would shortly begin writing off hundreds of billions of dollars in losses, their reserve ratio was near a twenty-year low. Banks had adequate levels of capital during the years leading to the crisis, and in fact this ratio improved. But that was in part due to the preferential capital treatment some assets received, including mortgages and mortgage backed securities. If banks had used the more old-fashioned leverage ratio, which required banks to have a set amount of capital no matter the type of assets, the assessment of capital adequacy would not been as sanguine. Banks, investment banks, and other lenders took full advantage of the capital rules to maximize lending during this period.

Both consumer and business confidence were comfortably positive, dispelling the general view that a collapse in confidence causes rather than follows the crisis. While confidence—false optimism—may have everything to do with runaway lending, no amount of confidence could have prevented the bad loans from unraveling and the lenders from tumbling. A lack of confidence does not cause a crisis but follows with grim logic from the horrid realization of how much damage has occurred.

By mid- to late 2007, as ARM introductory rates expired and a large number of loans moved to higher interest rates, they became unaffordable for many borrowers. A flood of delinquency followed. Bernanke assured markets that subprime losses would not exceed $100 billion,[42] but they would dwarf that estimate in the end. It slowly dawned on the broader financial world that the problem might reverberate far beyond the mortgage industry. Defying these emerging trends, the Dow reached an all-time high of 14,164 on October 9, 2007[43]—but soon took the first big tumble of the Great Recession, dropping almost 50 percent over the next fifteen months.

The CRE lending boom had lagged behind the mortgage boom, in some part because banks sought to increase other sources of earnings as mortgage problems emerged. Thus, the unraveling of CRE followed that of residential mortgages. Looser credit terms and increased loan volume had led to higher building valuations, but with insufficient actual tenant demand, CRE delinquency went from 1.02 percent in 2005 to 8.67 percent in 2009.[44] As lenders pulled back, the prices for buildings declined as well. In Manhattan, average per-square-foot prices for buildings went from $347 in 2002 to $947 in 2008, only to fall back to $404 by 2009.[45] In one notable case, a high-profile New York investor bought 6.5 million square feet of property for $7.5 billion, or $1,100 per square foot, financed almost entirely with debt. But he was unable to service the debt, and the lender moved to foreclose and sell many of these properties for $818 per foot, a 26 percent loss, only eighteen months later.[46] The CRE debt rout was on.

There was a similar pattern for home equity loans. Though far smaller in volume than mortgages, the peak loan totals were in the years 2008 to 2010, well after the decline in housing prices—and so reflected the compromised credit judgment of the industry. Some portion of this volume came from borrowers trying to cope with the crisis. On January 10, 2008, Ben Bernanke bravely dismissed concerns of a recession.[47] However, not long after, the Fed reported that a recession—defined as two consecutive quarters of GDP decline—had officially begun. The next day, Bank of America announced its purchase of troubled Countrywide on terms it mistakenly viewed as favorable.[48] Before long, the purchase would cost Bank of America more than $40 billion and push it to the brink of failure. Regulators would take over and sell or dispose of other major subprime lenders, including Washington Mutual and Indy Mac, later that same year.

In mid-February, President George W. Bush, who presided over the mortgage lending frenzy, signed the Economic Stimulus Act of 2008, which was an attempt to battle the burgeoning crisis by giving individual tax rebates and encouraging businesses to invest. It was far too little, far too late, and the government now had to step up the rescue of banks. Rampant mortgage lending hadn't just implicated mortgage brokers, such as New Century and Countrywide, or even banks, such as JPMorgan Chase and Citibank. Investment banks, including Goldman Sachs, Merrill Lynch, Bear Stearns, and Lehman Brothers, had been buying and selling MBSs and CDOs, and in many cases had billions of dollars of those securities on their own balance sheets. Like any lender, these institutions were dependent on funding, and their funders were anxious.

The first of these investment banks to lose its funding and thus succumb was Bear Stearns, which collapsed in March and was bought out by JPMorgan

Chase with substantial government assistance. At this point, the government was dealing with the crisis on an ad hoc basis, believing that if it could successfully deal with a few big problems, then the overall market would right itself.

Bear Stearns had participated aggressively in the mortgage securities market and was holding over $30 billion in rapidly deteriorating mortgage-backed securities.[49] Rumors of this were flying, and the company's short-term creditors were both refusing to lend more and demanding repayment of existing loans—the modern equivalent of a run on the bank. On March 14, 2008, Bear received a much-needed twenty-eight-day loan from JPMorgan[50] but was denied its hoped-for funding from the Federal Reserve, and, by Sunday, the circumstance was sufficiently dire that it had agreed to be acquired by JPMorgan Chase for $2 a share,[51] revised to $10 two weeks later.[52] The stock had been trading at more than $40 just days before. Integral to the deal was the Fed's agreement to fund and backstop losses on nearly $30 billion of Bear's mortgage-backed securities.

Fannie Mae and Freddie Mac were, catastrophically as it turned out, the largest institutional holders of mortgages in the United States. They held a combined $4.81 trillion in mortgages out of a total of $10.6 trillion U.S. mortgages.[53] By 2007, they held $227 billion in nonprime mortgage pools and altogether an approximate $1.6 trillion in low-quality loans, the credit quality of which was turning out to be much worse than forecast.[54] A tidal wave of bad credit engulfed them both. They bravely sought to stave off failure but had historically held little capital for that purpose. Their funders became increasingly reluctant to buy their bonds, which then plummeted in value. Starting in 2007, they began reporting huge quarterly losses—$6.1 billion in the fourth quarter of 2007 and $54.3 billion in the third quarter of 2008—which fatally impaired their limited capital. On September 7, the government, seeking to limit the rapidly expanding crisis, stepped in to take over these institutions.[55]

Seeing this, lenders to other companies with large holdings of mortgages became increasingly alarmed. The collapse of Fannie and Freddie and the fire-sale price of Bear Stearns brought into question the value of every other investment bank, most notably Lehman Brothers, which was the fourth largest investment bank in the United States. Lehman had gone "all in" on the mortgage business. In an overall mortgage market that was burgeoning in size and laden with compromised credit, the executives at Lehman failed to see the risk and, more than any other firm, were very literally betting their company on the success of that market. In the elation of the times, Lehman had acquired five mortgage loan companies to increase its stake in the industry. Two of these mortgage lenders were specialists in subprime lending, and so Lehman had $76.28 billion in MBSs, much of which was subprime.[56]

In 2007, Lehman's net income reached a titanic $4.2 billion on revenues of only $19.3 billion. It made huge fees on its mortgage transactions. Its market value reached $60 billion.[57] The nature of financial institutions is such that if they do not foresee and make proper provision for loan losses, their reported earnings are huge over the short term. That fact has misled many an executive and investor. As the dark clouds of 2007 gathered, Lehman reassured its investors. During that year, even as it began to pare back some areas of its subprime operations, Lehman continued to aggressively underwrite in this sector, with $85 billion more MBSs, which was quadruple its equity. With this, its assets were now thirty-one times higher than its equity in an industry where ten to twenty times is viewed by many as the limit of prudence.[58]

In March 2008, after the announcement of Bear Stearns, Lehman's shares fell more than 40 percent on concerns about its MBS exposure. But investors were blind and gave Lehman new investment support over the next few months. These new investors reasoned that if the company had been worth $60 billion and now was worth only $20 billion, then this was a buying opportunity. And so, in April, Lehman got $4 billion in new preferred stock; in June, though it had reported a $2.8 billion loss, it raised another $6 billion, and decreased its leverage. This was Chicken Little in reverse. The sky was falling, but no one involved had truly noticed.

In September, even with the new equity, Lehman's stock dove 77 percent, and, more important, its short-term lenders began to pull its credit lines. At this point the game was over. Though Lehman announced further restructuring as it preannounced another major loss on September 10, it was down to $1 billion in cash, which for an institution of that size and hemorrhaging money would only last weeks. That same day, Moody's announced another ratings downgrade for Lehman unless a major firm took significant stake in the company. Lehman spent the weekend in discussions with Bank of America and Barclays, trying without success to craft such an investment.

And so, on Monday, September 15, 2008, with a reported but likely overstated $639 billion in assets along with $619 billion in debt and more than 20,000 employees, and just days after the rescue of Fannie Mae and Freddie Mac, Lehman filed for bankruptcy. It was the largest bankruptcy in history to that point. The decision stunned the market. The government decided against rescuing Lehman as it had Bear Stearns and let it fail. Some cynics argued that Treasury secretary Hank Paulson, who had formerly worked at Goldman Sachs, would not deign to assist a firm that had been a lifelong competitor.

Some consider the Lehman failure the defining moment in the unraveling of the U.S. economy, but the crisis was inevitable well before that moment. The Lehman failure shattered the market's faith that the government was going to contain the crisis. If the government was not going to save major institutions, the future was dire. The reverberating fear made the government newly aware of the danger, and so its intervention accelerated to lightspeed.

On that same day, Bank of America, having already taken on unrecognized risk with its acquisition of Countrywide, announced that it had agreed to buy Merrill Lynch. It was a major and important transaction, although the frenzy drowned it out. Merrill Lynch too had plunged perilously deep into the mortgage market and was facing failure, and Bank of America was unwittingly assuming billions of additional dollars in mortgage-related losses. Bank of America's acquisitions of Countrywide and Merrill were in part opportunistic and in part a desire to mask the deterioration of its *own* loan portfolio. The Fed was an eager accomplice because it was increasingly desperate to find homes, any homes, for the growing list of troubled problem institutions.

The very next day, on September 16, the government stepped in to rescue the insurance giant AIG. AIG had been a major seller of CDSs to investors betting against the mortgage market from 2005 to 2007. If those underlying mortgages were good, which, given their high ratings, AIG executives assumed they would be, then AIG would have made millions in fees. If they went bad, then AIG would have to pay the buyers of those swaps in proportion to the amount of the losses. What was unrecognized at the highest level of AIG management was that it had sold such an extraordinary volume of CDSs that the entire company would go under if they went bad. Unwittingly, and in an activity that was largely unrecognized and unsupervised by its executive management, AIG had bet the company. And they lost the bet.

The previous day, recognizing this and concerned with rapidly emerging mortgage trends, all three rating agencies had downgraded AIG's credit rating, which meant, under the terms of the swaps, that it was obligated to post more collateral—in other words, fork over money—to the firms that had bought these swaps. In fact, calls for this collateral rose to $32 billion, and the company's shortfall quickly totaled $12.4 billion. But AIG simply didn't have the cash. Goldman Sachs was a key funder of AIG and thus had much to lose if AIG failed. Again, some viewed this government rescue as Secretary Paulson looking out for the best interests of his former employer.

In the chaotic and contradictory spirit of the times, the Fed's rescue of AIG came not long after Secretary Paulson had said there would not be any more Wall Street bailouts, not long after the government had rescued Fannie and Freddie, and only six months after the rescue of Bear Stearns. It stepped in with an $85 billion two-year loan and took ownership of 79.9 percent of AIG's equity, revised in the soon-to-be-enacted Troubled Asset Relief Program (TARP) to a $40 billion purchase of preferred shares and a $52.5 billion purchase of mortgage-backed securities.

Short-term rates had been 5.25 percent a year earlier. The Fed had knocked them down to 4.25 percent in January, then all the way down to 3 percent in February, and then to 2 percent in April. It now lowered rates to 1 percent.

The magnitude of these rescues was unprecedented yet extemporized. It was now time for a more comprehensive structure to deal with what was clearly a nationwide, systemic crisis. So days later, Paulson and Bernanke went to Congress to formally ask for $700 billion to rescue the entire U.S. economy. That emergency rescue legislation, enacted in a whirlwind and signed by President Bush on October 3, 2008, was called the Emergency Economic Stabilization Act of 2008, and created TARP, which authorized the government to spend up to $700 billion for stabilization. The government would now invest directly in the stock of troubled banks and in effect provide a guarantee to the creditors and counterparties of that bank. (On November 25, this was augmented with the Term Asset-Backed Securities Lending Facility, or TALF, to support owners of securities backed by credit card debt, student loans, auto loans, and small-business loans.)[59]

Within days of its passage, the Treasury secretary called a meeting of nine leading lending institutions and required them to accept its investment and the associated implicit guarantee. Those institutions were JPMorgan Chase & Company, Citigroup Inc., Goldman Sachs Group Inc., Morgan Stanley, Wells Fargo & Company, State Street Corporation, Bank of New York Mellon, and Bank of America Corporation, including the soon-to-be-acquired Merrill Lynch. Some protested because they objected to the implication that they were near failure. But most were, not just because of their impaired credit but also because of their liquidity risk. Paulson required that they accept the funds because he wanted to restore confidence in the entire market and felt if all these high-profile institutions took the funds, it would make an emphatic statement to the market and encourage others to do the same.

The Treasury soon had invested in a total of 214 financial institutions. Eventually, $427 billion was disbursed, but over time the government claimed that most or all of that was recovered through the sale of stock and other assets. TARP largely achieved the objective of stabilizing the financial institution markets. It gave banks and other financial institutions the certainty of liquidity and funding, and, with that, it gave them the time to determine the extent of their problems, to raise capital, and to begin the disposition of bad loans in a more orderly manner. The stock market ended its decline only two months later, and employment finally started to rise ten months later.

But the pain and turbulence were not over. The era had its sideshow of fraud, and the Great Recession's biggest came to light on December 11 with the arrest of Bernie Madoff. His Ponzi scheme, possibly the biggest financial fraud of all time, had lasted over fifteen years and cost investors tens of billions of dollars.[60] It was the stock market crash that unmasked the fraud as his investors scrambled to withdraw funds. As investor Warren Buffett said, only when the tide goes out do you discover who has been swimming naked.[61]

On December 16, for the first time in history, the Fed lowered its benchmark interest rate to zero, where it would remain for the next seven years—as evidence of the critically weak economy and the Fed's desire to give interest rate relief to the private-sector borrowers, who, despite some improvement, had remained highly leveraged.[62] The Fed also stepped up its effort to provide liquidity to lenders.

On December 19, the government intervened to prop up General Motors and Chrysler, offering an initial $13.4 billion loan from the TARP fund, but they remained on the verge of bankruptcy. In the face of considerable criticism and opposition, the Obama administration continued the rescue efforts. Counting the $13.4 billion in loans already made, the government invested a total of $49.5 billion in GM, eventually recovering $39 billion, and $12.5 billion in Chrysler, recovering $11.2 billion.

The Eurozone was contending with its part of the global meltdown. By November 14, 2008, it had officially slipped into a recession for the first time since its creation in 1999, pushed down by recessions in Germany and Italy. In the United Kingdom, by the fall of 2008, housing prices had dropped 15 percent from the previous year, and over 500,000 mortgage holders found

Table 6.2. U.K. Crisis Matrix: 2000s

Billions of British Pounds	2003	2008	2009	2003–2008 Change
GDP	1,191	1,519	1,482	328
Public Debt	444	786	976	342
Private Debt	1,910	2,946	2,871	1,036
Business Debt	921	1,470	1,397	549
CRE	127	247	237	120
All Other	794	1,223	1,160	429
Household Debt	988	1,477	1,474	489
Mortgage	773	1,185	1,192	412
All Other	215	292	282	77
As Percentage of GDP				2003–2008 Change
Public Debt	37%	52%	66%	14%
Private Debt	160%	194%	194%	34%
Business Debt	77%	97%	94%	19%
CRE	11%	16%	16%	6%
All Other	67%	81%	78%	14%
Household Debt	83%	97%	99%	14%
Mortgage	65%	78%	80%	13%
All Other	18%	19%	19%	1%

In the five years leading to 2008, Britain's private debt grew by 54 percent. Mortgage and commercial real estate comprised 51 percent of the increase, but non-CRE business debt was a large category that increased rapidly as well.

they had negative equity in their houses, "with another 700,000 mortgage holders facing the same risk if prices continue to fall."[63] The United Kingdom officially fell into a recession in the third quarter of 2008, and unemployment took its first big step up to 6.1 percent that fall.[64] (Notably, in Britain, mortgage and rent payments could be made for the unemployed under its social security program.)

Greece, whose troubles grabbed outsized attention, had its own massive private lending burst, with private debt growing from 54 percent to 118 percent of GDP between 2000 and 2008. Its problematic government debt growth *followed* that private debt burst. The same was true in Italy. Spain, having been perhaps the most profligate lender of all in this era, suffered the most drastic fall. Spain's acceleration had begun in 1999, and by the early 2000s, it already had crossed the private debt growth thresholds identified in this

Table 6.3. Spain Crisis Matrix: 2000s

Billions of Euros	2002	2007	2008	2009	2002–2007 Change
GDP	749	1,081	1,116	1,079	332
Public Debt	384	384	440	569	(0)
Private Debt	1,003	2,221	2,337	2,312	1,218
Business Debt	623	1,345	1,423	1,406	722
CRE	115	401	415	421	286
Household Debt	380	877	914	906	497
Mortgage	262	647	674	679	385
As Percentage of GDP					2002–2007 Change
Public Debt	51%	36%	39%	53%	−16%
Private Debt	134%	205%	209%	214%	72%
Business Debt	83%	124%	127%	130%	41%
CRE	15%	37%	37%	39%	22%
Household Debt	51%	81%	82%	84%	30%
Mortgage	35%	60%	60%	63%	25%

In the five years leading to 2007, Spain's private debt grew by 121 percent, and outgrew GDP by almost 4 to 1.

book as a harbinger of crisis. But the nation didn't have its crisis until 2008—largely because it kept lending. There are any number of ways lenders can keep companies afloat long after troubling trends have emerged. For example, a lender can keep a real estate company with poor sales afloat by allowing it to continually renew maturing loans and pay interest only or no interest, and even by increasing the amount of the loan. This has happened repeatedly for any number of companies in the late phases of lending booms. Spain's continued boom was further abetted by countries around it that were beginning their acceleration of lending. The party is often over only when lenders stop lending and the crisis, deferred, finally arrives. However, by keeping that party going for so long, Spain had only expanded the size and dimension of its eventual problem.

Construction spending in Spain plunged, GDP fell by 3.3 percent in 2009, and unemployment began its upward march to a painful 26 percent. Some housing developments began to resemble ghost towns. One airport, the €1.1 billion Ciudad Real Central Airport, stood almost empty. In 2015, a group of international investors bought it for a pittance of €10,000.

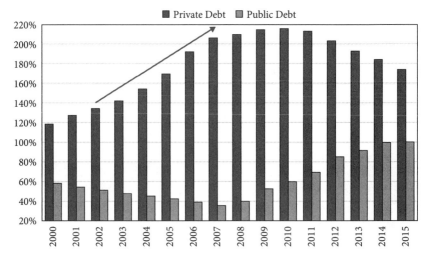

Figure 6.8. Spain: Private and Public Debt as a Percentage of GDP, 2000–2015
In Spain, private debt increased by 1.2 trillion Euros (or 121.5%) from 2002 to 2007.

Back in the United States, by January 2009, the government had to step in
with $100 billion in guarantees and a fresh $20 billion in bailout funds for
Bank of America, the hapless buyer of Countrywide Mortgage and Merrill
Lynch. Barack Obama was sworn in as president with a Democratic majority in
Congress on January 20, 2009, little more than three months after Bush signed
the epic TARP legislation. But the economy was still losing 800,000 jobs per
month, and unemployment had reached 7.8 percent; so in less than thirty days,
the $787 billion American Recovery and Reinvestment Act of 2009 (ARRA)
was enacted, a stimulus bill later revised to a total of $831 billion. It included
tax cuts and funding for infrastructure, green energy, schools, and health care
to save and create jobs. Its effectiveness has been debated ever since. Opponents
note the huge increase in the nation's debt that is in part due to this bill. Its ad-
vocates note that U.S. employment rebounded more quickly than that in other
countries where similar stimulus was not as quickly or fully employed.

On February 25, 2009, the Fed and other regulatory agencies announced
they would conduct "stress tests," simulating a potential future crisis, to as-
certain if banks now had adequate capital. Though skeptics questioned
whether these tests were sufficiently rigorous, when completed, they had the
effect of reassuring markets on the soundness of the overall financial system.
In March, AIG reported the largest loss in U.S. corporate history, a record

$62 billion for the December quarter of 2008.[65] The Dow took another tumble. But the events of 2009 turned out to be the beginning of the end. In June 2009, the Great Recession technically ended after eighteen turbulent months, making it the longest downturn in postwar history. The painful effects would linger. On October 2, 2009, the unemployment rate peaked at 10 percent, hitting double digits for the first time in twenty-six years.

In July 2010, Congress passed the Dodd-Frank bill, designed to minimize the risk of future crises. It passed into law those stress tests for banks, created a Consumer Financial Protection Bureau to protect Americans from abusive lending practices, increased liquidity requirements for banks, established some parameters for mortgage lending, and set higher regulatory standards for "systemically important" institutions. Some criticized Dodd-Frank as too much; others criticized it as too little. Home foreclosures hit a painful peak in 2010 at 2.9 million properties and ultimately a reported 9 million Americans lost their homes.[66] Over 8 million people lost their jobs. But by March 2011, unemployment was below 9 percent,[67] and in August 2013, the Dow hit a new high of 15,658.[68] A month later, unemployment fell to 7.2 percent.

One of the most pervasive, enduring legacies of the Great Recession was underwater mortgages. By late 2009 to early 2010, an estimated 10 million of the country's 53 million mortgages had a principal balance significantly greater than the market value of the home, largely because home prices had reached a lending-induced peak and then fallen significantly.[69] This brought heartache and suffering to these households and led to constrained consumer spending over the ensuing years. On some of these loans, an artificially low ARM rate had adjusted to a higher rate, and these homeowners struggled to make payments. This was one key factor in the Fed's moves to reduce interest rates. Others found that they could have made these payments if their income had stayed at the boom-era highs, but now they were making less and so were also struggling to make payments. Many families kept up their payments but spent years without taking vacations or buying new cars, and continually resorting to all other types of austerity. This was a key to understanding why the economic growth remained tepid years after the crisis.

Government debt skyrocketed in the wake of the crisis as tax revenues dropped and government stimulus programs were enacted, and the dramatic increase alarmed many. This is worth noting, because in the crisis fog, some observers conflated rapid growth in government debt, or too much government debt, with the cause of the financial crisis. Even in 2018, after it was abundantly well established that in the 2008 crisis it was not government debt but runaway growth in private debt that brought the fall, many still believed government deficits and debt were part of the problem. But U.S. government debt growth had been benign in the period before the crisis in comparison to private debt growth and was not a part of the cause. Looking across all countries since World War II, most financial crises are not preceded by rapid government debt growth, and most rapid buildups in government debt are not followed by financial crises. In fact, as we have seen, the government debt–to–GDP ratio often improves in years leading to crisis.

In Europe, the governance of the recovery process among so many different countries was more difficult and fragmented than in the United States. Germany, the European Union's most influential member, was guided by fear of inflation, a wholly misplaced fear given the pervasive deflation inherent in a financial crisis, and it therefore constrained the effectiveness of Europe's Central Bank in righting Europe's economy. Nevertheless, Europe, too, muddled forward.

The United States had learned its lesson from the Great Depression. It intervened to prevent contraction, a vastly better response than in 1929. Neither the Federal Reserve, nor the Office of the Comptroller of the Currency, nor the Treasury, nor the president, nor the Congress had foreseen the crisis, but when the economy began to unravel, they did enough things correctly enough and swiftly enough to avoid a deeper crisis. However, because the government intervened to stop loan contraction, the United States emerged from its 2008 crisis with still-high levels of private debt. This burden dampened growth.

The United States focused its government largesse on banks and corporations, and it largely neglected individuals. The executives of many large institutions that had helped cause the crisis kept their jobs, with trillions in taxpayer aid quickly provided to their institutions. But the Obama administration made no broadly targeted effort to address those whose extended unemployment hurt their chances to return to the job market nor to help those with underwater mortgages. Some advisers to Donald Trump attributed his presidential victory directly to the crisis of 2008 and the lingering impact on the lives of middle-class voters.

Most economists missed forecasting the great Global Crisis of 2008. The forecasting blunder was so widely noted that policymakers and economists, including former Federal Reserve chair Alan Greenspan and former U.S. Treasury secretary Timothy Geithner hurried to assert how impossible it was, and is, to predict crises. Some characterized 2008 as a black swan event—too rare to predict yet catastrophic.[70]

Ben Bernanke exemplified this blindness. In February 2004, he gave a speech known as "The Great Moderation," which was enthusiastically received and frequently referenced. In it, he stated that "one of the most striking features of the economic landscape over the past twenty years or so has been a substantial decline in macroeconomic volatility.... My view is that improvements in monetary policy, though certainly not the only factor, have probably been an important source of [this] Great Moderation."[71]

At the very moment he spoke these words, the mortgage lending craze was in high gear. The past twenty years of moderation he cited had been anything but moderate. It had included the S&L crisis, the junk bond crisis, and many other crises of the 1980s (see Chapter 2), as well as the first collapse of high-flying Internet stocks in the late 1990s and early 2000s. Bernanke's obliviousness continued over the next three years. Shortly before housing prices fell and the lending industry crumbled, in July 2005, he said, "We've never had a decline in house prices on a nationwide basis."[72] His statement conveniently overlooked the dramatic fall in house prices in the Great Depression. Three months later, on October 20, 2005, he conceded that "speculative activity" in houses had increased but asserted that "at a national level these price increases largely reflect strong economic fundamentals."[73] And a short time later, on February 15, 2006, he said, "Housing markets are cooling a bit. Our expectation is that the decline in activity or the slowing in activity will be moderate, that house prices will probably continue to rise."[74] This was followed by another statement on March 28, 2007: "At this juncture, however, the impact on the broader economy and financial markets of the problems in the subprime market seems likely to be contained."[75] On January 10, 2008, a point when we would later learn the recession had already begun, he intoned that "the Federal Reserve is not currently forecasting a recession."[76]

Whatever the case, it wasn't true that the 2008 crisis couldn't be foreseen or predicated—or even prevented. To do so, however, forecasters would have had to look elsewhere to data not included in prevailing models: private debt. In fact, a small coterie of heterodox economists, including Steve Keen, Wynne Godley, and Ann Pettifor, had done precisely that. But their analysis and warnings had gone unheeded.

Conclusion

The Crisis Next Time—and Policy Solutions

When I talk to noneconomists about my work on financial crises, I usually get these questions: where and when are the next financial crises, and what can we do to prevent them?

At the time of this writing, the winter of 2018, while overall U.S. private debt is still high, private debt-to-GDP *growth* is not occurring at a pace that indicates a pending national financial crisis. Overall household debt growth, especially mortgages, is benign, though there are segments within household debt, such as student loans, where overly rapid growth suggests problems. Corporate debt-to-GDP is growing, and high growth within certain segments does merit concern, notably the "highly leveraged" segment. But in aggregate, it remains below the level that would cause concern about a near-term system-wide financial crisis.

Globally, however, there are a small number of countries that do have both very high private debt growth and overall private debt levels that together are above the thresholds of concern. There is, therefore, a good chance of a financial crisis in these countries, although it is beyond the scope of this book to examine this in greater detail. They are potential or pending crises because private debt there is still growing, and, as we've seen, continued private debt growth, however improvident, can in some cases unnaturally extend the life of the boom well past the point of overcapacity.

The largest potential concern is China, but, as we saw in Chapter 3, China has remarkable and demonstrated expertise in finding ways to remediate its lending institutions when they have excessive bad debt. In fact, China's massive, innovative intervention to rescue its major banks in the 1999 crisis would suggest an almost boundless willingness and ability to prevent their failure—uniquely feasible since China's government owns or controls almost all the entities involved in any rescue equation—banks, major companies, regulators, and more. Still, private debt growth (or, more accurately, nongovernment debt growth) in China is the largest such growth in history. In the United States, when a major lender gets in trouble, depositors, funders, and investors have no ultimate certainty that the government will step in to rescue that lender. In China, the opposite assumption holds.

But preventing institutional failure does not mean that the accumulation of overcapacity will stop, and China's continued growth relentlessly adds to its already massive overcapacity. There are fifty million empty homes in China, most owned as largely unused second homes by its citizens. How many millions more can be added? Can this go on indefinitely if China keeps using money creation that comes from lending to fuel it and accounting legerdemain to prop up its institutions? If not, it means that China's GDP growth will slow markedly in the next several years.

This is a multitrillion-dollar question and in my view the greatest global economic question of the moment. A major portion of the world's economic growth over the last decade has come from China, and therefore much hinges on the answer. The timeline of Japan's 1900s crisis is instructive when considering China. Japan reached a point of significant overcapacity in the late 1980s but did not truly begin to intervene on behalf of troubled banks until 1998, a process that continued until the mid-2000s. And even though Japan already had excess capacity by the end of the 1980s, loan growth continued to create still more overcapacity until the late 1990s. Japan then struggled with that overcapacity for a generation.

Some of the other countries that risk crisis are well within China's economic orbit and tend to follow trends there. They have concerning private debt growth and are particularly vulnerable to a slowdown in China, but they don't have the same broad government control as China to deal with a crisis and therefore have greater risk for a widespread calamity.

As for the United States, do we now have the regulations necessary to prevent the next crisis?

The answer is no. As this book has shown, lending markets have repeatedly succumbed to financial crisis and in fact are prone to those crises. They have occurred in every environment: under different types of governments, different tax and regulatory regimes, in the presence and absence of a central bank, and with and without a gold standard.

Regulations often do not adequately address the problems they target. A case in point is the Sarbanes-Oxley Act, passed in 2002 in the wake of the WorldCom and Enron financial scandals. It was enacted to help prevent corporate misbehavior and was massive in scope and highly expensive to implement and maintain. However, it did nothing to mitigate the misbehavior just two to three short years later of any number of subprime lenders, conventional lenders, mortgage banks, and investment banks—misbehavior that led to the crisis of 2008.

Dodd-Frank, the 2010 law passed in hopes of preventing the next crisis, is in many respects helpful. Dodd-Frank did a number of things designed to increase the safety of the banks and the financial system, including increasing capital and leverage ratio requirements, increasing liquidity requirements, adding rules to curb abusive lending practices, increasing scrutiny of financial institutions deemed "too big to fail" (including a plan for more orderly shutdown of troubled institutions), extending oversight to certain nonbank financial firms, limiting banks' proprietary trading operations, regulating certain derivatives, and regulating credit ratings agencies.

But it will not prevent the next crisis.

To speak to just one aspect of Dodd-Frank, the increases in capital and liquidity levels it requires at banks are not enough to be truly effective. Banks are inherently very highly leveraged and therefore highly fragile institutions, and Dodd-Frank's modest changes in capital and liquidity requirements will do little to change that. Truly meaningful capital level changes would be so large as to completely change the profitability and pricing requirements of the industry. As regards liquidity, it always disappears in a crisis, even if it has been plentiful, unless it is locked in a quantity and for a period that extends beyond the crisis, which is more than the new requirements mandate.

Furthermore, banks are expert in designing ways to sidestep such requirements, not as a matter of bad faith but simply to maximize returns. To top it off, increasing these requirements simply pushes more lending to nonbank institutions outside the banking system, where these requirements don't apply.

It's like the old saying that accuses military generals of always fighting the last war. With Dodd-Frank, we have probably prevented any crisis that would take the form of the 2008 crisis but not a crisis that would take a different form. Next time, the lending industry may very well overlend using a different form or structure, through different types of institutions, or in different sectors than in the 2008 crisis.

Given enough time, the lending industry has shown that it is capable of innovating its way around legislative barriers or mounting the necessary lobbying efforts to remove those barriers, as with the 2018 Economic Growth,

Regulatory Relief, and Consumer Protection Act, which took many steps in that direction. The industry makes those efforts not because of any malicious intent but instead as a function of its responsibility and desire to increase the earnings performance at its firms or in an effort to meet a need of its customers, even if sometimes ill advisedly.

In any event, neither Dodd-Frank nor any regulatory policies took the one step I consider most effective and necessary to prevent financial crises: measuring growth in the ratio of private debt–to–GDP as an early warning sign. The surest strategy for early detection of a financial crisis is this: *monitor the aggregates.* More specifically, monitor the growth in aggregate lending totals. And in a world where derivative use has grown so markedly, monitoring should include the aggregate derivative growth. As these chapters have shown, widespread overlending leads to widespread overcapacity that leads to widespread bank (and other lender) failures. That is the essence of most financial crises.

The policy implications of this are clear and straightforward.

Policymakers and regulators should also monitor credit growth in individual lending sectors, including real estate, energy, student loans, and more. They should establish thresholds that, based on historical analysis, signal concern. This implies that a central authority is keeping careful, ongoing records of all lending activity, including aggregate and sector-level information on instruments that are derivatives of loans. Even today, there are emerging forms of loans that may not be included in government-reported national loan totals, as well as incomplete sector information and incomplete information about derivatives. One of the highest priorities of regulators should be to ensure that lending and derivative information is comprehensive and complete.

In my historical review, I have yet to find a financial crisis where the unsound lending practices that led to it were difficult to see. They were major, obvious, and egregiously imprudent, never minor and subtle.

The mortgage loan policies in 2003 to 2005 that led to the U.S. crisis of 2008 were not a modest reduction in the required down-payment amount and a minor reduction in borrowers' income verification. Instead, it was the wholesale elimination of down payments and income verification for billions upon billions of dollars of loans. The purchase of savings institutions in the 1920s and 1980s by real estate developers to make loans for their own real estate projects was a conflict of interest of the worst sort. The list goes on.

The surest method to detect these dangers has not been to dissect the minutiae of a lender's credit policy or the exact structure of securitization and collateral, as these are always mutating beyond the ability of laws and regulations to contain them. Instead, the surest method is to measure aggregate lending totals in the whole and by sector. Where loan growth is extraordinary in relation to GDP, it is almost certain that lending standards have been relaxed. It should then be a straightforward matter for regulators to intervene as needed.

Surely, regulators with broader powers with respect to the type, amount, and form of loan and debt growth can identify and intervene to curb risky practices before they threaten an entire economy. The biggest problem, of course, is that both banks and borrowers chafe at more attention and intervention. But this does not mean that regulations can or should be avoided. There is always a powerful tension between the benefits and dangers of lending, between wealth and prudence.

This book has also shown that highly risky lending practices at the outset of a lending boom usually emanate from secondary and tertiary types of financial institutions that are less regulated and where regulators with the most resources are often legally constrained or precluded from intervening. Therefore, one of the most important antidotes to financial crisis is a central, robust, and independent regulator that has a broad enough mandate both to monitor and intervene as necessary in all material lending sectors in the economy, including instruments that are derivatives of loans. Some of this authority has come with Dodd-Frank, but it is an area that requires ongoing vigilance.

Central bankers often say that their job is to "take away the punch bowl" by raising interest rates to curb a boom. But time has shown that when they do raise rates for this purpose, it is usually long after too much reckless lending has already occurred, and the action of raising rates only hastens or compounds the damage. Raising rates is a blunt and clumsy instrument, indiscriminate in its effects and not especially effective as a remedy for large numbers of ill-advised loans.

Private-sector growth is an important and beneficial thing. Private-sector growth built on unsound lending practices is not. Politicians should take special care to avoid being coopted by fast-growing sectors of the financial institution industry and refrain from intervening on behalf of those very institutions whose practices are bringing the concern.

When an overly risky loan is made, surely both the lender and the borrower are to blame. Surely the individuals who took the no-down-payment loan with the artificially low interest rate could have and should have performed the analysis and concluded that when the rate adjusted upward, they would no longer be able to afford the payment, or if housing values declined, they would no longer be able to pay off the loan by selling the house. (I would note, however, that some lenders acted to exploit the trust of borrowers in those situations, reassuring them that even though payments exceeded their capacity to pay, prices always rose, and they would be able to sell for a profit.) In any event, while laws, regulations, and policies should be in place to protect both the lender and the borrower, from my perspective, the more important priority of government is to protect the individual, and the balance of the law should reflect that.

Finally, if a crisis has not been prevented, and there is risk of widespread damage, a government should face up to the full cost of a crisis earlier rather than later. Regulators have sometimes been precluded from acting to address the full problem because of limited funds and resources. Ignoring or minimizing the estimate of the full cost of the problem as a political expedient has only increased the ultimate cost and damage of the crisis.

Some readers might wonder how a country with a high private debt ratio could reduce that ratio (or to use the technical word, deleverage). In theory, a country with a high private debt–to–GDP ratio could simply be disciplined and grow that debt no faster than GDP. If so, the ratio would improve.

However, that has almost never happened—especially over a long span.

Instead, private deleveraging in a given country has almost always occurred through one of three means: offsetting very high growth in public debt, which brings its own concerns; very high and sustained inflation, which is painful; or a very large net export position, which is hard to sustain without trade repercussions. Private debt deleveraging, absent any of these three things, reduces asset values (since increased debt is a key driver of those values) and has a contracting impact on GDP, bringing duress.

However, this deleveraging could be achieved through a broader strategy of debt restructuring or forgiveness. Yet approaches such as this are highly controversial, politically fraught, and laden with questions of fairness and redistribution—and have therefore almost never been widely used. Nevertheless, in 2009, a broad policy could have been put in place to allow lenders to write down the underwater portion of mortgages on terms that provided relief to borrowers, perhaps in exchange for participation in the gain on any future sale, and at the same time softened the impact to lenders through accounting and regulatory benefits. If implemented, it would have made a profound and positive difference in the pace of recovery *and* the resulting political environment.

In fact, the long-term secular trend for developed economies is toward ever-higher levels of debt, and this trend appears to be related to increasing inequality. Both are core, fundamental issues for policymakers, which makes the study of strategies for deleveraging all the more urgent. (Note that essentially the same conclusions are true of government debt deleveraging. Political promises notwithstanding, countries almost never grow their way out of high government debt without either very high growth in private debt, very high and sustained inflation, or a very large net export position.)

With what we know of financial crises, they can be foreseen and prevented, through data that are available by quarter, while the boom is growing. Some have asked me, Why bother—shouldn't we let the free market run its course, and aren't those who misbehave getting their just deserts?

No. It is never just those who misbehave that suffer the consequences. Thousands upon thousands of innocent people get hurt along the way. It is true that life does go on after a crisis, and solutions, however partial, are crafted. It is true that economies recover and go on, often robustly. It is also true that life is about much more than financial matters. Nevertheless, the effects of a financial crisis are devastating. Lives are ruined. Political parties and governmental systems are often overturned.

At the outset of this book, I contended that lending booms are caused by an intense desire to win, to prevail, and to increase wealth—by a ferocity of ambition that is ever present and incites, compels, and pervades these booms. I contended that this ambition is the equivalent of a computer company's desire to sell more computers, a coach's desire to win championships, or, for that matter, a king's desire to conquer new territories. Yet I would add one thought: because of the lending industry's scope, its high leverage and inherent risk, its privileged ability to create vast amounts of new money and with it new demand, and its ability to bring the risk of overextension and default to its customers, this ambition in the lending industry can almost uniquely lead to much greater harm than the same ambition in any other arena. That is the message of this book.

It is our responsibility to understand, predict, and prevent financial crises; this is our duty to our fellow citizens and to the well-being of our country.

NOTES

Introduction

1. Carmen M. Reinhart and Kenneth S. Rogoff, *This Time Is Different* (Princeton: Princeton University Press, 2009).

2. I developed a list of the major financial crises in these six countries over the last two hundred years, starting with seven excellent lists that I modified based on my own research and judgment. These lists come from the following scholars: Carmen Reinhart and Kenneth Rogoff; Moritz Schularick, Alan Taylor, and Òscar Jordà; Christina Romer and David Romer; Luc Laeven and Fabian Valencia; Michael Bordo, Barry Eichengreen, Daniela Klingbiel, and Maria Soledad Martinez-Peria; Gerard Caprio and Daniela Klingbiel; Matthew Baron, Emil Verner, and Wei Xiong.

In their work, Laeven and Valencia develop a useful definition of a financial crisis. For them, a financial crisis includes extensive bank failures or nationalization, extensive liquidity support for lenders, high bank restructuring gross costs, large government credit guarantees or bank asset purchases, and deposit freezes or bank holidays.

In this book, I use the terms *financial crisis* and *banking crisis* interchangeably and use them in the general sense of Laeven and Valencia's definition. The term *banking crisis* is intended to encompass crises involving all types of lenders, not just banks.

This is not an exhaustive list, but these are the crises that I view as the most major and worthy of study. For example, Rogoff correctly counts the failure of the French Comptoir d'Escompte in 1889 as a crisis. It had a large share of the French banking market, collapsed spectacularly after colluding with another firm to corner the copper market, and was rescued by the French central bank, the Banque de France. But the crisis did not extend far beyond this single bank. Since it does not appear to have been symptomatic of a broader trend in the French economy, I did not include it in my list.

3. Steve Keen, "The Macroeconomics of Endogenous Money: Response to Fiebiger, Palley and Lavoie," *Review of Keynesian Economics* 3, no. 4 (2015): 602–11.

4. Hyman P. Minsky, *Stabilizing an Unstable Economy* (New York: McGraw-Hill, 2008).

5. In addition to private debt, the worksheets for our analysis included, where available, bank balance sheet data, such as loans, deposits, capital, specie (gold and other precious metals), bank failures, charge-offs, delinquency rates, foreclosures, loans from secondary lenders, interest rates, stock market indices, inflation, exchange rates, trade, unemployment, sector spending and debt information, and commodity prices. Databases included data from each country's central bank, the International Monetary Fund, the World Bank, the Bank for International Settlements, the U.S. Census, and the *American Railroad Journal*, Moody's, and Poor's. Invaluable help has come from the research of the National Bureau of Economic Research and the extraordinary work of Schularick, Taylor, and Jordà. Many studies of

historical debt booms only use bank loan data, which is a piece of private debt, but does not capture all forms, such as corporate bonds and nonbank lenders.

6. This is the state many Western economies found themselves in during the years following the 2008 crisis and Japan found itself in after its 1990s crisis because the deleveraging that occurred after these crises was modest. This overhang of debt dampens growth because, with still-high levels of debt, both business and household borrowers use funds to pay interest and principal that would likely otherwise have gone to spending on goods and services. Being highly leveraged also curbs their willingness to borrow more, no matter how attractive the terms.

Chapter 1

1. Adam Hochschild, *Spain in Our Hearts: Americans in the Spanish Civil War, 1936–1939* (New York: Houghton Mifflin Harcourt, 2016), 6–8.

2. Milton Friedman and Anna Jacobson Schwartz, *A Monetary History of the United States, 1867–1960* (Princeton: Princeton University Press, 1993), 354–55.

3. John Kenneth Galbraith, *The Great Crash of 1929* (Boston: Mariner, 1954), 169.

4. According to Robert Fitch in *The Assassination of New York* (New York: Verso, 1993, p. 57), office vacancy rates ranged between 0 percent and 5 percent in 1929. By 1933, however, that figure had surpassed 30 percent. An astute reader might ask why a time four years past the stock market crash should be emphasized. As Fitch argues—and as Jason M. Barr demonstrates in his recent study of Manhattan skyscrapers—real estate development did not slow across all sectors in 1929. In fact, many real estate brokers saw their activity as completely separate (and therefore insulated) from the crash. Therefore, they saw no reason to halt construction. As the United States entered the worst economic depression in its history, the erection of skyscrapers in New York continued on an upward trajectory, ultimately peaking in 1931. See Jason M. Barr, *Building the Skyline: The Birth and Growth of Manhattan's Skyscrapers* (New York: Oxford University Press, 2016), 294.

5. Herbert Hoover, "Introduction," in John M. Gries and James S. Taylor, *How to Own Your Home: A Handbook for Prospective Home Owners* (Washington, DC: Government Printing Office, 1923), v.

6. Donald L. Miller, *Supreme City: How Jazz Age Manhattan Gave Birth to Modern America* (New York: Simon and Schuster, 2014), 170.

7. Robert M. Fogelson, *The Great Rent Wars: New York, 1917–1929* (New Haven, CT: Yale University Press, 2013), 35.

8. U.S. Bureau of the Census, "Selected Assets and Liabilities of Savings and Loan Associations: 1900 to 1970," in *Historical Statistics of the United States: Colonial Times to 1970, Part 2* (Washington, DC: Government Printing Office, 1975), 1047.

9. Exposing a scandal that had been covered for over seventy years, historian Raymond Vickers retrieved bank documents from the 1920s that demonstrated the ways in which a handful of lenders engaged in large-scale fraud and misappropriated depositors' funds in order to finance real estate projects. See Raymond Vickers, *Panic in Paradise* (Tuscaloosa: University of Alabama Press, 1994).

10. Jihad Dagher, "Regulatory Cycles: Revisiting the Political Economy of Financial Crises" (IMF Working Paper WP/18/8, January 2018), 18.

11. Earle Shultz and Walter Simmons, *Offices in the Sky* (Indianapolis: Bobbs-Merrill, 1959), 154 and 162, quoted in Barr, *Building the Skyline*, 281.

12. Daniel Okrent, *Great Fortune: The Epic of Rockefeller Center* (New York: Penguin, 2004), 251–52.

13. Fitch, *Assassination of New York*, 57.

14. Galbraith, *Great Crash*, 5–6.

15. Harold Bierman Jr., *The Causes of the 1929 Stock Market Crash: A Speculative Orgy or a New Era?* (Westport, CT: Greenwood, 1998), 85–102. Bierman also discusses the role of utility stocks in the 1929 crash in an article on the Economic History Association's website. See Harold Bierman Jr., "The 1929 Stock Market Crash," EH.net, accessed November 14, 2018, http://eh.net/encyclopedia/the-1929-stock-market-crash/.

16. Forrest McDonald, *Insull: The Rise and Fall of a Billionaire Utility Tycoon* (New York: Beard, 1962), 124–33.

17. The Federal Trade Commission hearings lasted seven years, from 1928 to 1935, and examined "29 holding companies, 70 sub-holding companies, and 278 operating companies having combined total assets of $19,038,698,378." The investigation concluded that these assets were overvalued by at least $1.5 billion. See *Annual Report of the Federal Trade Commission* (Washington, DC: Government Printing Office, 1936), 34.

18. McDonald, *Insull*, 278.

19. Following the news that President Coolidge would not run for a second term, then Secretary of Commerce Herbert Clark Hoover accepted the nomination at the 1928 Republican National Convention in Kansas City, Missouri. That Hoover's speech was replete with optimism about the prospect of soon eradicating poverty is ironic, considering the financial collapse a little over a year later and subsequent depression. See "Herbert Hoover's Acceptance Speech: Formally Accepting the Republican Nomination for President of the United States" (Washington, DC: Republican National Committee, 1928).

20. Infamous for their timing, these pronouncements have achieved an almost mythic status. Repeated across blogs, scholarly and commercial studies, and even in textbooks designed for undergraduates, Forbes and Fisher's statements have become emblematic of how blatantly out of touch supposed experts can be with financial trends. See Maureen Burton, Reynold F. Nesiba, and Bruce Brown, *An Introduction to Financial Markets and Institutions* (New York: Routledge, 2010), 300.

21. U.S. Department of Transportation, Federal Highway Administration, "Chart VMT-421C: Public Road Mileage–VMT–Lane Miles, 1920–2013," last modified November 7, 2014, https://www.fhwa.dot.gov/policyinformation/statistics/2013/vmt421c.cfm; Susan B. Carter (ed.), "Table Df956–963. Railroad passenger and freight operations-per-car and per-train traffic volume, and speed: 1890–1980," *Historical Statistics of the United States, Millennial Edition* (Cambridge, UK: Cambridge University Press, 2006).

22. Lendol Calder, *Financing the Great Depression* (Princeton: Princeton University Press, 1999), 262–90.

23. Not only the creator of the real estate bond market but also the most prominent financier of iconic skyscrapers—including the Westinghouse building, New York Athletic Club, Chrysler Building, and Ziegfeld Theaters—S. W. Straus was also, ironically, a moralizing "thrift" evangelist. His 1920 essay, "History of the Thrift Movement in America," is a condemnation of Americans' wastefulness, excess, and overindulgence. Recently, this essay has been made available in an illustrated book format. See S. W. Straus and Rollin Kerby, *The History of the Thrift Movement in America* (New York: Kessinger, 2010).

24. After evidence surfaced that Mitchell had engaged in illegal transactions, speculating on company stock, and tax evasion, he resigned his post at National City. As a result, he became a convenient target for government officials bent on tightening regulation. The Securities Act of 1933, alongside the Banking Acts of 1933 (popularly known as the Glass-Steagall Act) and 1935, are largely considered to be responses to the kind of behavior Mitchell emblematized. See Thomas F. Huertas and Joan L. Silverman, "Charles E. Mitchell: Scapegoat of the Crash?" *Business History Review* 60 (Spring 1986), 81–103.

25. Tom Nicholas and Anna Scherbina, "Real Estate Prices During the Roaring Twenties and the Great Depression," *Real Estate Economics* 41 (Summer 2013), 306.

26. Ibid.

27. A fairly well-known and oft-cited speech, this excerpt appears in many studies of real estate development during the Roaring Twenties. See Stephen L. Trampe, *The Queen of Lace: The Story of the Continental Life Building* (St. Louis: Virginia Publishing, 2013), 153.

28. Eugene N. White, "Lessons from the Great American Real Estate Boom and Bust of the 1920s," in *Housing and Mortgage Markets in Historical Perspective*, ed. Eugene N. White, Kenneth Snowden, and Price Fishback (Chicago: University of Chicago Press, 2014), page 126, note 15. White, in turn, cites Anna J. Schwartz, "The Misuse of the Fed's Discount Window," *Federal Reserve Bank of St. Louis Review* 74 (1992), 58–69.

29. For more information on Charles Ponzi, see Mitchell Zuckoff, *Ponzi's Scheme: The True Story of a Financial Legend* (New York: Random House, 2006).

30. Quoted in "Secretary of Treasury Andrew W. Mellon Looks for Revival of Industrial Activity in Spring and Steady Progress During 1830," *Commercial and Financial Chronicle* 130 (January 4, 1930), 21.

31. Robert F. Bruner et al., "Financial Innovation and the Consequences of Complexity: Insights from Major US Banking Crises," in *Complexity and Crisis in the Financial System: Critical Perspectives on the Evolution of American and British Banking*, ed. Matthew Hollow et al. (Cheltenham, UK: Edward Elgar, 2016), 28; Encyclopedia.com, "Banking Panics (1930–1933)," accessed November 14, 2018, https://www.encyclopedia.com/economics/encyclopedias -almanacs-transcripts-and-maps/banking-panics-1930-1933; Christopher Gray, "The First Domino in the Depression," *New York Times*, August 18, 1991.

32. Referenced in Kenneth A. Snowden Jr.'s essay, "The Anatomy of a Residential Mortgage Crisis: A Look Back to the 1930's," in *The Panic of 2008: Causes, Consequences, and Implications for Reform*, ed. Lawrence Mitchell and Arthur E. Wilmarth (Cheltenham, UK: Edgar Elgar, 2010), 60–61. For a full brief, see Henry Hoagland, "The Relation of the Work of the Federal Home Loan Bank Board to Home Security and Betterment," *Proceedings of the Academy of Political Science* 16, no. 3 (1935), 45–52.

33. Natacha Postel-Vinay, "What Caused Chicago Bank Failures in the Great Depression? A Look at the 1920s," *Journal of Economic History* 76 (June 2016), 480.

34. Irving Fisher, "The Debt-Deflation Theory of Great Depressions," *Econometrica* 1, no. 4 (1933), 337–57.

35. Federal Housing Finance Agency, Office of Inspector General, "A Brief History of the Housing Government-Sponsored Enterprises," https://www.fhfaoig.gov/, accessed November 14, 2018, https://www.fhfaoig.gov/Content/Files/History%20of%20the%20Government%20Sponsored%20Enterprises.pdf.

36. Gary Richardson, Alejandro Komai, and Michael Gou, "Roosevelt's Gold Program," federalreservehistory.org, November 22, 2013.

37. Timothy Green, *Historical Gold Price Table*, World Gold Council (London prices converted to U.S. dollars), retrieved from the National Mining Association, "Historical Gold Prices, 1833–Present," https://nma.org/, accessed November 14, 2018, https://nma.org/wp -content/uploads/2017/02/his_gold_prices_1833_pres_2017.pdf.

38. Carl Mosk, *Japanese Economic Development: Markets, Norms, Structures* (New York: Routledge, 2008), 136.

39. Takashi Nanjo, "Developments in Land Prices and Bank Lending in Interwar Japan: Effects of the Real Estate Finance Problem on the Banking Industry," *Monetary and Economic Studies* 20, no. 3 (October 2002), 120.

40. Charles Kindleberger, *Historical Economics: Art or Science?* (Berkeley: University of California Press, 1990), 313.

Chapter 2

1. Board of Governors of the Federal Reserve System, "Z.1, Table D.3, Debt Outstanding by Sector," from Data Download Program, https://www.federalreserve.gov/datadownload /Choose.aspx?rel=Z.1; U.S. Bureau of Economic Analysis, National Data, National Income and Product Accounts, "Table 1.1.5. Gross Domestic Product," accessed November 14, 2018, https://apps.bea.gov/iTable/iTable.cfm?reqid=19&step=2#reqid=19&step=2&isuri=1&1921 =survey.

2. Board of Governors of the Federal Reserve System, "Z.1, Table D.3."

3. Ibid.

4. Internal Revenue Service, "1954 to 1999 Corporation Income Tax Returns Report," from "Mortgages, Notes, and Bonds Payable in Less than One Year" and "Mortgages, Notes, and Bonds Payable in One Year or More," https://www.irs.gov/statistics/soi-tax-stats-archive -1954-to-1999-corporation-income-tax-return-reports.

5. Edward I. Altman and Gonzalo Fanjul, "Defaults and Returns in the High Yield Bond Market: The Year 2003 in Review and Market Outlook" (Salomon Center for the Study of Financial Institutions Working Paper Series, 2004), p. 19.

6. U.S. Treasury, "Historical Debt Outstanding—Annual 1950–1999," accessed November 14, 2018, https://www.treasurydirect.gov/govt/reports/pd/histdebt/histdebt_histo4 .htm.; U.S. Bureau of Economic Analysis, "Table 1.1.5. Gross Domestic Product."

7. Federal Deposit Insurance Company (hereafter FDIC) Division of Research and Statistics, *History of the Eighties: Lessons for the Future, Volume 1: An Examination of the Banking Crises of the 1980s and Early 1990s* (Washington, DC: FDIC, 1997), 295.

8. David Lawrence Mason, *From Buildings and Loans to Bail-Outs: A History of the Savings and Loan Industry, 1831–1995* (Cambridge: Cambridge University Press, 2009), 214.

9. "In response to the disintermediation caused since 1979 by the combination of deposit interest-rate ceilings and the sharp rise in interest rates, the law also provided for the gradual removal by 1986 of Regulation Q ceilings on maximum allowable rates on deposit accounts. The removal of the ceilings was meant particularly to increase depository institutions' ability to compete against money market mutual funds, but the ceilings were also attacked for penalizing small savers who did not have access to instruments through which they could obtain market rates." FDIC, *History of the Eighties*, 92.

10. Mason, *From Buildings and Loans to Bail-Outs*, 222.

11. Ibid., 223.

12. Ibid., 221.

13. Deirdre Clarkin and David E. McBee, for the FDIC Library, "The S&L Crisis: A Chrono-Bibliography," FDIC, last updated December 20, 2002, https://www.fdic.gov/bank/historical/sandl/.

14. Ibid.

15. Ibid.; Mason, *From Buildings and Loans to Bail-Outs*, 219.

16. Board of Governors of the Federal Reserve System, "Z.1, Table L.217, Total Mortgages," from Data Download Program, https://www.federalreserve.gov/datadownload/Choose.aspx?rel=Z.1.

17. "In major markets, new completions exceeded absorptions every year from 1980 to 1992.... As a result, vacancy rates in major markets rose to unprecedented levels, nearly quadrupling between 1980 and 1991 from 4.9 percent to a peak of 18.9 percent." FDIC, *History of the Eighties*, 146.

18. Greg David, "New York City: Then and Now," *Crain's New York Business*, June 27, 2010, https://www.crainsnewyork.com/article/20100627/ANNIVERSARY/100629890/new-york-city-then-now.

19. Darren Karn and Joe Martin, "The Commercial Real Estate Crisis of the 1980s and 1990s," research paper, Rotman School of Management, University of Toronto, 2017, 2, 6, 8, 9, https://www.rotman.utoronto.ca/-/media/Files/Programs-and-Areas/CanadianBusinessHistory/Commercial-Real-Estate-Crisis-Research-Paper_Feb2017.pdf.

20. "S&P 500 PE Ratio by Month," S&P 500 PE Ratio, http://www.multpl.com/table?f=m.

21. The unemployment rate rose from 8.5 percent in 1981 to 10.8 percent in 1982. See U.S. Bureau of Labor Statistics, "Civilian Unemployment Rate [UNRATE]," retrieved from Federal Reserve Bank of St. Louis (hereafter FRED), https://fred.stlouisfed.org/series/UNRATE.

22. Wriston's argument was that "LDCs [less developed countries] don't go bankrupt ... the infrastructure doesn't go away, the productivity of the people doesn't go away, the natural resources don't go away. And so their assets always exceed their liabilities, which is the technical reason for bankruptcy. And that's very different from a company." See Ross P. Buckley, "The Bankruptcy of Nations: An Idea Whose Time Has Come," *International Lawyer* 43 (2009), 1189.

23. FDIC, *History of the Eighties*, 193.

24. Ibid., 199.

25. Jocelyn Sims and Jessie Romero, "Latin American Debt Crisis of the 1980s," Federal Reserve History, last updated November 22, 2013, https://www.federalreservehistory.org/essays/latin_american_debt_crisis.htm.

26. FDIC, *History of the Eighties*, 191, 206.

27. Ibid., 208.

28. Ibid., 209.

29. Ibid., 294.

30. Ibid., 39. The authors note that the "estimated total cost of FDIC failed-bank resolutions in 1980–94 is $36.3 billion. The estimated cost of the savings and loan debacle is $160.1 billion, of which an estimated $132.1 billion was borne by taxpayers."

31. Ibid., 180.

32. Clarkin and McBee, "The S&L Crisis."

33. Ibid.

34. Ibid.

35. Kenneth B. Noble, "Empire Savings of Texas Is Shut Down," *New York Times*, March 15, 1984.

36. Clarkin and McBee, "The S&L Crisis."

37. Ibid.

38. Ibid. In their timeline, Clarkin and McBee write that by August,1985, there was only "$4.6 billion in FSLIC insurance fund" and that "Chairman Gray tries to gain support for recapitalizing FSLIC on Capitol Hill." By the following year, the "GAO estimates the loss to the insurance fund to be around $20 billion."

39. FDIC, *History of the Eighties*, 39.

40. Ibid.

41. Ibid.

42. Ibid.; Mason, *From Buildings and Loans to Bail-Outs*, 233.

43. Clarkin and McBee, "The S&L Crisis."

44. Ibid.

45. Ibid.

46. Tom Furlong, "The Keating Indictment: Targets of Bond Sellers: The 'Weak, Meek, Ignorant,'" *Los Angeles Times*, September 19, 1990, http://articles.latimes.com/1990-09-19 /business/fi-692_1_bond-sales-program.

47. William K. Black, "We Were Regulators Once: Ed Gray's Finest Hour," *New Economic Perspectives*, April 2012, http://neweconomicperspectives.org/2012/04/we-were-regulators -once-ed-grays-finest-hour.html.

48. John F. Walker and Howard G. Vatter, *History of U.S. Economy Since World War II* (Florence, KY: Taylor and Francis, 2015), 431.

49. Mine Aysen Doyran, *Financial Crisis Management and the Pursuit of Power: American Pre-eminence and the Credit Crunch* (London: Routledge, 2011), 28.

50. FDIC, "Historical Timeline," Federal Deposit Insurance Corporation, 2014, https:// www.fdic.gov/about/history/timeline/1980s.html.

51. Clarkin and McBee, "The S&L Crisis"; FDIC, "Historical Timeline."

Chapter 3

1. Christopher Wood, *The Bubble Economy: Japan's Extraordinary Speculative Boom of the '80s and the Dramatic Bust of the '90s* (New York: Atlantic Monthly, 1992), 62–64.

2. "Your Next Boss May Be Japanese," *Newsweek*, February 1987, 42–48.

3. In his syndicated column from the first week of September 1988, Harvey noted that the trade deficit with Japan had reached $4.4 billion and described Japan as "choking us with goods." See Paul Harvey, "Japan Buys US with Our Money," *Kentucky New Era* (Hopkinsville, KY), September 6, 1988.

4. Wood, *Bubble Economy*, 23.

5. Ibid., 145.

6. William M. Tsutsui and Stefano Mazzotta, "The Bubble Economy and the Lost Decade: Learning from the Japanese Economic Experience," *Journal of Global Initiatives: Policy, Pedagogy, Perspective* 9, no. 1 (2014), 66.

7. Mitsuhiro Fukao, "Japanese Financial Crisis and Crisis Management" (presentation, Japan Center for Economic Research, Tokyo, September 21, 2009), 2.

8. Wood, *Bubble Economy*, 38.

9. Ibid.

10. Ibid.

11. Ibid., 39.

12. Bank of Japan, "Assets/Loans by private financial institutions/Nonbanks/Stock—series code FF'FOF_FFYS170A240," accessed January 23, 2019, http://www.stat-search.boj.or .jp/ssi/cgi-bin/famecgi2?cgi=$nme_s050_en.

13. Wood, *Bubble Economy*, 39.

14. Mariko Fujii and Masahiro Kawai, "Lessons from Japan's Banking Crisis, 1991–2005" (ADBI Working Paper No. 222, June 2010), 3.

15. Curtis J. Milhaupt and Geoffrey P. Miller, "Regulatory Failure and the Collapse of Japan's Home Mortgage Lending Industry: A Legal and Economic Analysis," *Law and Policy* 22, no. 3/4, (2000), 260.

16. Richard Koo and Masaya Sasaki, "Japan's Disposal of Bad Loans: Failure or Success?" (NRI Papers No. 151, March 1, 2010), 10.

17. Milhaupt and Miller, "Regulatory Failure," 263–65.

18. Charles Goodhart, Philipp Hartmann, David Llewellyn, Liliana Rojas-Suarez, and Steven Weisbrod, *Financial Regulation: Why, How and Where Now?* (London: Routledge, 2001), 124–25; Fujii and Kawai, "Lessons," 4.

19. Wood, *Bubble Economy*, 121, 127.

20. Richard Lloyd Parry, "Yakuza Settle Bad Debts with a Bullet as Japan Bubble Bursts," *Independent* (London), February 4, 1996.

21. Wood, *Bubble Economy*, 141.

22. Fukao, "Japanese Financial Crisis," 7.

23. Wood, *Bubble Economy*, 41.

24. Fujii and Kawai, "Lessons," 4.

25. Wood, *Bubble Economy*, 29.

26. Milhaupt and Miller, "Regulatory Failure," 267–68.

27. Ibid., 273.

28. Ibid.; Akihiro Kanaya and David Woo, "The Japanese Banking Crisis of the 1990s: Sources and Lessons," *Essays in International Economics* 222 (2001), 24.

29. Koo and Sasaki, "Japan's Disposal of Bad Loans," 11.

30. Fujii and Kawai, "Lessons," 8.

31. Fukao, "Japanese Financial Crisis," 7, 12.

32. Wood, *Bubble Economy*, 40.

33. Ibid., 41.

34. This term was first used in the United States in the 1980s to describe regulatory tolerance of effectively insolvent lenders; by 1993 it was also being used to refer to Japan's lenders. For a short but erudite examination of the term, see William Safire, "Zombie Banks," *New York Times Magazine*, May 14, 2009, 26.

35. Milhaupt and Miller, "Regulatory Failure," 269.

36. Ibid.

37. Guonan Ma, "Who Pays China's Restructuring Bill?" (Centre d'Études Prospectives et d'Informations Internationales Working Paper No. 2006-04, February 2006), 8.

38. Ibid., 15.

39. Ibid.

40. Ibid., 16.

41. Ibid., 17.

42. Fukao, "Japanese Financial Crisis," 8.

43. Fujii and Kawai, "Lessons," 5; Kanaya and Woo, "Japanese Banking Crisis of the 1990s," 28.

44. Fujii and Kawai, "Lessons," 5.

45. Fukao, "Japanese Financial Crisis," 8.

46. Ibid.; Edgardo Demaestri and Pietro Masci, *Financial Crises in Japan and Latin America* (Washington, DC: Inter-American Development Bank, 2003), 129.

47. Fujii and Kawai, "Lessons," 5.

48. Koo and Sasaki, "Japan's Disposal of Bad Loans," 5. The authors give the precise figure as ¥7,659.3 billion, though many sources offer the rounder number of ¥7.5 trillion; see Fujii and Kawai, "Lessons," 5; and Demaestri and Masci, *Financial Crises,* 129.

49. Fukao, "Japanese Financial Crisis," 11, 12.

50. Fujii and Kawai, "Lessons," 6.

51. Ibid.

52. All quotations in this paragraph are from Fukao, "Japanese Financial Crisis," 16.

53. Ibid., 15.

54. Tsutsui and Mazzotta, "Bubble Economy and the Lost Decade," 69.

55. Ibid., 67. The authors note that although the "official unemployment rate topped 5.5 percent," during 2003, most "economists estimated that the actual rate was closer to 9 percent."

56. Ibid., 68.

Chapter 4

1. Ralph Charles Henry Catterall, *The First Six Years of the Second Bank of the United States* (Chicago: University of Chicago Press, 1902), 65.

2. Otto C. Lightner, *The History of Business Depressions* (New York: Northeastern Press, 1922), 119.

3. David Sinclair, *The Land That Never Was: Sir Gregor MacGregor and the Most Audacious Fraud in History* (Cambridge, MA: Da Capo, 2004), 249.

4. Larry Neal, "The Financial Crisis of 1825 and the Restructuring of the British Financial System," *Review (Federal Reserve Bank of St. Louis)* 80 (May/June 1998), 66.

5. C. K. Hobson, *The Export of Capital* (London: Constable, 1914), 101.

6. Bishop Carleton Hunt, *The Development of the Business Corporation in England, 1800–1867* (Cambridge, MA: Harvard University Press, 1936), 32.

7. Henry English, *A General Guide to the Companies Formed for Working Foreign Mines* (London: Boosey, 1825), 1–70.

8. Henry English, *A Complete View of the Joint Stock Companies Formed During the Years 1824 and 1825* (London: Boosey, 1827), 16, 29–30.

9. Ibid., 30.

10. "Commercial Revulsions: The Late Crisis in the Money Market Impartially Considered," *Edinburgh Review* 46 (June 1826), 86; "An Account of the Number of Licenses Granted in Each Year to Country Bankers Since the Year 1780," in *Appendix to the Report from the Committee of Secrecy on the Bank of England Charter* (London: Hansard, 1832), 111.

11. "An Account of the Balances of the Advances for the Purchase of the Dead Weight Annuity, of the Loans on Mortgages, of the Loans on Stock, of the Loan to the East India Company, of Advances to Government to pay off Dissentients on Conversion of £5 per Cents, the Amount of Notes in Circulation, the Amount of Coin and Bullion held by the Bank of

England, also the Rate of Exchange on Paris (real prices) and the Premium of Gold at Paris at the undermentioned periods in the years 1822, 1823, 1824, and 1825," *Appendix to the Report from the Committee of Secrecy*, 26–27.

12. Frank Whitson Fetter, *Development of British Monetary Orthodoxy, 1797–1875* (Cambridge, MA: Harvard University Press, 1965), 113.

13. "An Account of the Balances of the Advances," 27.

14. Niall Ferguson, *The House of Rothschild: Money's Prophets, 1798–1848* (New York: Penguin, 1999), 136–37.

15. Hubert Bonin, "France, Financial Crisis and the 1848 Revolutions," in *Encyclopedia of Revolutions of 1848*, trans. James G. Chastain (Athens: Ohio University, 2005), https://www.ohio.edu/chastain/index.htm.

16. Frederick Engels, *Socialism: Utopian and Scientific*, trans. Edward Aveling (London: Swan Sonnenschein, 1892), 40.

17. Alexis de Tocqueville to Ernest de Chabrol, June 9, 1831, in *Selected Letters on Politics and Society*, trans. James Toupin (Berkeley: University of California Press, 1985), 39.

18. Harriet Martineau, *Society in America*, vol. 1 (London: Saunders and Otley, 1837), 350.

19. Richard L. Forstall, ed., *Population of States and Counties of the United States: 1790–1990* (Washington, DC: U.S. Bureau of the Census, 1996), 4.

20. James Smith Buck, *Pioneer History of Milwaukee from the First American Settlement in 1833, to 1841*, rev. ed. (Milwaukee: Swain & Tate, 1890), 81, quoted in Alasdair Roberts, *America's First Great Depression: Economic Crisis and Political Disorder After the Panic of 1837* (Ithaca, NY: Cornell University Press, 2012), 20.

21. "Betting the House," *Economist* 407 (April 6, 2013), 88. In 2012 dollars, these numbers would be $800 and $327,000, respectively.

22. Joseph Baldwin, *The Flush Times of Alabama and Mississippi: A Series of Sketches* (Americus, GA: Americus Book Company, 1853), 85, 89.

23. Quoted in Roberts, *America's First Great Depression*, 25.

24. Jessica M. Lepler, *The Many Panics of 1837: People, Politics, and the Creation of a Transatlantic Financial Crisis* (Cambridge: Cambridge University Press, 2013), 12–13.

25. These sources provided valuable insight on slave financing and collateral: Sven Beckert and Seth Rockman, eds., *Slavery's Capitalism: A New History of American Economic Development* (Philadelphia: University of Pennsylvania Press, 2016), especially Bonnie Martin's chapter, "Neighbor-to-Neighbor Capitalism: Local Credit Networks and the Mortgaging of Slaves," 107–21; Richard Holcombe Kilbourne Jr., *Debt, Investment, Slaves: Credit Relations in East Feliciana Parish, Louisiana, 1825–1885* (Tuscaloosa: University of Alabama Press, 1995); and Samuel H. Williamson and Louis Cain, "Measuring Slavery in 2016 Dollars," MeasuringWorth, 2018, www.measuringworth.com/slavery.php.

26. Bonnie Martin, "Slavery's Invisible Engine: Mortgaging Human Property," *Journal of Southern History* 76 (November 2010), 840.

27. Sharon Ann Murphy, "Banking on Slavery in the Antebellum South" (working paper, presented at the Yale University Economic History Workshop, May 1, 2017), 1, 4, 6.

28. Ibid., 15.

29. Frederick Law Olmsted, *The Cotton Kingdom: A Traveller's Observations on Cotton and Slavery in the United States*, vol. 1, 2nd ed. (New York: Mason Brothers, 1862), 321. Also quoted in Roberts, *America's First Great Depression*, 30.

30. R. Thomas and N. Dimsdale, "Tab A31: Nominal and Real Interest Rates, Asset Prices and Yields," in "A Millennium of Macroeconomic Data for the UK," *Bank of England OBRA Dataset*, from https://www.bankofengland.co.uk/statistics/research-datasets.

31. Stephen W. Campbell, "The Transatlantic Financial Crisis of 1837," in *Oxford Research Encyclopedia of Latin American History* (Oxford: Oxford University Press, 2017), 5, accessed June 7, 2018, http://latinamericanhistory.oxfordre.com/view/10.1093/acrefore /9780199366439.001.0001/acrefore-9780199366439-e-399.

32. Roberts, *America's First Great Depression*, 36.

33. Joshua D. Rothman, "The Contours of Cotton Capitalism: Speculation, Slavery, and Economic Panic in Mississippi, 1832–1841," in *Slavery's Capitalism: A New History of American Economic Development*, ed. Sven Beckert and Seth Rockman (Philadelphia: University of Pennsylvania Press, 2016), 127.

34. Ibid.

35. Baldwin, *Flush Times of Alabama and Mississippi*, 50, 83.

36. Frederick M. Peck and Henry H. Earl, *Fall River and Its Industries: An Historical and Statistical Record of the Village, Town, and City* (New York: Atlantic Publishing and Engraving, 1877), 72.

37. Leland Hamilton Jenks, *The Migration of British Capital to 1875* (New York: Alfred A. Knopf, 1927), 67.

38. Roberts, *America's First Great Depression*, 28.

39. Harry N. Scheiber, "The Pet Banks in Jacksonian Politics and Finance, 1833–1841," *Journal of Economic History* 23 (June 1963), 202–3.

40. John Joseph Wallis, "The Depression of 1839 to 1843: States, Debts, and Banks" (working paper, 2008), p. 4, http://startabankca.com/history/200809_TheDepression/depression 1839.pdf.

41. Roberts, *America's First Great Depression*, 37.

42. John Clapham, *The Bank of England: A History*, vol. 2 (Cambridge: Cambridge University Press, 1944), 429.

43. Geoffrey Fain Williams, "'Lending Money to People Across the Water': The British Joint Stock Banking Acts of 1826 and 1833, and the Panic of 1837" (working paper, Transylvania University, Lexington, KY, 2016), p. 14, http://eh.net/eha/wp-content/uploads/2016/08 /Williams.pdf.

44. Lepler, *Many Panics of 1837*, 64; Campbell, "Transatlantic Financial Crisis of 1837," 7; James L. Watkins, *Production and Price of Cotton for One Hundred Years* (Washington, DC: Government Printing Office, 1895), 7.

45. Campbell, "Transatlantic Financial Crisis of 1837," 8; Lepler, *Many Panics of 1837*, 108–10.

46. Lepler, *Many Panics of 1837*, 109.

47. Quoted in Roberts, *America's First Great Depression*, 21.

48. Lepler, *Many Panics of 1837*, 198.

49. Ibid.

50. Charles Morris, "Events Preceding the Civil War," in *The Great Republic by the Master Historians*, vol. 3, ed. Charles Morris (New York: Great Republic, 1913), 136.

51. Henry Graff, *The Presidents: A Reference History* (New York: Simon & Schuster, 2002), quoted in Roberts, *America's First Great Depression*, 7.

52. Clapham, *Bank of England*, 429.

53. Henry Dunning MacLeod, "A History of Banking in Great Britain," in *A History of Banking in All the Leading Nations*, vol. 2, ed. *Journal of Commerce and Commercial Bulletin* (New York: Journal of Commerce and Commercial Bulletin, 1896), 135–36.

54. Roberts, *America's First Great Depression*, 47.

55. Namsuk Kim and John Joseph Wallis, "The Market for American State Government Bonds in Britain and the United States, 1830 to 1843" (National Bureau of Economic Research [hereafter NBER] Working Paper 10108, November 2003), 1–2; Mira Wilkins, *The History of Foreign Investment in the United States to 1914* (Cambridge, MA: Harvard University Press, 1989), 68.

56. Kim and Wallis, "Market for American State Government Bonds," 2.

57. Larry Schweikart and Lynne Pierson Doti, *American Entrepreneur: A History of Business in the United States* (New York: AMACOM, 2010), 90.

58. Roberts, *America's First Great Depression*, 63–64, 19.

59. Ibid., 22.

60. Robert Sobel, *Panic on Wall Street: A History of America's Financial Disasters* (New York: Macmillan, 1968; repr. Washington, DC: Beard Books, 1999), 72.

Chapter 5

1. Elroy Dimson et al., *Triumph of the Optimists: 101 Years of Global Investment Returns* (Princeton: Princeton University Press, 2002), 24.

2. As of October 31, 2018, information technology made up 20.7 percent of the S&P 500. See S&P Dow Jones Indices, "S&P 500," accessed November 6, 2018, https://us.spindices.com /indices/equity/sp-500.

3. For an account of the involvement of these men in railways and other industries in the nineteenth century, see Matthew Josephson, *The Robber Barons: The Great American Capitalists, 1861–1901* (San Diego: Harcourt, 1934).

4. Maury Klein, *Union Pacific, Volume 1, 1862–1893* (Minneapolis: University of Minnesota Press, 1987), 226, 285–305.

5. Maury Klein, *Union Pacific, Volume 2, 1894–1969* (Minneapolis: University of Minnesota Press, 2006), 12; "UP Falls into Bankruptcy," 1893, Union Pacific Railroad Timeline, accessed November 8, 2018, https://www.up.com/timeline/index.cfm/up-bankruptcy.

6. E. V. Grabill, "The Periodicity of Commercial Crises as Exemplified in the United States," *American Magazine of Civics* 13 (April 1896), 371.

7. For more on the first English steam railway, see Maurice W. Kirby, *The Origins of Railway Enterprise: The Stockton and Darlington Railway, 1821–1863* (Cambridge: Cambridge University Press, 2002).

8. Ira Ryner, *On the Crises of 1837, 1847, and 1857, in England, France, and the United States: An Analysis and Comparison* (Lincoln: University of Nebraska Press, 1905), 9.

9. William Frederick Spackman, *An Analysis of the Railway Interest of the United Kingdom* (London: Longman, 1845), 41–44.

10. "The Beauty of Bubbles, Booms and Busts," *Economist* (December 20, 2008), 116.

11. "Fraudulent Schemes—Capital Required for the Bubbles," *Bankers' Magazine* 4 (November 1845), 101.

12. "Opinion and Editorial," *Times*, July 1, 1845, 4.

13. Arthur D. Gayer, W. W. Rostow, and Anna Jacobson Schwartz, *The Growth and Fluctuation of the British Economy, 1790–1850: An Historical, Statistical, and Theoretical Study of Britain's Economic Development* (Oxford: Clarendon, 1953), 375.

14. J. T. Danson, "On the Accounts of the Bank of England Under the Operation of the Act 7 & 8 Vict., c. 32," *Journal of the Statistical Society of London* 10 (May 1847), 152.

15. R. Thomas and N. Dimsdale, "Tab A9: Nominal compromise/balanced estimates of GDP–'GDP(A),' 1700–2016 including estimates of Irish GDP," in "A Millennium of Macroeconomic Data for the UK," *Bank of England OBRA Dataset*, from https://www.bankofengland.co.uk/statistics/research-datasets.

16. W. T. C. King, *History of the London Discount Market* (1936; repr. London: Routledge, 2006), 103, 130.

17. Gareth Campbell and John Turner, "'The Greatest Bubble in History': Stock Prices During the British Railway Mania" (MPRA Paper No. 21820, 2010), 4–5.

18. "The Railway Crisis—Its Cause and Its Cure," *Economist* 6 (October 21, 1848), 1187.

19. For an account of the evolution of the transatlantic grain trade in the nineteenth century, including the role of railroads, see Morton Rothstein, "Centralizing Firms and Spreading Markets: The World of International Grain Traders, 1846–1914," *Business and Economic History*, n.s. 17 (1988), 103–13.

20. John Clapham, *The Bank of England: A History*, vol. 2 (Cambridge: Cambridge University Press, 1966), 202.

21. D. Morier Evans, *The Commercial Crisis, 1847–1848* (London: Letts, Son, and Steer, 1848), 69.

22. Ibid., 90–92.

23. King, *History of the London Discount Market*, 145.

24. Hubert Bonin, "France, Financial Crisis and the 1848 Revolutions," in *Encyclopedia of Revolutions of 1848*, trans. James G. Chastain (Athens: Ohio University Press, 2005), https://www.ohio.edu/chastain/dh/franfin.htm.

25. Richard Spree, *Die Wachstumszyklen der deutschen Wirtschaft von 1840 bis 1880* (Berlin: Duncker & Humblot, 1977), 471.

26. Albert Boime, *Art in an Age of Civil Struggle, 1848–1871* (Chicago: University of Chicago Press, 2008), 324.

27. Bonin, "France, Financial Crisis and the 1848 Revolutions."

28. David H. Pinkney, *Decisive Years in France, 1840–1847* (Princeton: Princeton University Press, 1986), 33–36; Rocio Robles Tardio, "Economic Investors and Railway Advertising," in *Across the Borders: Financing the World's Railways in the Nineteenth and Twentieth Centuries*, ed. Ralf Rotha and Gunter Dinhobl (Aldershot, UK: Ashgate, 2008), 63.

29. Mark Traugott, "The Mid-Nineteenth-Century Crisis in France and England," *Theory and Society* 12, no. 4 (July 1983), 457.

30. Ibid., 457–58.

31. Larry Allen, *The Global Financial System, 1750–2000* (London: Reaktion, 2001), 214; Charles P. Kindleberger and Robert T. Aliber, *Manias, Crashes, and Panics: A History of Financial Crises*, 5th ed. (Hoboken, NJ: John Wiley, 2005), 135.

32. Alan Brinkley and Davis Dyer, *The American Presidency* (Boston: Houghton Mifflin, 2004), 129–38.

33. *Second Report of the State Mineralogist of California* (Sacramento: State Office of California, 1882), 148.

34. "Opening of the Spring Trade," *New York Herald*, February 5, 1857, 4.

35. C. K. Hobson, *The Export of Capital* (London: Constable, 1914), 128.

36. Gavin Wright, *Slavery and American Economic Development* (Baton Rouge: Louisiana State University Press, 2006), 60.

37. Roger Ransom and Richard Sutch, "Capitalists Without Capital: The Burden of Slavery and the Impact of Emancipation," *Agricultural History* 62, no. 3 (1988), 133–60, http://www.jstor.org/stable/3743211.

38. Bonnie Martin, "Slavery's Invisible Engine: Mortgaging Human Property," *Journal of Southern History* 76 (November 2010), 857.

39. Scott Reynolds Nelson, *A Nation of Deadbeats: An Uncommon History of America's Financial Disasters* (New York: Vintage, 2013), 134–35.

40. Kenneth M. Stampp, *America in 1857: A Nation on the Brink* (New York: Oxford University Press, 1990), 215–18.

41. Timothy J. Riddiough and Howard E. Thompson, "Dèjá Vu All Over Again: Agency, Uncertainty, Leverage, and the Panic of 1857" (Hong Kong Institute for Monetary Research Working Paper No. 10/2012, April 2012), 21–23.

42. Ibid., 20–22.

43. Evans, *Commercial Crisis, 1847–1848*, 32. Improvements in the British economy are described in more detail in King, *History of the London Discount Market*, 171.

44. King, *History of the London Discount Market*, 171.

45. Clapham, *Bank of England*, 223.

46. Michael Collins, "Long-Term Growth of the English Banking Sector and Money Stock, 1844–80," *The Economic History Review* 36, no. 3 (August 1983), 376.

47. D. Morier Evans, *The History of the Commercial Crisis, 1857–58: And the Stock Exchange Panic of 1859* (London: Groombridge, 1859), 32–34. Evans was an early financial journalist who published several books, most notably on the financial crises of 1847 and 1857, and was also a principal contributor to the *Bankers' Magazine*. See Alsager Vian, "Evans, David Morier," in *The Dictionary of National Biography, 1885–1900*, vol. 18 (London: Smith, Elder, 1889), 59.

48. Evans, *History of the Commercial Crisis, 1857–58*, 33.

49. King, *History of the London Discount Market*, 182–83, 185.

50. Riddiough and Thompson, "Déjà Vu All Over Again," 16.

51. Nelson, *Nation of Deadbeats*, 144.

52. Ibid., 148.

53. For an account of Forbes and Thayer's political activities and their connection with Lincoln, see Nelson, *Nation of Deadbeats*, 139–48, 151.

54. George Van Vleck, *The Panic of 1857: An Analytic Study* (New York: Columbia University Press, 1943), 60.

55. NBER, "Wholesale Price of Wheat, Chicago, Six Markets for Chicago, IL [M04F1 AUS16980M260NNBR] and Wheat Prices for Great Britain [M04002GBM523NNBR]," retrieved from FRED, https://fred.stlouisfed.org/series/M04F1AUS16980MZ60NNBR.

56. The "thunder" quote comes from the *Cincinnati Daily Gazette*, August 25, 1857, as quoted in James L. Huston, *The Panic of 1857 and the Coming of the Civil War* (Baton Rouge: Louisiana State University Press, 1987), 14. The emotional impact is further described in J. S. Gibbons, *The Banks of New-York, Their Dealers, the Clearing House, and the Panic of 1857* (New York: Appleton, 1858), 344. For data reflecting the Ohio Life Insurance and Trust Company failure's effects on the stock market, see Riddiough and Thompson, "Déjà Vu All Over Again," 11.

57. Charles Franklin Dunbar, *Economic Essays*, ed. O. M. W. Sprague (New York: Mac-Millan, 1904), 279; Huston, *The Panic of 1857*, 14; and Van Vleck, *Panic of 1857*, 65–66.

58. Riddiough and Thompson, "Déjà Vu All Over Again," 7–8.

59. Huston, *Panic of 1857 and the Coming of the Civil War*, 15.

60. Michael A. Ross, *Justice of Shattered Dreams: Samuel Freeman Miller and the Supreme Court During the Civil War Era* (Baton Rouge: Louisiana State University Press, 2003), 41, 45.

61. Timothy J. Riddiough, "The First Sub-Prime Mortgage Crisis and Its Aftermath" (Bank for International Settlements Papers No. 64, 2012), 15–17.

62. Riddiough and Thompson, "Déjà Vu All Over Again," 24–28.

63. For the reasoning behind this conclusion, see Riddiough and Thompson, "Déjà Vu All Over Again," 13.

64. Dunbar, *Economic Essays*, 279; Gibbons, *Banks of New-York*, 363–64.

65. "News of the Day," *New York Times*, September 18, 1857, 4; E. Merton Coulter, "The Loss of the Steamship Central America, in 1857," *Georgia History Quarterly* 54 (Winter 1970), 467–68; Charles W. Calomiris and Larry Schweikart, "The Panic of 1857: Origins, Transmission, and Containment," *Journal of Economic History* 51 (December 1991), 819.

66. Van Vleck, *Panic of 1857*, 71.

67. "News of the Day," *New York Times*, October 14, 1857, 4. Numbers on the total value of outstanding loans are from Chamber of Commerce of the State of New York, *Annual Report for the Year 1858* (New York: Wheeler and Williams, 1859), 249.

68. "Business Failures in the Panic of 1857," *Business History Review* 37 (Winter 1963), 437–440; Evans, *History of the Commercial Crisis, 1857–58*, 134–37.

69. "The Clergy and the Crisis," *New York Times*, October 14, 1857, 4.

70. Clapham, *Bank of England*, 226–27.

71. "America," *Times*, September 7, 1857, 8.

72. Evans, *History of the Commercial Crisis, 1857–58* 35; Clapham, *Bank of England*, 226–27.

73. For Scotland, Wales, and England, see H. M. Hyndman, *Commercial Crisis of the Nineteenth Century* (London: Swan Sonnenschein, 1902), 82–83. In the United States, President James Buchanan reflected on the iron industry standstill in James Buchanan, "Second Annual Message to Congress on the State of the Union," December 6, 1858, in John Bassett Moore, ed., *The Works of James Buchanan: Comprising His Speeches, State Papers, and Private Correspondence*, vol. 10 (1856–1860) (Philadelphia: J. B. Lippincott, 1910), 264.

74. Evans, *History of the Commercial Crisis, 1857–58*, 8, 40; Hyndman, *Commercial Crisis of the Nineteenth Century*, 85.

75. Hyndman, *Commercial Crisis of the Nineteenth Century*, 86.

76. William Newmarch, "On the Recent History of the Credit Mobilier," *Journal of the Statistical Society of London* 21 (December 1858), 447–48.

77. Hyndman, *Commercial Crisis of the Nineteenth Century*, 87.

78. John Ramsay McCulloch, "Hamburg," in *A Dictionary, Practical, Theoretical, and Historical, of Commerce and Commercial Navigation*, new ed. (London: Longman, Green, Longman & Roberts, 1859), 651.

79. Evans, *History of the Commercial Crisis, 1857–58*, 190–92.

80. Office of the Mercantile Agency, "The Failures in America," reprinted in Evans, *History of the Commercial Crisis, 1857–58*, 123.

81. "Failures in America," 122–24.

82. This relationship between the 1857 panic and the Civil War is deeply analyzed in James L. Huston's *The Panic of 1857 and the Coming of the Civil War.*

83. "The Foreign News—The 'Credit System' at Home and Abroad," reprinted in *Washington Union* (October 15, 1857), 3.

84. Karl Marx, *Dispatches for the New York Tribune: Selected Journalism of Karl Marx* (London: Penguin, 2007), 201, 170.

85. Rhiannon Sowerbutts, Marco Schneebalg, and Florence Hubert, "The Demise of Overend, Gurney," *Bank of England Quarterly Bulletin* 56 (2016), 95.

86. David Foucaud, "L'impact de la loi de 1862 généralisant la responsabilité limitée au secteur bancaire et financier sur la crise anglaise de 1866," *Revue Économique* 62, no. 5 (2011), 878.

87. "Overend, Gurney and Co., Limited," *Bankers' Magazine and Journal of the Money Market* 25 (August 1865), 905–6.

88. King, *History of the London Discount Market*, 240–41; Sowerbutts, Schneebalg, and Hubert, "Demise of Overend, Gurney," 97.

89. King, *History of the London Discount Market*, 239–40.

90. "The Situation of the Discount Companies," *Bankers' Magazine and Journal of the Money Market* 20 (October 1860), 694.

91. King, *History of the London Discount Market*, 237–40.

92. Sowerbutts, Schneebalg, and Hubert, "Demise of Overend, Gurney," 98.

93. King, *History of the London Discount Market*, 240–44; "Overend, Gurney, and Co., Limited and Unlimited," *Economist* 24 (June 16, 1866), 698.

94. Sowerbutts, Schneebalg, and Hubert, "Demise of Overend, Gurney," 99.

95. When it did fail, the *Economist*'s Walter Bagehot wrote, "We have thought [its failure] possible any time this three months." See Bagehot, "The State of the City," *Economist* 24 (May 12, 1866), 553.

96. King, *History of the London Discount Market*, 242; "Failures, Embarrassments, and Windings-Up," *Economist* 24 (May 26, 1866), 183.

97. Sowerbutts, Schneebalg, and Hubert, "Demise of Overend, Gurney," 99.

98. King, *History of the London Discount Market*, 253; Clapham, *Bank of England*, 263. King expands on the firm's sloppy accounting and overall "rottenness," writing that the "tangle of financial intrigue and almost unbelievable graft is so complex that complete unravelling will probably never be possible" (King, 248).

99. King, *History of the London Discount Market*, 253; Sowerbutts, Schneebalg, and Hubert, "Demise of Overend, Gurney," 100–101.

100. Clapham, *Bank of England*, 269.

101. Sowerbutts, Schneebalg, and Hubert, "Demise of Overend, Gurney," 104.

102. Bank of England, "Daily Account Book for 1866, Bank of England Archive (C1/14)," https://www.bankofengland.co.uk/-/media/boe/files/archive/daily-account-books/1800 /1866.pdf.

103. Clapham, *Bank of England*, 268.

104. Marc Flandreau and Stefano Ugolini, "Where It All Began: Lending of Last Resort and the Bank of England During the Overend-Gurney Panic of 1866" (Norges Bank Working Papers 2011), 4. For an analysis of how Bagehot's principle emerged out of the intellectual climate in the 1860s and 1870s, see Vincent Bignon et al., "Bagehot for Beginners: The

Making of Lender-of-Last-Resort Operations in the Mid-Nineteenth Century," *Economic History Review* 65 (2012), 580–608. For a discussion of how widely shared this principle was at the time, see p. 598.

105. Rondo E. Cameron, *France and the Economic Development of Europe, 1800–1914: Conquests of Peace and Seeds of War* (Princeton: Princeton University Press, 1961), 195.

106. For perspectives along these lines, see Karl Brunner and Allan H. Meltzer, "Money and Credit in the Monetary Transmission Process," *American Economic Review* 78 (May 1988), 448; and Thomas M. Humphrey, "Lender of Last Resort: The Concept in History," *FRB Richmond Economic Review* 75 (1989), 8. This was the consensus in the early twentieth century as well, as shown by Flandreau and Ugolini, "Where It All Began," 2.

107. Walter Bagehot, "The Panic," *Economist* 24 (May 19, 1866), 581.

108. "Series Q 23–32—Railroad Passenger and Freight Service: 1865 to 1890," *Historical Statistics of the United States, Colonial Times to 1957* (Washington DC: Government Printing Office, 1960), 428.

109. Thorstein B. Veblen, "The Price of Wheat Since 1867," *Journal of Political Economy* 1 (December 1892), 73–75; National Agricultural Statistics Service, "All Wheat Area Planted and Harvested, Yield, Production, Price, and Value—United States: 1866–2017," *Crop Production Historical Track Records* (Washington, DC: U.S. Department of Agriculture, April 2018), 206, https://www.nass.usda.gov/Publications/Todays_Reports/reports/croptr18.pdf.

110. *American Railroad Journal* 38–46 (1865–1873); U.S. Bureau of the Census, "Railroads Before 1890—Capital, Property Investment, Income, and Expenses: 1850 to 1890," in *Historical Statistics of the United States, 1789–1945: A Supplement to the Statistical Abstract of the United States* (Washington, DC: Government Printing Office, 1949), 201.

111. Nelson, *Nation of Deadbeats*, 162; Arthur Arnold, "Russia in Europe," *Fraser's Magazine* n.s. 14 (August 1876), 142. Wheat prices in Chicago doubled during the two years ending in May 1867 and quadrupled over the previous four years. In Britain, wheat prices rose 72.5 percent between January 1864 and January 1868. In fact, the U.S. price reached a record $2.88 per bushel in May 1867, a number not seen again until the latter months of World War I. See NBER, "Wholesale Price of Wheat, Chicago, Six Markets for Chicago, IL," NBER Macrohistory Database Series 04001, http://www.nber.org/databases/macrohistory/data/04/m04001a.db; and NBER, "Wheat Prices for Great Britain," NBER Macrohistory Database Series 04002, http://www.nber.org/databases/macrohistory/data/04/m04002.db.

112. W. G. Langworthy Taylor, "Promotion Before the Trusts," *Journal of Political Economy* 12 (June 1904), 386–87.

113. NBER, "Germany Index of Stock Prices 01/1870–12/1913," NBER Macrohistory Database Series m11023a, http://www.nber.org/databases/macrohistory/data/11/m11023a.db.

114. John B. Lyon, *Out of Place: German Realism, Displacement and Modernity* (New York: Bloomsbury Academic, 2013), 42.

115. Monika Leopold-Rieks, *Ein Viertel in Bewegung: Hausbesitz, Mobilität und Wohnverhalten in der suedlichen Vorstadt Bremens zwischen 1875 und 1914* (Frankfurt: Peter Lang, 1998), 110.

116. Sebastian Kohl, "Homeowner Nations or Nations of Tenants: How Historical Institutions in Urban Politics, Housing Finance and Construction Set Germany, France and the

US on Different Housing Paths" (PhD dissertation, University of Cologne, 2014), 76, https://kups.ub.uni-koeln.de/6161/1/Diss-final-deutsch2.pdf.

117. Taylor, "Promotion Before the Trusts," 386–87.

118. Kilian Rieder, "A Historic(al) Run on Repo? Causes of Bank Distress During the Austro-Hungarian 'Grunderkrach' of 1873" (working paper, November 26, 2015), 4, https://www.banque-france.fr/sites/default/files/8-rieder-paper.pdf.

119. Charles P. Kindleberger, *Historical Economics: Art of Science?* (Berkeley: University of California Press, 1990), 314.

120. David C. Goodman and Colin Chant, *European Cities and Technology: Industrial to Post-Industrial City* (New York: Routledge, 1998), 228.

121. David Clay Large, *Berlin* (New York: Basic, 2000), 12.

122. Albert Boime, *Art in an Age of Civil Struggle, 1848–1871* (Chicago: University of Chicago Press, 2007), 795.

123. Erik F. Gerding, *Law, Bubbles, and Financial Regulation* (London: Routledge, 2014), 82.

124. Richard White, *Railroaded: The Transcontinentals and the Making of Modern America* (New York: W. W. Norton, 2011), 56; Ellis Paxon Oberholtzer, *Jay Cooke: Financier of the Civil War*, vol. 2 (Philadelphia: George W. Jacobs, 1907), 33–40.

125. White, *Railroaded*, 56.

126. "Issue of £4,000,000 Northern Pacific Railroad First Mortgage Land-Grant Bonds," *Times*, January 11, 1872, 10.

127. White, *Railroaded*, 77, 272.

128. Jonathan Levy, *Freaks of Fortune: The Emerging World of Capitalism and Risk in America* (Cambridge, MA: Harvard University Press, 2014), 141.

129. Nelson, *Nation of Deadbeats*, 162.

130. Ibid., 173.

131. Jeffrey Fear and Christopher Kobrak, "Origins of German Corporate Governance and Accounting, 1870–1914: Making Capitalism Respectable" (presentation, XIV International Economic History Congress, Session 96–Corporate Governance in Historical Perspective, Helsinki, 2006), 12, http://www.helsinki.fi/iehc2006/papers3/Kobrak.

132. E. C. Stedman and A. N. Easton, "History of the New York Stock Exchange," in *The New York Stock Exchange: Its History, Its Contribution to National Prosperity, and Its Relation to American Finance at the Outset of the Twentieth Century*, ed. Edmund Clarence Stedman (New York: Stock Exchange Historical Company, 1905), 265.

133. "The Week in Trade and Finance," *Nation* 17 (September 18, 1873), 200; Oberholtzer, *Jay Cooke*, 427.

134. "The Failures in Wall Street," *Commercial and Financial Chronicle* 17 (September 20, 1873), 375; Horace White, "The Financial Crisis in America," *Fortnightly Review* 19 n.s. (June 1, 1876), 815. For a detailed timeline of that September's failures, see *History of the Terrible Financial Panic of 1873* (Chicago: Western News Company, 1873).

135. White, "Financial Crisis in America," 815.

136. O. M. W. Sprague, *History of Crises Under the National Banking System* (Washington, DC: Government Printing Office, 1910), 83.

137. Fear and Kobrak, "Origins of German Corporate Governance," 12.

138. Jürgen Kocka and Marcel van der Linden, *Capitalism: The Reemergence of a Historical Concept* (New York: Bloomsbury, 2016), 16.

139. Fear and Kobrak, "Origins of German Corporate Governance," 12.

140. Vincent Bignon and Clemens Jobst, "Economic Crisis and the Eligibility for the Lender of Last Resort: Evidence from Nineteenth Century France," *Center for Economic Policy Research* vol. DP11737 (2017), 17.

141. White, *Railroaded*, 83–84.

142. U.S. Bureau of the Census, "Railroads Before 1890—Mileage, Equipment, and Passenger and Freight Service: 1830–1890," in *Historical Statistics of the United States, 1789–1945: A Supplement to the Statistical Abstract of the United States* (Washington, DC: Government Printing Office, 1949), 200.

143. White, *Railroaded*, 83.

144. Nelson, *Nation of Deadbeats*, 173–74, 176.

145. Eugene N. White, "The Krach of 1882, the Bourse de Paris and the Importance of Microstructure," *SSRN Electronic Journal* (2006), 14–15, http://dx.doi.org/10.2139/ssrn.948993.

146. Ibid., 14.

147. Eugene N. White, "The Krach of 1882 and the Bourse de Paris" (presentation, Sixth European Historical Economics Society Conference, Istanbul, Turkey, September 2005), 13.

148. White, "Krach of 1882" (2006), 20; Herbert R. Lottman, *Return of the Rothschilds: The Great Banking Dynasty Through Two Turbulent Centuries* (London: I. B. Tauris, 1995), 85.

149. Cindy King, "Paul Gauguin (1848–1903)," Metropolitan Museum of Art, accessed November 5, 2018, https://www.metmuseum.org/toah/hd/gaug/hd_gaug.htm.

150. Émile Zola, *Money [L'Argent],* trans. Ernest A. Vizetelly (London: Chatto & Windus, 1902), vii.

151. Arthur F. Burns, *The Frontiers of Economic Knowledge* (Princeton: Princeton University Press, 1954), 199.

152. Ibid., 311.

153. U.S. Bureau of the Census, "Series P 231-300. Physical Output of Selected Manufactured Commodities: 1860 to 1970," in *Historical Statistics of the United States: Colonical Times to 1970, Part 2* (Washington, DC: Government Printing Office, 1975), 689–697, collected in Thayer Watkins, "The Depression of 1893–1898," San José State University Department of Economics, accessed November 13, 2018, http://www.sjsu.edu/faculty/watkins/dep1893.htm.

154. Elmus Wicker, *Banking Panics of the Gilded Age* (Cambridge: Cambridge University Press, 2000), 40.

155. Douglas Steeples and David O. Whitten, *Democracy in Desperation* (Westport, CT: Greenwood, 1998), 32.

156. James L. Holton, *The Reading Railroad: History of a Coal Age Empire, Vol. 1: The Nineteenth Century* (Lewisburg, PA: Garrigues House, 1990), 323–25.

157. "Come to Grief: Receiver Appointed for the National Cordage Company," *Farm Implement News* 14 (May 11, 1893), 24.

158. Robert Sobel, *Panic on Wall Street: A History of America's Financial Disasters* (Washington, DC: BeardBooks, 1999), 258.

159. U.S. Department of Commerce, "Table No. 328: Commercial Failures—Number and Assets and Liabilities," *Statistical Abstract of the United States 1937* (Washington, DC: Government Printing Office, 1938), 291.

160. Steeples and Whitten, *Democracy in Desperation*, 21–22.

161. Nelson, *Nation of Deadbeats*, 188; Barry Eichengreen, "The Baring Crisis in a Mexican Mirror," *International Political Science Review* 20 (July 1999), 254; H. S. Ferns, "Invest-

ment and Trade with Argentina," *Economic History Review* n.s. 3 (1950), 216. Eichengreen notes that new issues of Argentine debt in Britain fell 78 percent in the two years from 1888 to 1890; Ferns points out the value of wheat imported into Britain from Argentina in 1890 was only £114,282—about 2 percent of the roughly £6 million annual average for the ten years from 1884 to 1893.

162. Steeples and Whitten, *Democracy in Desperation*, 84–85.

163. Ibid., 88–89; *The Daily News Almanac and Political Register for 1895* (Chicago: Chicago Daily News Company, 1895), 96. For more on the "Coxey's Army" movement, see Donald LeCrone McMurry, *Coxey's Army: A Study of the Industrial Army Movement of 1894* (Boston: Little, Brown, 1924).

164. Steeples and Whitten, *Democracy in Desperation*, 21–22.

165. Charles R. Geisst, *Wall Street: A History, Updated Edition* (Oxford: Oxford University Press, 2012), 103.

166. André Liesse, *Evolution of Credit and Banks in France: From the Founding of the Bank of France to the Present Time* (Washington, DC: Government Printing Office, 1909), 187.

167. David Blackbourn, *The Long Nineteenth Century: A History of Germany, 1780–1918* (New York: Oxford University Press, 1998), 313.

168. Toni Pierenkemper and Richard Tilly, *The German Economy During the Nineteenth Century* (New York: Berghahn, 2004), 116.

169. Arthur Raffalovich, *Le Marché Financier, 1901–1902* (Paris: Librairie Guillaumin, 1902), 45.

170. "Foreign Correspondence," *Economist* 58 (December 15, 1900), 1776.

171. "Foreign Correspondence," *Economist* 58 (July 7, 1900), 955.

172. "Foreign Correspondence," *Economist* 58 (September 8, 1900), 1277.

173. "Foreign Correspondence," *Economist* 58 (November 3, 1900), 1540.

174. "Foreign Correspondence," *Economist* 58 (1900), 1818.

175. Raffalovich, *Le Marché Financier*, 48.

176. "Foreign Correspondence," *Economist* 58 (October 27, 1900), 1504.

177. "Foreign Correspondence," *Economist* 58 (December 22, 1900), 1818.

178. Ibid.

179. Charles A. Conant, *A History of Modern Banks of Issue*, 5th ed. (New York: G. P. Putnam's Sons, 1915), 707.

180. "Germany's Industrial Crisis," *Scientific American* 85, no. 9 (1901), 130.

181. Marty Tone Rodgers and James E. Payne, "Was the Panic of 1907 a Global Crisis? Testing the Noyes Hypothesis" (presentation, Financial Crises Past and Present, Indiana University, September 25, 2014), 6.

182. Alexander D. Noyes, "A Year After the Panic of 1907," *Quarterly Journal of Economics* 23, no. 2 (February 1909), 203.

183. Nimura Kazuo, *The Ashio Riot of 1907: A Social History of Mining in Japan*, trans. Terry Broadman and Andrew Gordon (Durham, NC: Duke University Press, 1997), xi.

184. "The Ashio Riots," *Japan Times*, February 7, 1907, 3.

185. Liesse, *Evolution of Credit and Banks in France*, 222.

186. "Foreign Correspondence," *Economist* 65 (September 7, 1907), 105.

187. J. Riesser, *The German Great Banks and Their Concentration, in Connection with The Economic Development of Germany* (Washington, DC: Government Printing Office, 1911), 572.

188. Noyes, "A Year After the Panic of 1907," 200.

189. Ibid., 207–8.

190. Frank Fayant, "Fools and Their Money," *Success Magazine* 10, no. 1 (January 1907), 9.

191. Robert F. Bruner and Sean D. Carr, *The Panic of 1907: Lessons Learned from the Market's Perfect Storm* (Hoboken, NJ: John Wiley, 2007), xvii; Ellis W. Tallman and Jon Moen, "Lessons from the Panic of 1907," *Federal Reserve Bank of Atlanta Economic Review* 75 (May 1990), 7.

192. Bruner and Carr, *Panic of 1907*, 151.

193. Noyes, "A Year After the Panic of 1907," 188.

194. Bruner and Carr, *Panic of 1907*, 2.

195. Quentin R. Skrabec Jr., *H. J. Heinz: A Biography* (Jefferson, NC: McFarland, 2009), 168.

196. Stock exchange houses were private banks set up as partnerships, in which one or more partners is also a member of the NYSE, and were more common around the turn of the century. The following is a transcript from a hearing before the Senate Committee on Banking and Currency in 1914. Noted are Senator Henry F. Hollis, Democrat from New Hampshire, and John G. Milburn, a prominent New York attorney and a partner at the firm Carter, Ledyard & Milburn with prominent business clients. U.S. Congress, Senate, Committee on Banking and Currency, *Regulation of the Stock Exchange: Hearings Before the Committee on Banking and Currency*, 63rd Cong., 2nd sess., 1914, 362.

"Senator Hollis: There is one other thing I am quite anxious to know. So far as I am informed, members of the stock exchange representing private banking houses are members of those houses as partnerships. That is, so far as I know, none of these banking houses is a corporation but is a partnership; is that so?

"Mr. Milburn: Many banking houses have one or two partners who are members of the stock exchange.

"Senator Hollis: They are stock-exchange houses, so called?

"Mr. Milburn: Yes.

"Senator Hollis: All those with which I am at all familiar are partnerships. Now, is there any rule about that in the stock exchange?

"Mr. Milburn: A partnership which has a member who is a member of the stock exchange is a stock exchange house and its transactions on the exchange are subject to the jurisdiction of the exchange."

197. China's crises are a subject that deserves a great deal more research and analysis, and there were indeed financial crises, as part of an almost continuous maelstrom of every sort of crisis—inflation crises, currency crises, and sovereign debt crises—for a century or more. The financial histories of almost all crises from the pre–World War II era are difficult to reconstruct, but China's are especially difficult, with an acute scarcity of data in what was for most of this period a preindustrial and profoundly war-torn society. For much of this time, the country saw wars and rivalries—from the Taiping Rebellion, to the Boxer Rebellion, to the Xinhai Revolution, to the protracted struggle between Chiang Kai-Shek's Nationalist Party and the Communist Party of Mao Zedong.

China had a financial crisis in 1883 that emerged in the microeconomies that developed around the port cities the British had established, the so-called treaty ports, especially Shanghai. Stock market shares would crash after a panic, with the "average stock price decline . . . more than 70 percent for the 1883–84 period" (Zhiwu Chen, "Stock Market in China's Modernization Process—Its past, present, and future prospects," Yale School of Management, 2006, 12, http://

citeseerx.ist.psu.edu/viewdoc/download?doi=10.1.1.544.5311&rep=rep1&type=pdf). Few of the companies that were formed during the speculative mania leading to the crash would survive.

The main lenders at the time were the *qianzhuang*, who were close to the Chinese merchants. They worked on the "chop loan" system, borrowing from foreign banks and lending to native ones. The presence of the *qianzhuang* "was so pervasive that almost all of the Chinese merchants then engaged in Shanghai's foreign trade relied on qianzhuang loans" (Linsun Cheng, *Banking in Modern China: Entrepreneurs, Professional Managers, and the Development of Chinese Banks, 1897–1937* [New York: Cambridge University Press, 2003], 16). The total chop loans were often several times higher than the native banks' original capital, which created a very fragile capital structure and a complete vulnerability if a foreign bank were to call these loans (Zhaojin Ji, *A History of Modern Shanghai Banking: The Rise and Decline of China's Finance Capitalism* [New York: M. E. Sharpe, 2003], 66).

There was also a "mania for establishing native banks, and these in turn lent themselves to the starting of mines and other ventures, the result being so much excess that there was then a general collapse. Of some 60 or 70 banks of this nature which existed in Shanghai at the end of 1882 we learn that not more than 10 survived 1883" ("The Extent to Which Financially and Commercially We Are Interested in China," *Bankers' Magazine* 44 (1884), 1087–88).

By the early 1900s, China was haltingly entering the industrial age, with the introduction of railroads, which were at first largely built, owned, and run by foreigners. Globally, in the late 1880s and early 1890s, bicycles would explode in popularity, leading to a high demand for rubber. This was closely followed by the creation and rise of the automobile industry in the early 1900s. In 1906, "Shanghai interests took to launching rubber estates on the local market." Of course, this rapid growth wasn't without misbehavior. In order to bring these estates to the market, "promoters were prepared to mislead investors, and in the subsequent inquest three companies admitted that there were discrepancies between the prospectuses and the actual conditions of the estates. On one estate 'raw stumps were stuck into the ground and described as one year rubber'" (William Arthur Thomas, *Western Capitalism in China: A History of the Shanghai Stock Exchange* [Farnham, UK: Ashgate Publishing, 2001], 151–52). With what seemed like an infinite demand for rubber with the explosion of popularity of the automobile, issues were heavily oversubscribed, and there was a glut of people buying shares forward. "Some foreign banks also accepted mortgages on speculators' property to lend them cash for the stock.... Many Shanghai native banks also oversubscribed to the stock" (Ji, *A History of Modern Shanghai Banking,* 93).

The speculation was "riotous" in early 1910 and had everyone in a frenzy. Soon enough, stocks crashed, causing a chain reaction of bankruptcies and failures of native banks: "Zhengyuan, Qianyu, and Zhaokang were the first three native banks to declare bankruptcy, with debts of 1.4 million tael.... Yuanfengrun Yinhao ... close[d] its doors with debt of 20 million tael" (Ji, *A History of Modern Shanghai Banking,* 93). In the end, the Qing government would need to bail out the crisis by borrowing even more from foreign banks.

The Xinhai Revolution, or the Revolution of 1911, would see the fall of the Qing dynasty, the demise of which would "plunge Chinese banking and finance into chaos." The native banking system collapsed, the modern banking system was restructured, and the fearful public would make a run on the banks. The revolution also caused "a halt in commercial deposits and default on most loans," which was part of the collapse of the native banks (Ji, *A History of Modern Shanghai Banking,* 94).

Niv Horesh feels that the revolution itself was spurred on by the rubber crisis and issues with the manner in which railways were being renationalized, with the benefit given to the already wealthy, though does not specify any of these items as being directly blamable: "The stock exchange crash ramified into a national crisis that crippled nascent railway ventures, and was responsible in part for the provincial discontent that toppled the Qing" (Niv Horesh, *Shanghai's Bund and Beyond: British Banks, Banknote Issuance, and Monetary Policy in China, 1842–1937* [New Haven, CT: Yale University Press, 2009], 33).

The 1920s saw banking crises, and once again rubber shares and political upheaval were culprits, though not at the level of 1910. There was also a drop in commodity prices, which adversely affected gold speculators, "many of whom were merchants with ch'ien-chuang (qianzhuang) interests." Foreseeing a run on banks, those who were currency note-issuing stocked up on dollars, which increased the tael-dollar exchange rate. All of this, along with the refusal of modern banks to renew chop loans, led to seven *qianzhuang* being unable to meet their obligations in August 1924; they were saved only by the two bankers' guilds that took steps to prevent a panic (Andrea Lee McElderry, *Shanghai Old-Style Banks [Ch'ien-Chuang] 1800–1935* [Ann Arbor: Center for Chinese Studies, University of Michigan, 1976], 146).

The 1930s in China saw sovereign debt and currency crises; by the 1940s, this had extended to a prolonged inflation crisis that included warring factions continuing to print and use increasingly less valuable paper currency to pay and provision their armies. This inflation crisis was a factor in bringing the Communists to victory. Financial records are scarce in this period. In 1949, Mao's Communist Party prevailed, and capitalism came to an end in China, only to return, haltingly at first, in 1978 under the rule of Deng Xiaoping.

Chapter 6

1. U.S. Bureau of Labor Statistics, "Civilian Unemployment Rate [UNRATE]," FRED, last modified November 2, 2018, https://fred.stlouisfed.org/series/UNRATE.

2. Ibid.

3. For profiles on some of these investors and how they made fortunes betting against runaway lending, see Michael Lewis, *The Big Short: Inside the Doomsday Machine* (New York: W. W. Norton, 2011).

4. Board of Governors of the Federal Reserve System, "2.1, Table D.3, Debt Outstanding by Sector," from Data Download Program, https://www.federalreserve.gov/datadownload/choose.aspx?rel=21.

5. Securities Industry and Financial Markets Association (hereafter SIFMA), "Research & Data," https://www.sifma.org/resources/archive/research.

6. Organisation for Economic Co-Operation and Development (OECD), "Long-Term Iinterest Rates," https://data.oecd.org/interest/long-term-interest-rates.htm.

7. Ibid.

8. S&P Dow Jones Indices LLC, "S&P/Case-Shiller 20-City Composite Home Price Index," FRED, last modified October 30, 2018, https://fred.stlouisfed.org/series/SPCS20RSA.

9. This data is the sum of two FRED series: U.S. Bureau of the Census and U.S. Department of Housing and Urban Development, "New One Family Houses Sold: United States [HSN1F]," retrieved on May 17, 2016, https://fred.stlouisfed.org/series/HSN1F; and National Association of Realtors, "Existing Home Sales [EXHOSLUSM4955]," retrieved on May 17, 2016, https://fred.stlouisfed.org/series/EXHOSLUSM4955.

10. SIFMA, "Research & Data."

11. Joint Center for Housing Studies of Harvard University, "Table W-2: Ratio of Median House Price to Median Household Income by Metro Area: 1994–2005," in the Appendix Tables for "The State of the Nation's Housing 2006," http://www.jchs.harvard.edu/research-areas /reports/state-nations-housing-2006.

12. Board of Governors of the Federal Reserve System, "Z.1, Table L.217, Total Mortgages," from Data Download Program, https://www.federalreserve.gov/datadownload/Choose.aspx ?rel=Z.1.

13. Daniel C. Vaughan, "The Credit Crisis in Commercial Lending and the Effect on Your Real Estate Practice," *Washington State Bar Association Quarterly* (Summer 2008), 4.

14. Tomoeh Murakami Tse, "Down Payments' Downward Trend," *Washington Post*, January 21, 2006.

15. Bethany McLean and Joe Nocera, *All the Devils Are Here: The Hidden History of the Financial Crisis* (New York: Portfolio/Penguin, 2010), 20.

16. Ibid., 23–28.

17. "The Secret 'Friends of Angelo,'" *Wall Street Journal,* June 25, 2009, https://www.wsj .com/articles/SB124588865553750813.

18. SIFMA, "Research & Data."

19. McLean and Nocera, *All the Devils,* 251.

20. In an attempt to prevent depositors from withdrawing funds, former president George W. Bush signed legislation raising the amount insured by the FDIC. See FDIC, "Emergency Economic Stabilization Act of 2008 Temporarily Increases Basic FDIC Insurance Coverage from $100,000 to $250,000 Per Depositor," press release, October 7, 2008, https://www.fdic .gov/news/news/press/2008/pr08093.html.

21. Despite the fact that mortgage-backed securities certainly became popular in the 1980s, there is some disagreement over how far back they go. Some scholars, for instance, trace the earliest MBSs to 1968. See Frank J. Fabozzi and Franco Modigliani, *Mortgage and Mortgage-Backed Securities Markets* (Cambridge, MA: Harvard University Press, 1992).

22. Board of Governors of the Federal Reserve System, "2.1, Table L.218, Home Mortgages," specifically line 18 plus line 19 divided by line 2, from Data Download Program, https://www.federalreserve.gov/datadownload/choose.aspx?rel=2.1.

23. Vikas Bajaj, "Freddie Mac Tightens Standards," *New York Times,* February 28, 2007.

24. SIFMA, "US-Mortgage Related Securities Outstanding," https://www.sifma.org/wp -content/uploads/2017/06/sf-us-mortgage-related-sifma.xls.

25. Lewis, *Big Short,* 7.

26. Ibid., 72.

27. Bank for International Settlements (hereafter BIS), "Credit to the Non-Financial Sector" dataset, https://www.bis.org/statistics/totcredit/totcredit.xlsx.

28. Ibid.

29. Eurostat, *People in the EU: Who Are We and How Do We Live?* (Luxembourg: Publications Office of the European Union, 2015), 77.

30. International Monetary Fund, *Spain: Financial Sector Assessment Program: Technical Note: Housing Prices, Household Debt, and Financial Stability* (Washington, DC: International Monetary Fund, 2006), 5.

31. USA International Business Publications, *Spain Country Study Guide Volume 1: Strategic Information and Developments* (Washington, DC: International Business Publications, 2013), 194.

32. Ben Bernanke, "The Great Moderation," speech, meeting of the Eastern Economic Association, Washington, DC, February 20, 2004, https://www.federalreserve.gov/boarddocs/speeches/2004/20040220/.

33. Charles P. Kindleberger and Robert T. Aliber, *Manias, Crashes, and Panics: A History of Financial Crises*, 5th ed. (Hoboken, NJ: John Wiley, 2005), 3.

34. Maurice Obstfeld and Kenneth Rogoff maintain that "global imbalances" did not "cause the leverage and housing bubbles" but nonetheless insist such imbalances were "a critically important codeterminant." See their report, "Global Imbalances and the Financial Crisis: Products of Common Causes" (Federal Reserve Bank of San Francisco Asia Economic Policy Conference, October 18–20 2009, Santa Barbara, CA), 1, https://www.imf.org/external/np/res/seminars/2010/paris/pdf/obstfeld.pdf.

35. Writers at *Forbes* described the global financial crisis in terms of contagion. While it makes sense that in panic, many chose to refer to the unfolding crisis as such, the rhetoric and discourse of contagion presumes that if one sector or country is contaminated, then the infection, if left unchecked, will spread globally. However, as I have made clear throughout the book, financial crises caused by runaway lending practices are years in the making. A crisis is not like an infection that latches onto a perfectly healthy and unsuspecting host. If we insist on using the language of illness—and I am not saying that we necessarily ought to—then we at least should think of financial crises as conditions born of habit, the consequences of which can be catastrophic in the long run. Human behavior was responsible for the crisis, not a pathogen found in nature. See Oxford Analytica, "U.S. Financial Crisis Goes Global," *Forbes*, September 22, 2008, https://www.forbes.com/2008/09/19/banks-contagion-globalization-cx_0919oxford.html#559f5fc13ed9.

36. Teri Buhl and John Carney, "Deutsche Bank Also 'Victimized' Goldman 'Victim,'" *Atlantic: Business*, April 26, 2010, https://www.theatlantic.com/business/archive/2010/04/deutsche-bank-also-victimized-goldman-victim/39471/.

37. It would be three years before Burry learned AIG was the insurance company selling CDSs on subprime mortgages. However, his certainty that such an insurer existed led him to jump on the opportunity early on. See Lewis, *Big Short*, 68.

38. BIS, "OTC Derivatives Outstanding," October 2018, https://www.bis.org/statistics/derstats.htm.

39. Jenny Anderson, "Wall Street Winners Get Billion-Dollar Paydays," *New York Times*, April 17, 2008, https://www.nytimes.com/2008/04/16/business/16wall.html?mtrref=www.google.com&gwh=F206AE32678C6EEEC340792CC473E22A&gwt=pay.

40. Brooksley Born, "Testimony of Brooksley Born, Chairperson Commodity Futures Trading Comission Concerning the Over-the-Counter Derivatives Market: Before the U.S. House of Representatives Committee on Banking and Financial Services," July 24, 1998, https://www.cftc.gov/sites/default/files/opa/speeches/opaborn-33.htm.

41. Scott Horsley, "Huge Lender New Century Files for Bankruptcy," National Public Radio, April 2, 2007, https://www.npr.org/templates/story/story.php?storyId=9293451.

42. Emily Kaiser, "Subprime Losses Could Hit $100 Billion: Bernanke," *Reuters*, July, 19, 2007, https://www.reuters.com/article/businesspro-usa-fed-bernanke-dc/subprime-losses-could-hit-100-billion-bernanke-idUSN1933365020070719.

43. Alexandra Twinn, "Dow, S&P Break Records," CNN, October, 9, 2007, https://money.cnn.com/2007/10/09/markets/markets_0500/index.htm?postversion=2007100917.

44. Board of Governors of the Federal Reserve System, "Charge-Off and Delinquency Rates on Loans and Leases at Commercial Banks," https://www.federalreserve.gov/releases /chargeoff/.

45. Colliers International, "Manhattan Class A & Class B Price/SF" table, from "Manhattan Office Capital Markets Report 1Q 2014," 2, http://www.colliers.com/-/media/Images/UnitedStates /MARKETS/New%20York%20City/1Q-2014-Manhattan-Office-Capital-Markets.

46. Christopher Longinetti, "The Credit Crisis in Commercial Real Estate," *Center for Real Estate Quarterly* 3 (2009), 28–29.

47. Ben S. Bernanke, "Financial Markets, the Economic Outlook, and Monetary Policy," speech, Women in Housing and Finance and Exchequer Club Joint Luncheon, Washington, DC, January 10, 2008, https://www.federalreserve.gov/newsevents/speech/bernanke20080110a.htm.

48. David Ellis, "Countrywide Rescue: $4 Billion," *CNN Money*, January, 11, 2008, https://money.cnn.com/2008/01/11/news/companies/boa_countrywide/.

49. Edmund L. Andrews, "Fed Acts to Rescue Financial Markets," *New York Times*, March 17, 2008, https://www.nytimes.com/2008/03/17/business/17fed.html?dlbk.

50. "Bear Stearns Gets a Lifeline from Fed and JP Morgan," *New York Times*, March 14, 2008, https://www.nytimes.com/2008/03/14/business/worldbusiness/14iht-bear.4.11107180.html.

51. Scott Horsley, "Bear Stearns Collapse Costly to Many," National Public Radio, March 17, 2008, https://www.npr.org/templates/story/story.php?storyId=88415073.

52. Ibid. According to "Bear Stearns Gets a Lifeline," officials at the Federal Reserve claimed the Fed "voted unanimously to lend the funds through JP Morgan because it would be operationally simpler than a direct loan to Bear Stearns."

53. Board of Governors of the Federal Reserve System, "Z.1, Table L.218, Home Mortgages," Lines 18 (Government-sponsored enterprises; home mortgages; asset) and 19 (Agency-and GSE-backed mortgage pools; home mortgages; asset), from Data Download Program, https://www.federalreserve.gov/datadownload/Choose.aspx?rel=Z.1.

54. Peter J. Wallison and Edward J. Pinto, "A Government-Mandated Housing Bubble," *Forbes*, February 16, 2009, https://www.forbes.com/2009/02/13/housing-bubble-subprime -opinions-contributors_0216_peter_wallison_edward_pinto.html#2ef4bb46778b.

55. James R. Hagerty, Ruth Simon, and Damian Paletta, "U.S. Seizes Mortgage Giants," *Wall Street Journal*, September 8, 2008, https://www.wsj.com/articles/SB122079276849707821.

56. Lehman Brothers Holdings Inc., 10-K Form, U.S. Securities and Exchange Commission, Washington, DC, 104, https://www.sec.gov/Archives/edgar/data/806085/000110465908005476 /a08-3530_110k.htm.

57. Nick K. Lioudis, "The Collapse of Lehman Brothers: A Case Study," Investopedia.com, December 11, 2017, https://www.investopedia.com/articles/economics/09/lehman-brothers -collapse.asp.

58. Ibid.

59. Federal Reserve, "Federal Reserve Announces the Creation of the Term Asset-Backed Securities Loan Facility (TALF)," press release, November 25, 2008, https://www.federalreserve .gov/newsevents/pressreleases/monetary20081125a.htm.

60. Edith Honan and Dan Wilchins, "Bernard Madoff Arrested over Alleged $50 Billion Fraud," *Reuters*, December 11, 2008, https://www.reuters.com/article/us-madoff-arrest/bernard -madoff-arrested-over-alleged-50-billion-fraud-idUSTRE4BA7IK20081212.

61. An oft-repeated and cited saying of his, Buffett sometimes includes this quote in his newsletters to investors at Berkshire Hathaway.

62. Edmund L. Andrews and Jackie Calmes, "Fed Cuts Key Rate to a Record Low," *New York Times,* December 16, 2008, https://www.nytimes.com/2008/12/17/business/economy/17fed.html.

63. Jan Strupczewski, "Euro Zone Recession Confirmed," *Reuters,* December 4, 2008, http://www.reuters.com/article/us-eurozone-economy-gdp-sb/euro-zone-recession-confirmed=idU KTRE4B32JK20081204.

64. Edmund Conway, "Bank of England: 1.2 Million Face Negative Equity as Property Slumps," *The Telegraph,* October 28, 2008, http://www.telegraph.co.uk/finance/financialcrisis /3270886/Bank-of-England-1.2million-face-negative-equity-as-property-slumps.html.

65. Andrew Ross Sorkin and Mary Williams Walsh, "A.I.G. Reports Loss of $61.7 Billion as U.S. Gives More Aid," *New York Times,* March, 2, 2009, https://www.nytimes.com/2009/03 /03/business/03aig.html.

66. Susanna Kim, "2010 Had Record 2.9 Million Foreclosures," *ABC News,* January 13, 2011, https://abcnews.go.com/Business/2010-record-29-million-foreclosures/story?id=12602271.

67. TED: The Economics Daily, "Unemployment Rate, March 2008–March 2011," Bureau of Labor Statistics, April 6, 2011, https://www.bls.gov/opub/ted/2011/ted_20110406_data .htm.

68. Hibah Yousuf, "Dow Closes at 5-Year High," *CNN Business,* September 11, 2012, https://money.cnn.com/2012/09/11/investing/stocks-markets/index.html.

69. The Dow Jones Industrial Average reached this level on August 2, 2013. See S&P Dow Jones Indices LLC, Dow Jones Industrial Average (DJIA), FRED, https://fred.stlouisfed.org /series/DJIA.

70. See Nassim Nicholas Taleb, *The Black Swan: The Impact of the Highly Improbable* (New York: Random House, 2007).

71. Bernanke, "Great Moderation."

72. Ben S. Bernanke, CNBC interview, July 1, 2005, quoted in David Leonhardt, "Bernanke, Pro and Con," *New York Times,* December 3, 2009, https://economix.blogs.nytimes .com/2009/12/03/bernanke-pro-and-con/.

73. Ben S. Bernanke, "The Economic Outlook," testimony before the Joint Economic Committee, U.S. Congress, Washington, DC, October 20, 2005, 7, https://georgewbush-whitehouse .archives.gov/cea/econ-outlook20051020.html.

74. Ben S. Bernanke, U.S. House of Representatives Hearing, Washington, DC, February 15, 2006, quoted in "Greenspan and Bernanke: Evolving Views," *New York Times,* August 22, 2007, https://www.nytimes.com/2007/08/22/business/22leonsidebar-web.html.

75. Bernanke, "Economic Outlook."

76. Bernanke, "Financial Markets."

ACKNOWLEDGMENTS

Researching and writing this book was challenging, if for no other reason than the extraordinary amount of data that had to be retrieved, reconstructed, and assembled. But on top of that, the research led me to views that were often well outside the mainstream, which made the need to get data all the more acute and the challenge all the more daunting. However, I was aided by a group of full-time analysts and researchers who did exceptional work and whom I would now wager have as much or more expertise in reconstructing financial data from the past than anyone else. The team was led by the dedicated and dependable Dan McShane, with analysts Michael Grady and Menachem Hauser and researchers Nicole Amato and Gary Jarvis. The efforts of this group have been exceptional. We garnered additional help from a number of terrific individuals, including Don Steinberg, Talia Coutin, Eduard Saakashvili, Juan Gallardo, Anastasia Saverino, Grace Hylinski, and Francesca Robin. I was continually surprised and delighted by the discoveries they made.

The director of Penn Press, Eric Halpern, and my chief editor, Damon Linker, guided me and made all of this possible. They also introduced me to the inimitable editor and writer Pamela Haag, who waded deep into the project; provided firm, steady-handed guidance; and never hesitated to tell it to me like it was. I opened her emails with trepidation because I knew they would contain new lists of tasks and revisions that would be right on target but would require me to up my game.

Beyond this, I was guided by the great work of the Institute for New Economic Thinking, which is superbly led by its executive director, Robert Johnson, along with former chair Lord Adair Turner, who also happens to be one of the important voices on the subject of private debt.

My longest-standing adviser on economic matters is Sherle Schwenninger, who, among his many other duties, is executive director of the Private Debt Project. Sherle was the one I turned to if I needed the straight story or an unvarnished answer to a complex economic question. He also led the effort to assemble the readers noted below.

A number of key individuals agreed to read and comment on my manuscript at a point when it was still in very rough shape. They gave me feedback that transformed the work and corrected any number of errors. These readers were Moritz Schularick, Steve Keen, Matthew Baron, Patrick Lawrence, David Gerson, François-René Burnod, Nicholas Mulder, and Joerg Bibow. I can only shudder when I think how much worse the book would have been without their input. Moritz's work on the data in this field has been foundational. Much of what we have done would simply not have been possible without his groundbreaking efforts. Steve is an iconoclast who so presciently called the 2008 crisis; he has consistently confronted the misguided orthodoxy in his field. Matthew is a rising star whose work on reconstructing historical stock market data has been both important and inspiring, and whose helpfulness and fairness mask his intellectual daring. Joerg provided invaluable help on my first book, and he did so again here. Nicholas, Patrick, and François-René are more recent acquaintances whose insights advanced my learning considerably. David provided a boost at just the point I needed it most.

Certain institutions play an indispensable role in collecting and maintaining key economic data, as well as providing research leadership. Since our efforts have shown that key data have not always been maintained, even in fairly recent decades, we are particularly grateful to the following: the Federal Reserve, including the extraordinary Federal Reserve Economic Data (FRED) database maintained by the Federal Reserve Bank of St. Louis; the U.S. Bureau of Economic Analysis; the Bank of International Settlement; the International Monetary Fund; the World Bank; the United Nations Statistics Division; and the Bank of England. I would also like to thank Ray Boshara, William R. Emmons, and Lowell R. Ricketts of the Federal Reserve Bank of St. Louis's Center for Household Financial Stability for their leadership on issues relating to consumer debt.

Thanks to all my many friends near and far, but especially to Paul McGlasson, who read many a draft and provided ongoing encouragement, and to Kevin Kleinschmidt and Steve Clemons, who have been my partners in so many endeavors and a constant source of support.

Thanks too to my mom, sister Joanna, and brothers David and Steven. And a special thanks to my dear and recently departed dad who gave me my love of history.

Finally and most important, I wish to thank my amazing, wonderful, and beloved wife, Laura, who along with our family, Lauren, Victoria, Sophia, Eric, Davis, and Mikael, together formed a bedrock of love, tolerance, and encouragement.